Especially for

....

From

....

Date

....

THE

Heart-Shaped Life

DAILY DEVOTIONAL
JOURNAL

KAREN MOORE

THE
Heart-Shaped Life

DAILY DEVOTIONAL JOURNAL

BARBOUR BOOKS
An Imprint of Barbour Publishing, Inc.

Published by Barbour Books, an imprint of Barbour Publishing, Inc., 1810 Barbour Drive, Uhrichsville, Ohio 44683, www.barbourbooks.com

Our mission is to inspire the world with the life-changing message of the Bible.

ecpa Member of the
Evangelical Christian
Publishers Association

Printed in China.

Welcome to a fresh start. . .

. . .not just to the day, but to life! It's time to energize your spirit and realign your heart so you think more positively and lovingly about every circumstance you encounter.

God offers you His kind and generous Spirit so you can stay healthy in heart and mind. He nourishes your soul and shapes your heart so you become more like Jesus.

You are a recipient of the fullness of God's goodness and love. A little inspiration each day helps to change your perspective and lighten your heart to make life's journey easier. As it says in Proverbs 4:23 (MSG), "Keep vigilant watch over your heart; *that's* where life starts."

God commanded us to love Him, to make Him a priority, and to do so with the biggest love we can possibly muster. Right after that, He said to love each other, even as much as we love ourselves. Love is what motivates your heart every morning. . .what makes you see the world through His eyes.

Rejoice in your loving and generous Creator who knows you and who willingly shapes your heart to live in abundant joy. Offer Him your praise and thanks as your spirit grows stronger, lavished by His love!

May God grant your heart's desires and help you to live a heart-shaped life.

—Karen Moore

A Heart-Shaped Spirit

"So now I am giving you a new commandment: Love each other.
Just as I have loved you, you should love each other. Your love for
one another will prove to the world that you are my disciples."

JOHN 13:34–35 NLT

As a new year begins, we all make promises to ourselves—and sometimes even to God—to live better lives. We promise we'll pray more, love more, or give more to those around us. We truly hope to be better people, more aware of what motivates our thoughts and causes us to rejoice in life's goodness.

God always hears those promises and blesses the spirit in which we make them. He knows that right at that moment, we really mean to follow through. He knows we have good intentions as each day dawns to do better than we did the day before. That's why He works so hard to help shape us—body, mind, and spirit.

Perhaps today, you can really step into the world heart-first. Seek more of His Spirit to help you keep those heartfelt promises. Keep aligning yourself with God's direction, asking for a clean heart and a new way to share His love. Ask Him to give you the kind of eyes that focus on all that it means to love wholeheartedly.

You can make a heartfelt difference in someone's life today. . .even your own.

A HEART OF JOY

As I open the door to a new day, Lord, strengthen and renew my joy, my love, and my commitment to You. With every beat of my heart, let me seek Your will for my encounters with others. Amen.

In the Spirit of Love

Follow God's example, therefore, as dearly loved children and walk in the way of love, just as Christ loved us and gave himself up for us as a fragrant offering and sacrifice to God.
EPHESIANS 5:1–2 NIV

It's fun to watch young children as they play. They might pretend to play the guitar like Daddy or like their favorite rock star. They may pretend to bake a cake or work on the computer like Mommy does. Children are great at imitating those closest to them because they want to be like the ones they love. They love to be noticed for being so "grown up."

As we develop a spirit of love and grow more confident in our walk with the Lord, this passage from Ephesians invites us to imitate Jesus. He is someone we want to be close to, someone we love, so we want to please Him in every possible way, and we want to have Him see that we are "growing up" in faith.

As you put on a spirit of love today, see if you can imitate Jesus, be like Him in some special way, or be more like Him in a way that hasn't been easy for you in the past. . .more giving, more compassionate, or more patient. Follow Him wherever you go today, and if your heart is in it, He's sure to be pleased.

A HEART-SHAPED PRAYER

Lord, help me to put on childlike faith in You today, imitating Your love for others and creating a spirit of peace within my soul. Bless all I do this day. Amen.

Love Is an Action Word

Dear children, let us not love with words or speech but with actions and in truth.
1 JOHN 3:18 NIV

How do we understand the word *love*? What would love in action feel like, taste like, or smell like? How can we know if we are sharing love both in action and in truth?

Look back at yesterday. Think about every interaction you had with your spouse, a coworker, a child, or a neighbor. Run it through your mind on instant replay. Did that interaction create closeness, a sense of well-being, a moment shared that left you both feeling better than you did before? If so, you had a good day where your actions spoke louder than words.

Actions created in love feel good. They lift our spirits and encourage our hearts. If what you did yesterday doesn't bring you peace of mind today, then try again. Create meaningful interactions with the people around you, and let love guide all you do. You can do it because God put His spirit of love within you.

God is love because He sent Jesus to redeem us. You are love when you fit your words and your actions together for His glory.

A HEART OF LOVE

Lord, let me show Your love to everyone I meet today. Let me lift the spirits of others and strengthen their hearts in each thing that I do. Amen.

The Apple of His Eye

For the LORD's portion is his people, Jacob his allotted inheritance. . . .
He shielded him and cared for him; he guarded him as the apple of his eye.
DEUTERONOMY 32:9–10 NIV

When you're the "apple of someone's eye" you feel pretty special. Perhaps you were your grandmother's "apple," or your aunt Mary's special little one. Maybe you have someone in your life who is the "apple of your eye." What a delightful position to be in!

Imagine being the apple of God's eye. You might remember that Jacob was shielded and cared for by God's grace. He was guarded and protected. What joy it is to remember that we are cared for in the same way! We are shielded from things we don't even know He protected us from. We are cared for by angels with tender mercy wherever we happen to be. Why? Because we're loved so much! Remember today that you are the apple of God's eye and the joy of His heart.

When you feel good about yourself, you extend more mercy and love to others. If the Lord's portion is His people, then you are the reason He has joy, you are one of His beloved. See each person you meet today as the "apple of God's eye!" When you do, you'll see more clearly that each one is worthy of great love.

A HEART OF JOY

Lord, let me act today as though I understand what it truly means to be the "apple" of Your eye. Let me know Your protection, mercy, and love in all that comes my way. Amen.

How Do You Quench Love?

*Many waters cannot quench love; nor can rivers drown it. If a man
tried to buy love with all his wealth, his offer would be utterly scorned.*

SONG OF SONGS 8:7 NLT

One of the most passionate messages in the Bible says that we cannot quench love.
What does that mean? We might think we could quench a thirst by drinking water, or
quench a feeling by subduing it. However, what we see in this Scripture reminds us that
rivers cannot wash love away, nor waters quench it so that you ever feel you've had
enough. Therefore, love is here to stay, for nothing can drown it! Love continues on, and
that's why God places such a premium on the matters of the heart.

God's love is forever unquenchable! You will never get enough of it and you will
never use it up. Perhaps a way to capture a comparison is to think about someone in
your life whom you truly love.

You may think that nothing could change the love that you have for this person and
that you will always want more of it. You could never imagine that your love could dry
up. You know that your love will continue to flow, flooding the heart of your beloved with
every breath. It's amazing to think about this love. This thought may give you the initial
flavor of God's outpouring of love for you.

Now think again about those dearest to your heart. Promise those you love that
nothing will quench, or ever change, your love for them. Promise yourself that you will
seek love that shapes your heart with the kind of unconditional acceptance that you
receive from God. May your love for others simply overflow.

A HEART OF LOVE

*Lord, let me overflow with love today, drinking You in, breathing You out, so that
everyone around me will see more of You, less of me, and feel Your unquenchable love. Amen.*

....

....

....

....

....

....

....

Loving the Unlovable

"To you who are ready for the truth, I say this: Love your enemies. Let them bring out the best in you, not the worst. When someone gives you a hard time, respond with the energies of prayer for that person. If someone slaps you in the face, stand there and take it. If someone grabs your shirt, giftwrap your best coat and make a present of it. If someone takes unfair advantage of you, use the occasion to practice the servant life. No more tit-for-tat stuff. Live generously."

LUKE 6:27–30 MSG

It only seems right to be loving to the people you care about, but loving your enemies? Now, isn't that going just a bit too far? Pray for those who mistreat you? Well, that's a nice idea, but can you really do it?

Most of us treat others with compassion and kindness because we expect to be treated with compassion and kindness in return. It's not always easy because we're human, and so we have to lean on God's grace to help us have a heart-shaped life with His perspective, able to see beyond the situation at hand.

Sometimes you treat others with kindness and they still throw you under the bus or tell lies about you. It's possible that even your friends will betray you. When those things happen and your heart is broken, it's not easy to do it God's way. However, the scripture answer is pretty clear, "Love, do good, bless, and pray."

Abusive actions of others give us no excuses to be abusive in return. Instead, we are given opportunities in difficult moments to put Jesus into action, to show God's love, even if we can't quite show our own. May you find that your heart is so shaped by God's love that you can even embrace those who appear to be unlovable.

A HEART OF LOVE

Lord, let me out-love all those around me today. Let me be an example of Your care, Your gifts, and Your presence wherever I am. Amen.

Sing for Joy!

But let everyone who trusts you be happy; let them sing glad songs forever. Protect those who love you and who are happy because of you.

PSALM 5:11 NCV

Imagine what it would be like if you decided to rise every morning, maybe even this morning, rejoicing in the Lord. Picture it! You're singing for joy and living in peace. You know, without a doubt, that you are protected, loved, and meant to live fully and well. You are not going to let a negative thought anywhere near you because this is your day for joy! You've got the wings of an angel gently wrapped around your shoulders and you know God watches over you and protects you. It's an astounding day!

Okay, now coming back down to earth, take a serious look at the word *joy*. What can you do on any given day to find the best, most positive side of a situation? Maybe this will help. When you can't be happy in a circumstance, you can feel the joy of knowing you are known by your Creator, the One who wants only your good. Trusting that God wants only your good means that you can look to Him to help you rise above anything that ushers in the gray skies.

Step into the day with a smile for the world, renewed energy for those you love, and a decision in your heart that today you'll do it. You will live in joy. You will think joy! Sing joy!

A HEART OF JOY

Lord, I'm walking, I'm singing, I'm running with You all day today in great joy! Thanks for being with me and giving me the right spirit to see Your hand at work in all I do. Amen.

Put on a Happy Face

A happy heart makes the face cheerful,
but heartache crushes the spirit.
PROVERBS 15:13 NIV

When your spirit is crushed it's not easy to find your way back to the positive you. You may decide to put on a happy face, but that decision alone does not always change the way you feel inside.

Suffering, anguish, sadness, and other negative feelings come out of nowhere, ambushing you and leaving you feeling hopeless. The good news is that you don't have to embrace them. You don't have to carry them with you every place you go. In fact, you can't carry them because they are dead weights. So, how do you step around them and return to a happy heart? Try something like this. Pray about your sorrow and then imagine putting it outside yourself, wrapping it up and just setting it aside. Ask Jesus to carry it for you, and then go out for a walk, unburdened. You have given the burden to the only One who can make a difference in the situation. You are not meant to carry the load alone. Your Savior desires to do that for you.

Open your eyes to the world around you and focus your heart on the needs of others. Talk to a neighbor, reach out to a friend, and find a reason to laugh. By the time you return home, the burden you've been feeling will have lifted, your step will be lighter, and your face will shine with true joy.

A COMFORTING HEART

Lord, help me to realize that my sorrows are important to You and that I don't need to carry them alone. Bless this situation that concerns me today, and walk with me until the answers come. Amen.

Joyful, Patient, Faithful...Me?

*Be joyful because you have hope. Be patient when trouble comes,
and pray at all times. Share with God's people who need help.*
ROMANS 12:12–13 NCV

Hope is the thing that gives wings to the soul. It changes the way we perceive the world. When we have hope, our spirits are renewed and we have reason to rejoice. Hope is a matter of the heart; for with hope we see things differently, positively, and joyfully.

When affliction comes, though, our patience gets shorter and we lose hope. Sometimes we even lose our ability or our desire to pray. We wonder if God is still near. What do we do then?

The writer of Romans gives us a suggestion. When our hope is down, we can turn our attention to others. We can share with God's people in need and practice hospitality. We can take the opportunity to volunteer our services and our talents and take our minds away from our lagging spirits. In so doing, we may discover that hope returns. Giving from the heart produces wings of hope. Giving of ourselves brings patience and peace.

There's a great day ahead. Remember that you are an ambassador of hope because you have the love of Jesus tucked inside your soul. Let your heart return to that hope today.

A HEART OF HOPE

Lord, renew my hope today. Let my spirits rise as I work, live, and serve others in Your name. Let my heart find hope in You again. Amen.

Creating a Heart-Shaped Day

This is the day which the LORD has made; let us rejoice and be glad in it.
PSALM 118:24 NASB

Every sunrise brings a choice. You can choose to live in the light of God's love and blessing, or you can choose to crawl back under the covers and go it all alone. If you go it alone, you may not see the world with the same perspective that you will surely have under the guidance of God's Spirit.

Without a sense of your Spirit's connection to your heart and to God, your choices become limited. In a somewhat dimmed light you may see everyone around you as difficult and cruel. You may imagine an obstacle hides around every corner. You may even be blinded by worries that prevent you from realizing all that God has for you.

When you choose to view people as those that the Lord loves and has redeemed, and you choose to see life as a continual source of learning what is good, you'll be awake to the Spirit and able to see things in a more positive way. You'll see the light and not the darkness, the good and not the evil. Your heart will understand its purpose and shine a light through your smile and your kindness. The choice you make is significant.

This is the day the Lord has made. It was created for you to enjoy right now. This is the only day you have; it's the gift of the present. When the sun goes down on this day, will you have spent it in joy? Will you be the reason someone else can rejoice? You are the light of the world and this is your day to shine. Rejoice!

A LIGHT HEART

Lord, as I walk in Your light, help me to bless everyone that comes onto my path with Your love and compassion. Help me to keep choosing to see the good in all those I encounter. I offer You heartfelt thanks and praise in all things. Amen.

Living in Harmony

For God is not the author of confusion but of peace,
as in all the churches of the saints.

1 Corinthians 14:33 nkjv

Okay, brothers and sisters, kids and coworkers, this is your day to make peace with one another. Try something new! For one day, just today, live in harmony, forgiveness, and genuine contentment. No excuses! Are you ready to try it?

Harmony doesn't mean you have to sing the same note or even the same song as everyone else. It just means you have to hum along and help keep things running smoothly. You have to know when it's time to sing your own melody or when to sing your part loudly and happily to add a supportive note. You have to know when to listen with your heart for a song that may not be familiar to you.

Your job for one conversation at a time, moment by moment, is to make today orderly. You will not allow discord, chaos, apathy, or anger, for these are all notes of discontent. They'll keep you keyed up, with a high-pitched anxiety level, and cause your throat to get dry. The reason for great tension is often about the negative stories in your head, the ones you've allowed to have control. They don't have to have the last word though because you have other stories and they come from the love you have in your heart.

Clean up the chaos and get back to harmony. Let your song burst forth into praise for your God who loves you so and wants you to be at peace with everyone.

A HEART OF HARMONY

Lord, let me seek forgiveness from any that I may have offended. Renew my heart, and help me offer friendship to those I meet today. Cause me to live in harmony with Your Spirit and Your purpose for my life. Amen.

Messengers of Peace

*How beautiful on the mountains are the feet of those who
bring good news, who proclaim peace, who bring good tidings,
who proclaim salvation, who say to Zion, "Your God reigns!"*

ISAIAH 52:7 NIV

We live on a planet that nearly spins off-kilter on information overload. We know at a glance in the paper, on our tablet, or by the latest CNN news banners where the ugliest battle is being fought or where death and destruction are taking a toll. We are there, even more than we want to be. We carry the pain of those war-torn places and natural disasters, consciously or not, in the very fiber of our being.

Sometimes it becomes more than we can bear and we suffer an unspoken depression. In fact, it seems like the whole planet is depressed. We wonder where God is. Then, we hear good news! Peace is declared. People are safe again from the landslides of life, and we can breathe a bit more easily. We begin to hope that things will stay that way.

What if God sends you to be a voice of hope, a smile of cheer, a heart of compassion when everything else seems dreary? What if you are the only messenger who can bring good news to your family, your office, or your neighbors? God is sending you to do just that, and He has been preparing your heart for days such as this.

Bring everyone you meet the good news of God's love, and offer mountains of joy to lay at their feet. It will make your heart glad. . .and theirs!

A HEART OF PEACE

Lord, we may never know the peace of nations or of shifting continents for more than a moment at a time, but we can know Your peace and carry it with us to deliver to others. Help me to deliver Your good news today. Amen.

Love Truth and Peace

"Therefore love truth and peace."
ZECHARIAH 8:19 NIV

"Love truth and peace!" Well, that seems easy enough. "Of course!" we might say to ourselves. It makes total sense to us to tell the truth or to approach the world with love. However, if we're going to love truth today, that might mean there's no room for those little "white lies." You know, those quick things we say without even thinking, like: "You have been on my mind," or "I'll pray for you," or "I'll call you soon." We say a lot of things, and then we don't pray or we don't call.

Since we always want those who are dear to us to feel important, we may not admit that we haven't thought about them lately. In our hearts, we really do mean to pray for people even when we forget. *"I'll call you"* is just a polite version of procrastination. . .at least sometimes. Those little "untruths" sneak into our lives all day long and before we know it, any sense of peace is gone.

What does it mean to love truth? Perhaps it means that you are proud of whatever you do today, that you operate with a heart that is considerate and kind and recognizes the needs of others, even placing those needs above your own. Peace comes when your heart is in the right place and your love is genuine. God has put His truth in your heart, and it is shaped by His grace to keep you coming back for more.

AT THE HEART OF THE TRUTH

Lord, You know my truth even better than I do. Let me live in that truth and honor my friends and family with my words and my intentions. Let me seek real truth and peace today. Amen.

Please Pass the Salt

*"Salt is good for seasoning. But if it loses its flavor, how do you
make it salty again? You must have the qualities of salt
among yourselves and live in peace with each other."*

MARK 9:50 NLT

Salt makes your french fries taste better. It gives sauces and stews a bit more pizzazz.
It's so popular in fact, millions of people have to watch how much salt they actually add
to their foods. What would happen, though, if you added the salt to your favorite dish,
but it remained bland? What if it had no taste at all?

This passage from Mark reminds us that we as Christians are the "salt." We're the
salty spice, the ones who enhance life and flavor it with joy. It's the salt of God's love and
of the Holy Spirit that helps flavor our lives and those of others as well. The right amount
of salt, the kind you carry in your heart and your spirit, helps you bring the best out of
each person you meet.

The best way for others to see how desirable your faith is, is if you're willing to share.
Come on, don't be bland, spice things up and pass the salt!

AT THE HEART OF BEING THE SALT

*Lord, spice me up today, and let me show Your Spirit in ways that flavor the lives of
those around me. Help me truly be the "salt" that adds to the goodness of life. Amen.*

The Wisdom of the Heart

Real wisdom, God's wisdom, begins with a holy life and is characterized by getting along with others. It is gentle and reasonable, overflowing with mercy and blessings, not hot one day and cold the next, not two-faced. You can develop a healthy, robust community that lives right with God and enjoy its results only if you do the hard work of getting along with each other, treating each other with dignity and honor.

JAMES 3:17–18 MSG

We attribute wisdom to people in the world that we perceive as important. We might imagine that those in political office or religious leadership roles would be wise. We might hope that parents and teachers and those who have influence over others would operate with genuine knowledge and generous spirits.

Solomon asked God for wisdom to lead and rule over others. He was considered the wisest man of his day. What is wisdom? We may think the wisest people today are Rhodes Scholars or great scientists or inventors. We often equate wisdom with intellect or with being smart. We strive to be smarter than someone else, so we can stay slightly ahead of them. Does that mean we're wise?

The "wisdom of heaven" appears to be different, though. It is about being considerate and showing mercy or kindness. It's about being peaceful and leading with a heart shaped by love. This kind of wisdom, the kind that brings inner peace, is the one for which we pray,

Today, may your loving heart guide you into true wisdom in all of your relationships.

A HEART OF PEACE

Lord, grant me the wisdom of a loving heart, the kindness to extend to every living soul, and the mercy to realize we all need Your grace each day. Help me to live always in Your peace. Amen.

Please Help Me Wait!

I wait for the LORD, my soul waits, and in His word I do hope.
My soul waits for the Lord more than those who watch for the morning.

PSALM 130:5–6 NKJV

Imagine the lonely watchman waiting through the night for the rising sun to begin the day. Slip into those quiet hours as he's trying to stay awake, plan all that must be done, and prepare for the morning activities. The watchman can hardly wait for the dawn to break, for there's little to make his life interesting in those wee hours of the night. He waits patiently and with anticipation.

Yet, the psalmist stresses that waiting for the Lord requires even more patience than that of the watchman. The psalmist's soul longs for the Lord, living on the Word and passing the time in hope.

Most of us are neither the watchman, nor the psalmist. We don't have the patience to wait, night after night. You may recall that even Jesus couldn't get His disciples to wait with Him through that one lonely night in the garden.

Why do we grow weary of waiting so quickly? We pray for patience, but we want the waiting to be over now. Perhaps it is in the waiting where God can best shape our hearts to be more like His. Today, let us wait in anticipation, hope, and joy.

A HEART OF PATIENCE

Lord, help me to wait in hope with Your Word to feed my soul and Your grace to guide my spirit. Help me to wait and not get ahead of You today. Amen.

The Patient Heart

Patient people have great understanding,
but people with quick tempers show their foolishness.
PROVERBS 14:29 NCV

There's often a fine line between understanding and folly. The old adage that "patience is a virtue" comes to mind here. The reason patience is a virtue is that we recognize we don't seem to have it programmed into us. We like things to happen quickly, because we live in an "on demand" kind of world. Few of us would claim that we're good at being patient or that we truly make the effort to gain understanding before we act. Hence, folly looms everywhere.

Go back and think a moment about that last conversation you had with your teenager, the advice you gave your coworker, or the way you felt about the delay you experienced in this morning's traffic jam. For that matter, go back and consider those moments when you're not able to be patient with yourself. It could be as simple as misplacing your glasses or losing the car keys; it doesn't take much for your patience to wear thin.

Another old saying is "The hurrier I go, the behinder I get!" It's amusing, but it's the reason that folly has so much opportunity in our lives. We resist the waiting and the planning and the things that would help us to move wisely.

May your heart be guided and gently shaped with greater patience in every task you undertake today.

A HEART OF PATIENCE

Lord, rescue me from impatience. Help me to be willing to listen, to seek to understand, and to simply give things time to unfold according to Your will and the plans You have for my life. Amen.

Do Good Today

Live in peace with each other. We ask you, brothers and sisters, to warn those who do not work. Encourage the people who are afraid. Help those who are weak. Be patient with everyone. Be sure that no one pays back wrong for wrong, but always try to do what is good for each other and for all people.

1 THESSALONIANS 5:13–15 NCV

Let's try an experiment. Give yourself one point for every time you would be able to stay calm, and take away one point for every time you would not be very calm in situations like these:

- The car keys weren't put back on the rack and you're in a hurry to get to work.
- You got stopped at a red light for fifteen minutes because of a minor collision.
- Your mother-in-law calls before 7 a.m. on a Saturday morning.
- Your babysitter cancels at the last minute.
- You're having a bad hair day. Is that enough?

Are you ready for sainthood because you're so patient you don't even have to think about it? Bravo!

If not, remember to be patient with yourself and with others. Encourage the hearts of those who are weary, strengthen the spirits of those who are lost, and show genuine kindness to everyone you meet. Give yourself points for every effort you make to have a heart shaped by patience and a willingness to stay calm today. With a little more effort, you'll score big points with God.

A HEART OF PATIENCE

Lord, help me to see clearly those times when I can be a bit more patient and understanding. Help me to encourage each person I meet and to be willing to do the good I can do wherever I am. Amen.

Do You Really Know What Time It Is?

Do not forget this one thing, dear friends: With the Lord a day is like a thousand years, and a thousand years are like a day. The Lord is not slow in keeping his promise, as some understand slowness. Instead he is patient with you.

2 PETER 3:8–9 NIV

Did you ever wait in a long line for something you really wanted? Maybe you were anxious to get special theater tickets, or you were excited to ride your favorite roller coaster at the amusement park. Or perhaps you found yourself sitting in traffic that wouldn't budge and you thought you could have walked home faster.

We're all driven by the clock. We're in a hurry to get up, get to work, get the job done, get home, feed the kids, get to the store, get to Bible study, or watch our favorite TV show and then get to bed and start all over again. Whatever it is that we have to do or wherever it is we have to be, we're in a hurry to get there.

Today God seems to be saying, "Don't worry and don't hurry." If we believe that God is in the details of our lives, then we can afford to be a little more patient with others and with ourselves. As you stand in the endless lines of life, allow for His perfect timing, pray for inner peace, and be gracious. It will do your heart good.

THE HEART OF TIME

Lord, remind me that my time is always Yours. Let me move in the rhythm of Your divine timing for all that You would have me accomplish today. Amen.

Matters of the Heart

And be kind to one another, tenderhearted,
forgiving one another, even as God in Christ forgave you.
EPHESIANS 4:32 NKJV

The writer of Ephesians suggests that kindness and compassion may go hand in hand with forgiveness. Kindness matters. Compassion helps. Forgiveness heals.

How different would our lives be if people practiced random acts of compassion, crazy moments of forgiveness, and loving handfuls of kindness!

Compassion is one of those words that gets to the heart of the matter quickly. It is only needed when a situation is out of control. . .too much sorrow, too little money, too much need. . .it goes on and on. We prefer to share our compassionate hearts more than we want to be the recipients of other people's compassion. Yet life happens to us all, and at one time or another we each need the kindness, compassion, and forgiveness of someone else.

Today, make it your primary goal to have a soft heart, one that is kinder and more compassionate to everyone you meet. God is working with each of us, to give us more tender hearts.

A HEART OF KINDNESS

Lord, let me give from a heart of compassion, act with a desire toward kindness, and extend the hand of forgiveness to those I meet today. . .even so to me, the one I see in the mirror. Amen.

Be Kind to Your Soul

Your own soul is nourished when you are kind.

PROVERBS 11:17 TLB

We have all been blessed with defined talents and personality styles. We can be politicians, actors, mothers, or role models for others, but there is still more to us than any career path we might take or role we might play.

God places a special premium on our efforts to be kind. The feedback for your effort lies in your own soul, for it feels nourished and your heart feels light. You are deeply aware of God's presence and you are able to share His light with confident joy.

How sad it is when we think that in order to succeed in the world, we have to be aggressive in our dealings with others, perhaps even abusive or hateful. What greater success could we have than being considered both kind and compassionate? Your soul delights in your kindness and your heart does a happy dance as well.

May your heart be blessed by the kind deeds you do at every opportunity.

HEART-SHAPED KINDNESS

Lord, fill my soul with joy today as I share my heart and mind with others according to Your grace and mercy. Let kindness be the rule and not the exception in all I do. Amen.

Who's My Neighbor?

"Then the King will say to those on his right, 'Enter, you who are blessed by my Father! Take what's coming to you in this kingdom. It's been ready for you since the world's foundation. And here's why: I was hungry and you fed me, I was thirsty and you gave me a drink, I was homeless and you gave me a room, I was shivering and you gave me clothes, I was sick and you stopped to visit, I was in prison and you came to me.' "

MATTHEW 25:35–36 MSG

Doing good deeds and taking care of others is not just a nice idea, it's one of the key ways God sees your heart. He is pleased when you help in whatever ways you can to care for your community and your family. God asks you to love your neighbor as yourself. He asks you to care for others in the same way Jesus cares about you.

The world is shrinking. Your neighbors are no longer simply living on your same street or your same town. They live across the country, across the continent, and around the world. You have endless opportunities to show kindness and to give encouragement and love. God blesses those acts, the big ones and the small ones, and fills your heart with joy in the things you do to share His love with others.

Today, may you realize that every act of kindness, every word of encouragement, and every good deed you do makes the heart of your Father burst with joy.

A KIND HEART ——————————————————————

Lord, let me offer a kind heart and a compassionate word to any who might need me to strengthen and nourish their souls today. Amen.

When Kindness Meets Love

We love because God loved us first. But if we say we love God and don't love each other, we are liars. . . . The commandment that God has given us is: "Love God and love each other!"

1 JOHN 4:19–21 CEV

When God's Spirit works in our hearts, it blows the wind of kindness through our bodies and moves us into action. It fills us with a desire to be more loving and to literally become a source of inspiration and renewal for each other.

It demands that we show Jesus to everyone. It asks us to open our hands, lift up our hearts, and love like we may not have ever done before. We are brothers and sisters of His blood, and our heritage will take us through eternity. Let's love as He loved us.

Think of all the ways you love others. How can you create even more fulfilling and more loving relationships with everyone you know? It is always a blessing to your soul to share your love in new ways and refresh the spirit of those who are so weary around you. God wants you to embrace each person in your life with His love and with amazing acts of kindness.

A HEART OF LOVE

Lord, when I think of every person as being part of Your family, it helps me to see each one more clearly, through the eyes of my heart. Thank You for Your amazing love for me. Amen.

A Heart for Sharing

Make sure you don't take things for granted and go slack in working for the common good; share what you have with others. God takes particular pleasure in acts of worship—a different kind of "sacrifice"—that take place in kitchen and workplace and on the streets.

HEBREWS 13:16 MSG

Our own lives are enriched by the things we do to help everyone around us thrive. When we offer encouragement or the hand of fellowship, we make a difference. When we bless others by our willingness to talk, share our hearts, or fill a basic need of survival, God is pleased. It shows Him that we are responding to His Spirit in positive ways and that we take His commands seriously.

In the race between good and evil most people have the intention of being good and of being generous to others. If we open our hearts to that notion, God will continue to instruct us and give us guidance about how we can do good deeds in a variety of ways. He will lighten our hearts and give us joy. He will bless our efforts and make us glad.

May God help you have a heart for others in some very new ways today. Whether you bake brownies for the new neighbors, encourage a coworker, or give a generous tip to the waiter at lunch, God will see your work. . .and your heart!

HEART-SHAPED GOODNESS

Lord, let me honor You by sharing the goodness of my heart and my actions with others. Help me to recognize those who need me in some special way today. Amen.

Putting on the Glow

Light shines on those who do right; joy belongs to those who are honest.
PSALM 97:11 NCV

Most of us like things to be shiny and clean. We wash an apple and dry it and make it shine before we eat it. We take a dust cloth and make the tabletop glow once again. We put on our best smile when we're going to meet a friend. We like to shine.

Imagine that you have an assignment today to simply shine your light for the Lord wherever you go. You go to work and everyone notices how brilliant you seem to be today. You go to the grocery store and help a lady get a box from the shelf or you tell the cashier as you're leaving what a great job she is doing. You simply bring out the best in others wherever you are.

The reason God wants your light to shine is because the world has a lot of dark and dingy corners, places where few people even know a light exists. He wants you to share your heart and your light so that others can glow right along with you.

The best part of this is that your willingness to shine doesn't depend on the weather, your mood, or on the circumstances you might be in. It just depends on the strength of your relationship with God so that He can shine through you any time at all.

Shine on today!

A HEART THAT SHINES

Lord, help me to be mindful of Your presence in all I do today so that I can help someone else see Your light. Amen.

What Good Can You Do?

Serve wholeheartedly, as if you were serving the Lord, not people,
because you know that the Lord will reward each one for whatever good they do.
EPHESIANS 6:7–8 NIV

What if you were walking along the street one day and you saw a sign that said, "$5000 reward for anyone caught in the act of doing good?" Would you pay special attention to doing good deeds for the rest of the day? Would you keep looking over your shoulder for the reward police to come along and give you the money? Would you try to outdo others in your acts of goodness?

Of course, it would be interesting to see how we would respond to such a sign, but then God has already posted that sign for us. He said he would give the gift of eternal life (a rather awesome reward) for all those caught in the act of believing in His Son.

You show you believe in Him by serving others wholeheartedly. When you serve others, you are serving Him. You have a chance every day to do His good deeds. Your reward is absolutely guaranteed.

A HEART FOR DOING GOOD

Lord, help me to do good things for others without even thinking about it. Make it such a natural part of me to be an extension of You, that it's reward enough to have had the privilege to do it. Amen.

The Perfect Gift

Whatever is good and perfect is a gift coming down to us from God our Father, who created all the lights in the heavens. He never changes or casts a shifting shadow.

JAMES 1:17 NLT

Advertising influences your choices every day. When styles change, you're bombarded with messages that tell you to get with it, be cool, be in the now. Your once fine and dandy wardrobe becomes too drab and you need new clothes. You're behind the times just because a magazine said so. You may even become discouraged that you simply can't keep up with the trends. You start to wonder how everyone else does it.

The fact is that everyone else copes with styles and trends the same way you do. Change is a constant. If you lived through shag haircuts, bell-bottoms, or torn jeans as a fashion statement, you may agree that change is definitely a good thing. There's a gift in change, and there's a gift in recognizing the good things in what you have right now.

The One who is the same yesterday, today, and tomorrow keeps the good in our lives a constant. The gift of His Son will never go out of style.

A HEART SHAPED BY CHANGE

Lord, I may not always be up with the latest styles and trends or be in with those in the "know." Please be with me as I put on Your helmet of salvation. It may be somewhat outdated, but I know it will protect my heart and mind. Amen.

I Don't Have a Thing to Wear!

Therefore, as God's chosen people, holy and dearly loved, clothe yourselves with compassion, kindness, humility, gentleness and patience.

COLOSSIANS 3:12 NIV

Some days, looking into my closet really is a humbling experience. I see the sizes I want to be, the ones I used to be, the ones I am, and God forbid, the ones I hope not to be again. I select an outfit based more on what offends my pride the least, than for what I'm really doing or where I'm going at the moment. The struggle always leaves me feeling that I don't have a thing to wear. Looking at the closet so stuffed I can hardly add another hanger, reminds me that that certainly is not true.

So, I look again and determine that I must have something that will be okay, something that might even be good for the events of the day. I pick an outfit, and when I add the right accessory, I feel a bit better and go on about my business.

Today, make it your goal to stop judging yourself and choose your daily wardrobe as a beloved child of God. You can complement an outfit with a vivid hue of compassion, a fragrance of kindness, or the genuine heart-shaped style of goodwill. Then, each time you pass a mirror, you'll see the reflection of those holy accessories and see how amazing you really are. God has already clothed you in the gifts of His love. Sometimes, it's even okay to wear your heart on your sleeve.

HEART-SHAPED CHOICES

Lord, help me to dress well today. Let me put on gentleness in the way I treat others, add a belt of compassion in the things I say and do, and finish off my look with the smile of Your grace to share wherever I go. Amen.

You Are So Kind!

Love suffers long and is kind; love does not envy; love does not parade itself, is not puffed up; does not behave rudely, does not seek its own, is not provoked, thinks no evil; does not rejoice in iniquity, but rejoices in the truth; bears all things, believes all things, hopes all things, endures all things.

1 CORINTHIANS 13:4–7 NKJV

You are so kind. You offer encouragement to those around you. You smile at complete strangers to remind them that they've been noticed and that life is good. You lend a hand whenever duty calls, and you volunteer for the church social without batting an eye. Your kindness causes your spirit to rejoice. It causes your heart to be glad. Others notice you in positive ways.

Doing all those kind things gives you a glimpse of the way your heart is shaped by God. You can see how He causes you to think about others first and imagine what He is trying to accomplish in their lives. You see His light glow as a little ember in each person you encounter.

You know the kindness God holds toward you and all of His creation. Breathe it in. Share it. Be kind and shine the light of God's love to those in need. You'll find them waiting for you every place you go. You'll find that you have more spring in your step and a song in your heart when you let kindness lead the way.

HEART-SHAPED KINDNESS

Lord, when I forget to reach out, or when I am too busy to lend a hand; when I no longer have a moment to shine Your light, then be patient with me. Turn me again in the direction of Your love. Amen.

It's Time to Party

For seven days celebrate the festival to the LORD your God at the place the LORD will choose. For the LORD your God will bless you in all your harvest and in all the work of your hands, and your joy will be complete.

DEUTERONOMY 16:15 NIV

Believe it or not, sometimes we forget to party. We forget to stop and give thanks for all that we've accomplished with God's generous help and just celebrate with those who are near and dear to us. God commanded the Israelites to take a break and let God share in the good things they had done. What an idea!

God is the Creator of just plain fun, just as much as He is the Creator of all the other aspects of our humanity. Our days are quickly passing. We're moving at an incredible pace, doing, doing, and still doing!

Listen for God's voice today and see if He isn't nudging you, in fact, urging you to stop and take some time apart and discover the joy in your good work. See if He doesn't want you to simply celebrate all the good things He's already brought into your life. Maybe today is the day you pop into the local bakery, grab a sweet delight, and invite God to share it with you.

Are you listening? Are you having fun yet?

AT THE HEART OF FUN

Lord, help me to remember that You meant for us to live in joy, not in a rat race that never seems to have a finish line. Help me to look for the right moments to just live it up. . .that is, live in an upbeat, joyful way for all that You've done for me. Amen.

Giving and Lending

But love your enemies, do good, and lend, hoping for nothing in return;
and your reward will be great, and you will be sons of the Most
High. For He is kind to the unthankful and evil.

LUKE 6:35 NKJV

Did you ever stop to think about how kind God really is? On our worst days, when we've been selfish, inconsiderate, or grumpy to everyone we know, He is still kind to us. He doesn't demand that we let go of our frustrations or our anger or our bad hair days and just pretend they aren't happening. He hears us complain, and patiently waits in kindness for us to become more of the light He meant for us to be.

According to this sixth chapter of Luke, He's even kind to the ungrateful children and the wicked ones too. Some part of me wants to politely slip by that verse in case there's any chance that I've been one of those ungrateful children. The good news is that God is giving and not lending. . . . He's not waiting for us to pay back before He gives more. He just keeps on giving. Wouldn't it be something if we could be like that?

Today, imagine that you have no interest in getting anything from anyone. You don't need their praise, their help, or their money. All you need is an opportunity to be a giver, a giver with an amazing heart of love. May you give, and not even notice all you give, today.

HEART-SHAPED GIVING

Lord, help me to be more giving and less of a lender. Help me to give freely
without the need or thought of getting something back. Let me give
unconditionally, fully, and clearly to those in need. Amen.

Guided Forever

For this God is our God for ever and ever; he will be our guide even to the end.
PSALM 48:14 NIV

When you travel to an unfamiliar place and don't know the landscape or the best hotels and restaurants, you are apt to engage a tour guide or at least get a book or an app on the area to give you some direction so that you don't miss the best things about your adventure. It's more comfortable to know where you're going and what you can expect.

Psalm 48 is a reminder that you have the same opportunity for your travels across our planet. You have a God who has provided a Good Book to help you along the way. It's His personal GPS. He's ready to join you on the tour at any point you ask. He's prepared to show you new landscapes, and He'll stay with you until the whole trip is done.

When you use a guidebook, you may be surprised by the lack of details about an incredible, out-of-the-way place you discovered on your own. Your guidebook only shows endless descriptions about tourist favorites that aren't as fulfilling to your heart and soul. God's guidebook takes you past the usual places and brings you insights into the mysteries of life and love. He leads you to incredible places you never knew existed. You just have to have your heart focused on the direction you want to go and let Him know you're ready for the trip. He'll make sure you don't miss one beautiful site you were meant to see.

A HEART FOR DISCOVERY

Lord, help me travel today in the direction You would have me go, whether it's across town or out of the country. Please go before me and prepare my heart for the journey. Amen.

Just as You Believe

Then Jesus said to the Roman officer, "Go on home. What you have believed has happened." And the boy was healed that same hour!

MATTHEW 8:13 TLB

We're pretty good at being faithful sometimes. We read the Word, we pray, and we put our belief system into practice. We even feel we're doing a good job, at least when life is going along smoothly and most of our prayers are being answered. We're generous and content in those circumstances and we give God the glory.

However, when trials come or the limits of our faith are tested, our strength wavers. We're not as sure God is listening or even what it means to be faithful. . .full of faith. Our hearts need more encouragement. Our minds need comfort and more instruction.

According to the Bible story, the centurion reached Jesus after offering his own prayers and making an effort on behalf of his servant. When his own efforts failed, he went straight to the Source. He didn't give room for the idea that Jesus might not be able to help. He just believed that Jesus could save his servant. He just believed it!

Believe it! Your life can change too. . .with God's help. You do not have to rely on your own strength. Put all you are and all you want to be in God's hand today.

HEART-SHAPED BELIEF

Lord, it is not always easy to keep believing when I can't see anything changing or see any signs that You're near when I'm reaching out to You. Please help me to keep believing and to be trusting. Help me to be faithful today. Amen.

According to Your Faith

*When he had gone indoors, the blind men came to him, and he asked them,
"Do you believe that I am able to do this?" "Yes, Lord," they replied.
Then he touched their eyes and said, "According to your faith let it
be done to you"; and their sight was restored.*

MATTHEW 9:28–30 NIV

Most of us are not blind in the literal sense of the word. We can fumble for our glasses and get the right perspective of the world pretty quickly. We can get through the day without running into walls. . .or do we?

If Jesus could stand in front of you and answer a desire of your heart "according to your faith," would it happen? Would you overcome your own spiritual blindness enough to see His amazing grace for you?

Faithfulness requires us to believe that Jesus can restore our misty thoughts, our dark sides, and our uncertainties. He can shape our hearts to see Him more clearly and to see others with greater understanding and love. May Jesus touch some area of blindness in your life and shed His light on your darkness so that you may see His hand at work in your daily life. May His will be done "according to your faith."

A HEART-SHAPED FAITH

Lord, You know that my faithfulness wavers. No matter how hard I try, I go through spells when I'm not seeing things very clearly. Shape my heart today to be faithful and to be willing to overcome my own blind spots. Amen.

In Search of the Mustard Seed

"Because you're not yet taking God seriously," said Jesus. "The simple truth is that if you had a mere kernel of faith, a poppy seed, say, you would tell this mountain, 'Move!' and it would move. There is nothing you wouldn't be able to tackle."

MATTHEW 17:20–21 MSG

The fact that various mountain ranges around the world don't seem to be packing up their flora and fauna and moving to higher ground begs a few questions about our faith. If just a tiny, teeny seedling of faith is all that we need to launch such a marvel of nature, our seeds must not be very well rooted. If we're thinking we have seed faith the size of pumpkin seeds, or maybe even a good-sized squash seed, something is wrong.

Somehow we have to move from the ground of impossible faith, to the heights of the always possible faith. Possible faith allows us to move the mountains of doubt, despair, and uncertainty that arise in our lives. Possible faith says we can hike that "fourteener," as some of those great Colorado mountains are called, and keep on going. Possible faith says that we trust God to help us become more than we could ever be alone.

May your heart-shaped faith keep you moving in the direction of all things possible today! Give your heart and your faith a chance to grow in God's grace and mercy.

A HEART FOR THE POSSIBLE

Lord, I know I've created more mountains than I've moved. I've fallen down more mountains than I've scaled. Help me today to have possible faith and overcome any obstacles in my path. Amen.

Childlike Faithfulness

"I tell you the truth, anyone who doesn't receive the kingdom of God like a little child will never enter it."

MARK 10:15 NLT

Sometimes we're a bit too "adult." We lose our sense of amusement at the little challenges life brings our way. We forget that we have lots of options when it comes to solving a problem. In short, we take all our toys and go home when we don't think others are playing quite fairly.

Corporations breed tired adults. . .adults who are overworked, under-validated, and seldom rewarded. Those same adults then go home and feel overwhelmed by too much responsibility where no one is saying, "thank you." When adults need time to play, we call it "taking a vacation." We need a vacation from chaos, tumult, and uproar. We need a change of heart.

Sometimes your faith-walk challenges you in the same way. Your adult side struggles to make sense of all the theology put in front of you, and your child side wants to get out and just run free to believe in the simple truths of Jesus' love. Let your kingdom be ruled by your childlike faith, by your more innocent heart, and it will endure forever. You'll grow up in Jesus' love, and it will sustain you to be a fulfilled and happy adult.

A HEART-SHAPED, CHILDLIKE FAITH

Lord, I've lost my innocence. I've traded it all for knowledge and rightness (oh, not righteousness), and humorless living. Help me to find You, Jesus, the way I did so long ago when I first gave You my heart. Amen.

Child of God

And the Spirit himself joins with our spirits to say we are God's children.
ROMANS 8:16 NCV

When babies are born, the adoring mommies, daddies, and glowing grandmas have great fun discussing the tiny infant's beautiful features. He has Mommy's fingers, Daddy's chin, or Grandma's reddish hair. She's clearly brilliant and has the smile of a saint. That family resemblance is the beginning of establishing the place where this child belongs, and the family is happy to adopt such sweet innocence and joy.

When you were born into God's family, you started taking on a resemblance to your spiritual family. Perhaps angels said, "She has her Father's eyes, her Creator's gift for joy, or her Savior's gift of grace. She has a heart for God." It was another scene where love was happening at first sight.

God never makes you wonder who your Father is, for He testifies within you, establishing Himself in your spirit, to let you know that you are His. He wants very much for you to have your Father's heart and your Father's love. He wants you to be a spitting image of Him.

May your Father's heart guide you in all you do today so that others may see Him reflected in your face.

YOUR FATHER'S HEART

Lord, thanks for reminding me that I am Your child and that You have already claimed me in Your love. Help me to show You to those I meet who may need a fresh glimpse of Your generous love within their spirits today. Amen.

An "F" Might Be Better Than An "A"

*God's Spirit and God's power did it, which made it clear that your
life of faith is a response to God's power, not to some fancy
mental or emotional footwork by me or anyone else.*

1 CORINTHIANS 2:4–5 MSG

It's a good thing our faith does not depend on how smart we are. It doesn't ask us to be president of the women's circle, vice president of General Motors, or even the best singer in the choir at church. Our faith doesn't seem to depend on anything our brains can think about.

Does the faith of a great preacher like Billy Graham mean more to God than the faith of a woman with two children at home and only a little Bible training? Is there a difference in the way God receives a public expression of faith over a private one? How big is your faith?

If it feels to you like you need to be an A student to get into the program, it's time to look again. God takes on a lot of students who have managed to get an F now and then. The good news is that He takes that F from failure to faith and demonstrates not only His power to change lives, but His steadfast love as well. He helps you to understand that your faith is not a matter of enormous brain activity, but of infinite heart activity. Be persuaded by His love, and seek opportunities today to grow in your knowledge and love for Him and your willingness to share His love with others.

A HEART SHAPED BY FAITH

Lord, sometimes I get so caught up in trying to better myself and my circumstances that I almost don't have time for You. I may be getting As in life, but I'm getting Fs in faith. Shape my heart so that I can turn that around and pay more attention to You. Amen.

Wallflower Faith

For God has not given us a spirit of timidity, but of power and love and discipline.
2 TIMOTHY 1:7 NASB

Remember those dances in high school, or maybe even junior high that you attended with your friends? One by one, they got up on the dance floor, but for some reason, you hung back in the shadows. For you, nothing was more important than getting another cup of punch. You were always waiting in the wings, wishing your shyness away. If this wasn't you, then you probably knew someone like this who just didn't dare to get into the dance.

Things are different now, not just because you're older, but because God has invited you to the dance. No matter what music is playing, He knows you can follow Him because He's already adorned you with His love. He knows you're a powerful dancer, and He doesn't want you waiting in the wings any longer. He wants you to be His partner for a lifetime, connected in every move you make, heart to heart.

Get out there then and strut your stuff for Him today. After all, He gave you great moves for a reason.

A HEART SHAPED BY SELF-CONTROL

Lord, let me rise and shine today according to Your grace and mercy. Let me take my wallflower faith and turn it into bouquets of blessing. Amen.

Playing the Part

*People who think they are religious but say things they should not say are just
fooling themselves. Their "religion" is worth nothing. Religion that God accepts as
pure and without fault is this: caring for orphans or widows who need help,
and keeping yourself free from the world's evil influence.*

JAMES 1:26–27 NCV

My sister used to create characters through a one-woman show. She played the roles of certain personality types of women. She memorized stories and poems and taking on their persona, shared their lives with the audience.

One of her stories depicted a woman and her husband, standing at St. Peter's door trying to get in. The woman looks perfect in her Sunday clothes, clutching her little purse and wearing her hat just so, as she rambles on about all she did at the church and how worthless her husband was in all of that. She picks at him, while reminding St. Peter what a wonderfully religious woman she has been and that *surely* she should get into heaven. Her husband is quietly standing by, not saying a word in his own defense and awaiting his fate.

After listening to the woman complain about everyone else, her scathing comments about her husband, and her insistence on her own goodness, St. Peter makes his decision. He concludes that the husband deserves a break and sends him on alone through the pearly gates. The woman is totally stunned because she had not even considered that she never engaged her heart in the things she did in life.

Most of us aren't quite in league with this woman, but this comment from the book of James might remind us that the biggest challenge we have sometimes is simply to keep quiet. When we're quiet, we can reflect on the truth of who we are and who we want to be, and God who searches the heart will move us forward.

AT THE HEART OF SELF-CONTROL

Lord, please help me to remember that every word out of my mouth either helps and encourages someone else, or hurts and diminishes someone's spirit. Challenge me to use my words wisely today. Amen.

Divine Discipline

No discipline seems pleasant at the time, but painful. Later on, however, it produces a harvest of righteousness and peace for those who have been trained by it.
HEBREWS 12:11 NIV

We aren't exactly ready to say "thank you" when someone tells us where we've fallen short, or what we need to do to improve our skills. In our work environment, we tolerate job reviews as necessary evils that somehow determine whether we'll get a raise in the coming year.

Discipline of any sort is not easy. During Lent, you may try not to eat chocolate, or at the New Year you may make a commitment to exercise or to be more consistent about your prayer life. As children of God, we sometimes need reminders of His hopes and expectations for us. Those reminders can feel like discipline. If we know in our hearts that we deserve that discipline, it doesn't feel good.

Divine discipline offers us a new perspective that can renew our hearts and minds. We may even see the value of the trial we just passed through. Divine discipline is given with the intention of helping to reshape us and remold us to become more of what God wants us to be. If we see it in that light, it can do our hearts good.

Today, discipline yourself in ways that serve to strengthen your heart and mind.

A HEART SHAPED BY DISCIPLINE

Lord, ever since I was a child I've resisted anything that makes me feel I'm being chastised, especially if I don't understand what I did wrong. Help me now as an adult, to receive discipline in a more positive light, as a way to become a better person in Your eyes. Amen.

Hoping and Praying

Be joyful because you have hope. Be patient when
trouble comes, and pray at all times.

ROMANS 12:12 NCV

Trouble is a very interesting teacher. We learn a lot about ourselves when we face adversity. We discover new fears, unlimited ways to worry, and renewed self-doubt. We're good at dealing with trouble in every negative way possible.

This short verse from Romans wants us to take another view. What if we faced trouble with gladness? What if we renewed our efforts to pray with greater fervor because we believed so well in the hope that springs forth from our faith?

Your friends might look at you strangely, might even think you need some quick counseling if you smile through adversity. Yet could you? If you really believed in the hope that is yours as a child of God, could you?

This may be your day to move patiently through adversity and let hope radiate its light into your spirit. God will see you through and strengthen you in the process.

A HEART SHAPED BY HOPE

Lord, I know I'm at my worst when I'm facing a difficult situation. I try too hard to be in control and find all the right solutions, and I work so hard that I forget to even pray. Help me, Lord, to find my hope in You today. Amen.

What Is World Peace?

I give you peace, the kind of peace that only I can give. It isn't like the peace that this world can give. So don't be worried or afraid.

JOHN 14:27 CEV

If you listen to CNN or other news programs with any regularity, it doesn't take long to recognize that we're a long way from world peace. It's interesting to even try to imagine world peace. What would that look like and how would it be achieved?

It's a pretty good bet that even if the world could give you a sense of peace, it would disappear again with the next news broadcast.

So what kind of peace does Jesus give? It's the kind that passes all understanding, the kind that keeps you calm and content no matter what is playing out on the world stage. How can you tell if you have that kind of peace?

If you're looking for peace with your mind, your intellect, or anything but your spirit and your heart, you may not find it. Peace comes from knowing who you are, where you're headed, and from knowing the One who walks beside you and guides your steps every day.

The peace the world gives may not even be possible. Thankfully you have the peace that takes away fear and worry, the kind that allows your heart to be shaped by Jesus.

A HEART OF PEACE

Lord, I get caught up in the troubles of the world and feel totally unable to control anything beyond the borders of my own home. Help me to find peace through Your Spirit each day. Amen.

Let Your Light Shine

If you extend your soul to the hungry and satisfy the afflicted soul, then your light
shall dawn in the darkness, and your darkness shall be as the noonday.

ISAIAH 58:10 NKJV

Millions of Good Samaritans live around the world. It's easy to think of people like Mother Teresa or Oprah Winfrey as women who have gone beyond the call of duty to let their light shine. These women, along with many others, feed the hungry, clothe the poor, or help in any way they can. Sometimes, with examples like that, we can get complacent and think there are lots of institutions, food banks, caregivers, and missionaries taking care of the hungry and giving aid to those in trouble. We can begin to imagine no one really needs what little we could do, that our contribution would be insignificant.

That's unlikely! The hungry and the ones in trouble in the world well outnumber the caregivers. Each city and village, in the state you live in or around the world, has people desperately in need. Each of us can be the light. Reach out in the darkness and help a neighbor to stand on his own.

You don't have to be a celebrity to make a difference. You just have to touch one life beyond your own. You just have to offer your hand to one person at a time, heart to heart, anywhere you are. Shine on!

A HEART SHAPED BY LIGHT

Lord, help me remember that each day there's someone right near me who is hungrier than I am, in deeper trouble than I am, and if I just look into the warehouse of my abundance, I can surely shine Your light. Amen.

What Is This Thing Called Love?

*"Let me give you a new command: Love one another. In the same way I loved you,
you love one another. This is how everyone will recognize that you are my
disciples—when they see the love you have for each other."*

JOHN 13:34–35 MSG

If you celebrate Valentine's Day, you may be looking for ways to send a little more love to those around you to remind them how special they are. It's a nice tradition, and I imagine if this holiday had existed in Jesus' time His friends would have sent Him encouraging thoughts and good wishes or special thanks for the things He had done.

God gave you a physical heart to help your body function well and to sustain the gift of life. He also gave you an emotional heart to help you see the world with love. He wants you to see every person around you with the eyes of compassion, mercy, and grace.

The thing is that love is the key to everything we do. It is the very reason Jesus came to earth. He is the embodiment of our understanding of the phrase "God is love." Wouldn't it be wonderful if we could show that kind of love to each person we meet today and every day? Spread a little love right where you are. You can be someone's valentine every day of the year.

HEART-SHAPED LOVE

Lord, You were the gift of love to Your followers. Now You have millions more who look to You to lead the way and guide our efforts toward love. Help us be Your examples of love and treat everyone as a special valentine, no matter what day of the year it is. Amen.

The World Needs More Heroes

And let us consider how we may spur one another on toward love and good deeds.
HEBREWS 10:24 NIV

Nothing stimulates and motivates us more than seeing the underdog win, or applauding as Spiderman tosses out his web and comes to the rescue of some hapless victim. It's important for all of us to create heroes because we need those we can emulate and those who can rescue us when we can't rescue ourselves.

Jesus was a hero to many people in His day. He is still our hero today. He reached out with kindness, healed those in great need, and He loved the underdog. He motivated people to want to do better and be better and to want to give more of themselves.

In our own culture, we gave much deserved recognition to the New York City police officers who worked heroically to rescue the living from the shocking attack on the World Trade Center towers in 2001. Those heroes served as a beacon to the kind of light God wants any of us to be in the world when it comes to helping others. He wants us to go into any situation, heart-first, armed with His power and strength to do all the good we can.

You can be a hero today. You can share the lifeline you draw upon in Jesus and help restore someone to a sense of hope and grace. Come on, there may even be a cape in it for you.

HEART-SHAPED MOTIVATION

Lord, motivate me to lead. Help me to reach out, or sit quietly by, dig deeper, or whatever is needed to help someone in trouble. Help my work be shaped by a hero's heart today. Amen.

Somebody Has to Lead

What I say is true: Anyone wanting to become an overseer desires a good work.

1 TIMOTHY 3:1 NCV

The call to leadership, whether you're male or female, is not one to take lightly. Whether your role is religious or political, or you're a teacher or the head of your household, your leadership is important to the success of those around you. Being in authority and being a leader are not necessarily the same things, however. Some people come into a power position but still do not lead for the benefit of their group. Presidents may have great authority, but they are not all great leaders.

Leaders look out for those in their care. A great leader is often a great servant, and a leader with a great heart shepherds his flock. As believers, we have the authority of Jesus who leads us only with His love. He calls us to draw near to Him so that we can better understand the wisdom of the Spirit and the generosity that comes with a loving heart.

May we be called to the leadership of love wherever we are, so that our hearts are prepared and shaped to serve. You're already a leader somewhere in your own circle of influence. May your heart lead you to greater levels of kindness and generosity in all you do.

A HEART FOR LEADERSHIP

Lord, I don't know how much I'm longing to lead those around me, but I know that as a parent, a friend, a sibling, and as a coworker, I am often placed in that role. Help me to lead with Your love. Amen.

Follow the Light

Your word is a lamp for my feet, a light on my path.
PSALM 119:105 NIV

We're not very comfortable with darkness. If you've ever been walking alone on a dark street, or come into the house when the day is spent and fumbled for the light switch, you know that you feel profoundly better when the light comes on.

As a child, I lived on a country road that we sometimes found ourselves walking along at night after being at choir practice at church or at the neighbor's house. It was a dirt road and the cemetery was just a short distance from it. I can remember praying for God to light my way home more than once. It's funny because it always seemed like the moon got ever so much brighter and I would reach our house at the top of the hill so much faster. It always seemed like God heard my prayer to keep me safe in the dark.

The good news is that God always keeps the light on for us because He wants us to be sure of where we're going. He keeps us safely on the path. Just keep in mind that wherever you go, God always has His light shining for you.

A HEART-SHAPED LIGHT

Lord, help me to walk in Your light today, being sure of every step and breathing in the comfort that comes from knowing You're just ahead of me. Amen.

Save the Planet

"I will also make you a light for the Gentiles,
that my salvation may reach to the ends of the earth."
ISAIAH 49:6 NIV

We love those days when we're just "on" and we can almost feel our light shining, people are receptive to us, everyone is our friend, and somehow we can do no wrong. Then we wake up. . .okay, it's an old joke, but the point is that we give a lot of lip service to letting our light shine or being a light to others. Yet do we have a worldview so that we're really poised to go out and save the planet, or at least our little corner of it?

If you're not hiding your light under a bushel, but letting it shine over all those around you, then you have the right idea. You become a light to your family, your church, your community, your state, and in some way, to the world. Now the interesting aspect of the verse from Isaiah is that it says "I."

God tells Isaiah that He will make him a light to the nations so that the world can be saved. Seems like a small detail, but it is an important one. Just as the moon has no light of its own, but merely reflects the light of the sun, so you have no light of your own. You merely reflect the light of the Son. He makes you shine! He will help you act in the ways that bring His light to others. He will shape your thoughts, your words, and your deeds.

You're His moonbeam!

A HEART SHAPED BY LIGHT

Lord, help me to reflect Your light in all that I do today. Give me a heart that reflects You—always. Amen.

....

....

....

....

....

....

....

....

A New Necktie

Don't ever forget kindness and truth. Wear them like a necklace.
Write them on your heart as if on a tablet. Then you will be
respected and will please both God and people.

PROVERBS 3:3–4 NCV

When you get a new scarf, or perhaps a necktie, you might enjoy the fact that it is very colorful or a sharp accent to the outfit you're wearing. Perhaps this added piece even gives you an air of sophistication, so that other people consider you well-dressed or simply good-looking. A scarf or a necktie is a rather prominent piece that rests just under your chin and crosses over your heart. It may even accentuate your smile and the light in your eyes.

This proverb reminds us, though, of something more significant to wear around our necks. . .faithful love and constancy. It suggests that if you keep your faithful love tightly wrapped around your neck, you'll be so aware of it that nothing will get in the way of the things your heart sees. You will continually think about others because you will literally have each person wrapped around your neck.

Whether you want faithful love with your partner, or faithful love with your Savior, the more you keep close to your loved one, the better off you are. If a necktie, a scarf, or something else helps you to keep closely tied to the people around you, reminding you that God wants you to love them and bless their lives, then go out today adorned in every way. Blessed be the tie that binds.

A HEART SHAPED BY LOVE

Lord, help me to be faithful in all that I do today, in the love I share, the love I receive, and the love I give to You. Amen.

Marvelous Meditation

I meditate on your precepts and consider your ways.
PSALM 119:15 NIV

I've been a prayer person my whole life, but in recent years I've gained an appreciation for meditation as an addition to my prayer life. The beauty of meditation is that it allows me to focus on one major issue, joy, concern, or request, and oftentimes new insights come into view. For example, in one of my recent meditations, I was asking Jesus how I could be a better light for Him. During the meditation, I found myself following Jesus up a mountain path, and I asked Him again, "How do I shine my light?"

At that point, He turned toward me, holding what looked like a virtual ball of light and He tossed it at me. I caught it in my now glowing, shaky hands and He said, "Just *BE* the light."

The insight I received from that meditation was that I didn't need to keep asking how to shine my light, I simply had to allow His light to shine through me and *BE* the light. I've been working on that ever since.

If you're interested in shining your light for God, then step in front of the mirror and see the person God created with great love. Then send that person out with a joyful heart to be all that God created you to be.

SHAPED BY THE LIGHT

Lord, thank You for being the light for each of us and especially for me. Help me to share that amazing light and shine for those around me today. Amen.

Mindfulness

*You will keep him in perfect peace, whose mind is
stayed on You, because he trusts in You.*

ISAIAH 26:3 NKJV

Do you ever think about that old cliché about "mind over matter" or "if you don't mind, it doesn't matter"? One thing I do know is that what's on my mind, matters. How I am processing things, whether I'm going slightly off the deep end, doing my best to stay calm, or feeling all out of whack, I've discovered that things change when I change.

As soon as I give up the thing I feel concerned about, let it rest where it belongs in God's care, and keep my mind steadfastly trusting Him, then I'm more together and peace returns to my spirit.

We're not always ready to be mindful, to be trusting, or even to be in a state of believing when things are going haywire in our lives. If we need peace in our souls, then the lesson is to trust. . .trust that your well-being matters to God. Trust that He holds the matter in His hands and wants you to be filled with peace as things are worked out. Trust brings peace. What's in your mind really matters, and not just to you, but to God!

A HEART OF PEACE AND MINDFULNESS

Lord, I'm not always the best at handing my troubles over to You, trusting that You'll take care of them without me interfering. I've gone through endless worry beads in that process. Today, help me throw out the worry beads and throw my heart in the ring with You. Amen.

The Peace of God

The peace of God, which surpasses all comprehension,
will guard your hearts and your minds in Christ Jesus.
PHILIPPIANS 4:7 NASB

We are so schooled in the fine art of asking "Why?" that we sometimes forget that we don't always need to know the answer. It's actually uncomfortable for us to be in a situation where we can't intellectually reason what is going on and come out with a full understanding of the events before us. We assume that we are smart enough to figure things out.

The frustration then comes from doing all that work and getting back to the fact that we still don't have the answers. We don't know why our spouse left, why our kids made bad choices, or why we didn't choose another path so long ago. We don't even understand why people simply can't get along.

One thing we do know is that we can have peace in any situation. We have been offered the peace that passes all understanding and protects our hearts and minds in Christ Jesus. That's a pretty amazing offer and one we might want to run to receive. It's even better than knowing "why."

Today, may all your answers be ones that give your heart peace and joy.

A HEART AT PEACE

Lord, You know how much I struggle with trying to understand things, and trying to problem-solve so that I can come up with answers. Help me today to just rest in Your arms and let Your peace guard my soul. Amen.

Put on a Happy Face

"The LORD bless you and keep you; the LORD make His face shine upon you, and be gracious to you; the LORD lift up His countenance upon you, and give you peace."
NUMBERS 6:24–26 NKJV

You may remember having a circumstance where you were at your limit as a parent with every nerve jangled and stretched as far as nerves can go, only to have the doorbell ring and some seemingly well-adjusted adult is standing there. Somehow you have to dredge up a smile.

Or maybe you have an interview with your boss at work and you just know it's not going to go well through no real fault of your own, and you have to work hard to be strong, stay positive, and put on a happy face.

Whatever the situation, we spend a lot of time masking our feelings, creating faces that we hope will get us safely out of a room, or beyond the current crisis. Yet, the reverse of that, the one where we genuinely can offer our joy, our smiles, our best selves, helps us to understand this blessing from Numbers more easily. Receiving a smile from the Lord, sharing in His favor, makes any day brighter.

As you decide what face to wear today, check your anxieties at the door, and leave with a peaceful smile because you are in God's favor. He knows your heart, and He will guide all that you do.

A HEART OF JOY

Lord, help me to share the joy I have in You with those near me today. Remind me that whatever face I choose to put on, I'm reflecting my faith in Your love for me. Amen.

Discover Your Good Side

Your love must be real. Hate what is evil, and hold on to what is good.
ROMANS 12:9 NCV

We're blessed to live in a world where we can speak out against injustice in any of its angry forms. We can write newspaper articles, we can march in parades, picket businesses, and stand on the side of what we believe to be good. We can, but how often do we take the opportunity?

Sometimes, even when we agree with a cause, we decide that we cannot get involved, or we assume other people are already taking care of the problem and have it well in hand. Other times we imagine we can't solve the troubles of the world because it's such an overwhelming task. That kind of thinking is certainly valid.

However, somewhere in your own sphere of influence, opportunity will knock and ask you to stand on the side of good. It will ask you to show others that you really do love them because you're willing to stand up for something. The old adage that "if you don't stand for something, you'll fall for anything" isn't totally off the mark. Stand up for love and discover more of what you can really do to be a champion for the good side!

A HEART OF GOODNESS

Lord, thank You for the freedom to express ourselves about things we believe in. Thank You for watching over the efforts of millions of activists as they strive to stand on the side of good. Help me to stand with them when You lead me to do so. Amen.

Simplifying Success

Commit your actions to the LORD, and your plans will succeed.
PROVERBS 16:3 NLT

We all enjoy success and aspire to achieve our goals. We may want to become the CEO of the "Be Good Company," the teacher of the year, or the best spouse on the planet. Whatever it is, we have goals and those goals are very important to us.

How we achieve success can make a difference to our spirit, our health, and our family. We can become a workaholic, be envied for our bulletin boards, or make the best omelet in town, but we may lose sight of the other significant things around us. This proverb suggests that it can be much simpler to be successful if we just do one thing.

Our primary work is to commit what we want to the Lord. The promise is that when we do, our plans will succeed. This commitment is more than a quick prayer as we start something new. It's deeper than that.

Our commitment means those prayers must go on without ceasing, because commitment continues and grows over time. Marriage wouldn't be a commitment if you were going to walk away from it the week after the wedding. Commit your work to the Lord. He alone knows every step you should take. Put your heart into it and your faith will guide you.

A HEART FOR SUCCESS

Lord, I'm making a commitment to You today to keep the work I do in Your hands. May all my work be done for You, and then whatever the outcome, I will have succeeded in Your eyes. Amen.

Out of Control!

Patience is better than strength.
Controlling your temper is better than capturing a city.
PROVERBS 16:32 NCV

I wonder what images we would choose today to help us understand the significance of maintaining self-control. The proverb says having self-control is a better thing than conquering a city. Warriors of old, or even warriors today, may not agree with that, but what does it really mean to us?

Most of us don't have any plans to stampede Chicago or take over New York. Conquering a city took a lot of soldiers, a lot of strength and muscle power. Perhaps conquering the self is more similar than we think. Perhaps overcoming our own weaknesses takes more discipline, exercise, and shaping up to maintain self-control than we've stopped to consider.

If patience is power, then self-control is what conquers the city of our discontent and offers us true strength. Today, look at the temptations around you that may inspire a response of self-control. Let God help you to maintain the kind of control that will benefit your life in the best ways.

A HEART'S DESIRE FOR SELF-CONTROL

Lord, as I go about conquering my own worlds today, stand beside me and remind me to move patiently toward winning those places that overwhelm my spirit and cause me to do things that simply are wrong for me. Help me to stay in Your loving control. Amen.

Shake the Dust Off

"Whenever you enter a city or village, search for a worthy person and stay in his home until you leave town. When you enter the home, give it your blessing. If it turns out to be a worthy home, let your blessing stand; if it is not, take back the blessing. If any household or town refuses to welcome you or listen to your message, shake its dust from your feet as you leave."

MATTHEW 10:11–14 NLT

You have probably been in the position of offering advice, sharing opinions, or giving guidance more times than you're even comfortable to admit. When your advice is not well received, you may carry the weight of that conversation with you for a long time. Your intent was to be helpful and it's hard to know what to do when you see no result from your efforts.

Matthew is speaking in this scripture of carrying the Gospel to others, but perhaps there's wisdom for us today as we seek to help others who may not acknowledge our help. When you've done your best to share your heart and your insights about a situation to someone else, but they simply don't receive your advice, then it's time to let it go and move on. You have done your best and God will free you from taking responsibility for someone else's actions.

Sometimes you just have to shake the dust off and give yourself permission to move on.

AT THE HEART OF SELF-CONTROL

Lord, help me today to hold on to those things that are really mine to deal with and to shake the dust off those that are not. Let the winds of Your love carry me forward according to Your will and purpose. Amen.

Holy Ground

*"Do not come any closer," the LORD warned. "Take off your sandals, for you are
standing on holy ground. I am the God of your father—the God of Abraham,
the God of Isaac, and the God of Jacob." When Moses heard this,
he covered his face because he was afraid to look at God.*

EXODUS 3:5–6 NLT

Have you ever stood somewhere that felt to you like holy ground? I remember a visit
to Westminster Abbey in London where I was awed to be in a room where great kings
were buried. I stopped to put my feet in the same place where Sir Thomas More was
sentenced to death. The Poet's Corner was nearly mystical in its ability to take me back
to ancient times.

On another occasion I was standing on board the warship, *Arizona*, outside of Hono-
lulu. Oil still spills from its engines after some seventy years of floating in those waters
after the event that exploded World War II. It was awesome. For me, it was even somewhat holy.

In a broader sense, I've learned that we are often on holy ground. We stand there in
our churches taking communion, we stand at altars making wedding vows, or we deliver
babies into a world of sorrows. God has placed us on holy ground any time we draw near
to Him, no matter where we are.

May you take off your shoes and acknowledge His presence in a very real way today.
Thank God for putting you on holy ground.

A HEART OF HOLINESS

*Lord, help me to see the holy places that are built into my heart this day. Help
me to stand in Your presence and marvel at Your works in all I do. Amen.*

Notable Noah

*Noah was a righteous man, blameless among the people of his time,
and he walked faithfully with God.*
GENESIS 6:9 NIV

In order to understand the impact of this verse from Genesis, I tried substituting my name in place of Noah. Giving it the proper gender needs, it becomes "Karen is a righteous woman, blameless among the people of her time, and she walks faithfully with God." Wow! I don't know about you, but that sounds like an amazing, yet unattainable goal. Try it! It will give you a new perspective on this passage and make the words come alive.

Doing that exercise literally puts me in awe of Noah and what an incredible man he must have been. Personally, I'm grateful for Jesus. He is the one reason that I can even read the sentence above with my name in it. Because of His love, I can walk with God. It's interesting how many mistakes I've made in a few short decades, and Noah lived to be 950 years old. I can only imagine what havoc I could wreak on the world in that length of time.

On the other hand, perhaps it helps me to see what good I can do in my own time, if I choose to do so with great heart and intention. Regardless of the number of days we share the pathways of earth, our challenge is to walk with God. I may not be out building a boat, but I am hanging on to the anchor. You can too!

A RIGHTEOUS HEART

Lord, thank You for the example of those who go before us to help us see Your goodness and mercy. Help me to try a little harder to become more of what You would have me be, and in the meantime, please, keep walking with me. Amen.

The Principle of Peter

Peter fairly exploded with his good news: "It's God's own truth, nothing could be plainer: God plays no favorites! It makes no difference who you are or where you're from—if you want God and are ready to do as he says, the door is open. The Message he sent to the children of Israel—that through Jesus Christ everything is being put together again—well, he's doing it everywhere, among everyone."

ACTS 10:34–36 MSG

We live in a culture that loves to put labels on everything. We label schoolkids as gifted, special needs, or any number of classifications. We label adults as company presidents, blue-collar workers, aggressive, or lazy. We label our foods and we label our clothes and we label our churches and, well, we hardly miss putting a label on anything. Sometimes I wonder what would happen if we took off the labels. Would anyone really know whether the suit you wore was an Armani or Calvin Klein? Would it matter whether it came from Neiman Marcus or Walmart?

Chances are, taking away the labels would put a lot of things back on neutral ground. Peter's description of those who are acceptable to God reminds us that sometimes we get a little too caught up in the labels. God-fearing people are everywhere…all over the world. God has labeled those people as His.

As you go out into the world today, meet people heart-first, extend the hand of fellowship and forget about worrying about their title or position in life.

A HEART FOR GOD

Lord, we know that You have people on every corner of the globe that You call Your own. Help us to remember that You're not playing favorites, for You created every one of us and gave us all a way to be part of Your family. Amen.

Goodness, What's Wrong?

In those days there was no king in Israel;
every man did what was right in his own eyes.
JUDGES 17:6 NASB

We all like to think we know right from wrong, good from evil, and love from hate. This passage from Judges, though, could have been written about life today. Many people appear to be living according to what they believe to be right in their own eyes, perhaps with no regard as to whether the thing they believe is actually "right in God's eyes."

Living according to the "gospel of you" breaks down if you believe it's okay to steal a car from the driveway, kidnap a child, or steal someone's identity online. Some people live as though there was no king in Israel, that is, no Jesus, or no God of this universe.

How can you live with Jesus in your heart then? By believing that there is indeed a King who rules over you. You can seek Him and do all you can to spend your life on earth in ways that please Him, in ways that are right in His eyes. If you wonder if something you may do is right or wrong for you, consult with the One who still reigns. . .yesterday, today, and forever.

A HEART FOR RIGHT AND GOODNESS

Lord, help me to live according to the commands of Jesus, the King of my heart, and to step aside from those things that would bring You sorrow. May Your will be done today in every place on the globe. Amen.

What Did You Say?

"You can be sure that on the Judgment Day you will have to give account of every useless word you have ever spoken."
MATTHEW 12:36 GNT

Do you remember every word you said today. . .this morning. . .yesterday? The words we speak to one another are always significant. Not just the words, of course, but the intention of them, because often they bring more than information, they bring healing or sorrow to someone's heart.

This passage from Matthew is downright scary. It reminds us that God does not take our words lightly, that what we say matters. Are you ready to give an accounting of every useless word you've ever spoken? God have mercy!

Going forward, it might be good for all of us to take a little more notice of what we say and how we say it. The old phrase that you may have to eat those words, be forced to digest the things you once said, might not be too far from the truth. Let the words you speak today be sweet and refreshing!

Keep in mind that it's not just about your good words to others but the words others speak to you as well. Encourage kind words any way you can.

A HEART OF GOOD WORDS

Lord, help me to remember that everything I say to lift another person up is meaningful. I understand the old adage "If you can't say something nice, don't say anything at all" might just be close to what You want us to understand. Let me speak only words of love today. Amen.

The Hope Within

But sanctify the Lord God in your hearts, and always be ready to give a defense to everyone who asks you a reason for the hope that is in you, with meekness and fear; having a good conscience, that when they defame you as evildoers, those who revile your good conduct in Christ may be ashamed.

1 PETER 3:15–16 NKJV

In the Christian community, we talk a lot about witnessing to our faith. Some of us do it with great gusto, wearing our faith on our clothing, dropping it into our answering machines, practically flaunting it without actually waiting for just the right moment. We're loudspeakers and little can stop us from sharing what we believe.

Some of us share our hearts in quieter ways. We do it by lending a hand any time we're needed, without waiting for a thank-you. We do it by encouraging those around us with our positive spirits and our generous hearts. We do it by praying faithfully for people everywhere and by adding one more potato to the pot when someone comes by unexpectedly at dinnertime. All of those things help us to be steadfast defenders of our faith. All of those things serve as an example of our love for the Lord.

Being ready to defend your faith is not always about standing up to bullies or mockers, although it may be. More often, it's about standing up for what you believe in every circumstance with love and compassion. It's about showing God's heart as it is reflected through your voice and your spirit. The hope within you is the Great Defender Himself.

A HEART OF HOPE

Lord, since I know my hope rests in You, help me to share that hope with others today with a simple breath of human kindness. Amen.

Tender Words

A soft answer turns away wrath, but a harsh word stirs up anger.
PROVERBS 15:1 NKJV

We've all experienced the angry words of another person, whether justified or not. In receiving those same words, we've had to choose how to respond. Should we come back with more anger and harsh words? Or should we respond gently, offering the olive branch of peace?

Further in the reading of Proverbs, it says, "Gentle words bring life and health." What we say is so important to the well-being of others, and to the spirit within each of us, that we must be very conscious of our words, our tone, and our intentions any time we speak. We must remember to protect the hearts of others in our interactions. Today, let us recognize the amazing power of words and how we can offer them in kindness, gentleness, and a spirit of healing.

Francis de Sales said, "Nothing is so strong as gentleness, nothing so gentle as real strength." Let your words always be shared for the good of another. What you say really matters, so be sure to let your heart speak into any situation. Let your words always be full of grace and blessing.

A HEART FOR GENTLE WORDS

Lord, in every conversation that I am part of today, may Your Spirit prevail to bring gentleness and self-control. According to Your gifts of love and mercy, may I learn to speak with Your kindness. Amen.

Thinking Clearly

So prepare your minds for action and exercise self-control.
1 PETER 1:13 NLT

If you're like most people, you have great days and then you have days when you feel like everything in your life is simply out of control. You wonder how things got so messy and if God sees what has happened to you.

Controlling what you say and do, in large measure is about controlling what you think. What you think is controlled by what you believe about yourself and about the world around you. What you believe is based on the actual center of your life, in other words on your faith in God as the Source of all things. What you believe is a matter of the heart, and from your heart you make important choices.

Your thoughts help you or hurt you as you respond to the world. You can pay more attention to your thoughts and beliefs. You can be clear with yourself and with others about what really motivates the things you say and do. You can do these things because of the grace of God within you.

When you lead with your heart, and follow in the footsteps of your Savior, everything feels more balanced, more blessed, and in control.

A HEART OF POSITIVE THOUGHTS

Lord, be in control of my thoughts and actions today, so that each thought comes from a heart focused on You. Help me to think clearly and to act with love in all that I do. Amen.

The Protection of Faith and Love

*We belong to the day, so we should control ourselves. We should wear faith
and love to protect us, and the hope of salvation should be our helmet.*

1 THESSALONIANS 5:8 NCV

As you get ready for the day, imagine that you are going to go out into the world wearing faith and love. Faith and love protect you and allow your light to shine. You'll have a greater desire to help other people, and without saying a word, offer them the hope of salvation.

When you wear something new, a new suit or new shoes, you may expect others to notice and even make a comment. If you wear faith and love, others will take notice too. They will see something about your positive spirit that will linger with them long after you've left the room, kind of like a fragrance that permeates the air on a spring day.

Since you belong to the day, boost the spirits of others simply by your fresh-faced eagerness to wear every aspect of your faith and love with great joy. Not only will you experience God's protection, you'll be strengthened in your own heart and mind.

A HEART FOR FAITH AND LOVE

*Lord, help me today to wear a brighter smile, shine Your light with greater
enthusiasm, and let others know what joy I have in You. Help me to be someone
who can make a difference in a world that is weary and worn out. Amen.*

Always Be Joyful

Always be joyful. Never stop praying. Be thankful in all circumstances,
for this is God's will for you who belong to Christ Jesus.
1 THESSALONIANS 5:16–19 NLT

Learning to *always* be joyful is no simple task. In fact, most of us would say that it is an impossible idea. Why? Perhaps it's a matter of attitude. Marcus Aurelius said, "Find joy in simplicity, self-respect, and indifference to what lies between virtue and vice. Love the human race. Follow the divine."

You may agree that you can find joy in simplicity. After all, it's the little things about the day that are often the highlights: a warm conversation with a friend, a favorite cup of hot chocolate, or even a great prayer time in the morning.

Joy is often a result of having a sense of well-being and self-respect. It is a divine attribute and a divine gift. One way to keep joyful is to honor your connection to Christ in everything you do. Seek His will for your life and you may find continual gifts of joy and a heart that overflows with His grace and goodness.

Keep on praying, keep on following, keep on being joyful, for that is your divine calling.

A PURE HEART OF JOY

Lord, thank You for bringing Your Son, Jesus, into the world to offer us an abundance of joy so that our spirits thrive. Help me to look for His divine presence in all I do and to share Your joy with others. Amen.

It's Time for a Hug!

For I hope to visit you soon and to talk with you face to face.
Then our joy will be complete.

2 JOHN 12 NLT

We all love to be with the people who mean the most to us. When Paul was traveling, he was always grateful when he returned to a city where he had many friends to share his time and his thoughts. Since most of us live far away from our families of origin, the same is true for us. We pine for the days when we were all in each other's presence.

Since connection and relationship are so important to us, we welcome friends into our homes, visit shut-ins who may need our help, or spend time with those in our church family. We have greater joy when we are aligned with people who understand us and who share the things that matter most to our hearts.

Your personal relationships are matters of the heart. Whenever you can, make plans to get together with people you love, make a few phone calls, or make a comment on Facebook so the people you love know they are often on your mind and always in your heart. A face-to-face hug is always the best, but a hug from the heart, reminding others you are still there can change a drab day into a sparkling one.

A HEART FOR OTHERS

Lord, remind me today how important my friends are and how special my family is. Bring us together at every opportunity to share in the fullness of Your joy and blessing. Give us a chance for more big hugs. Amen.

Let's Be Friends!

"I've told you these things for a purpose: that my joy might be your joy, and your joy wholly mature. This is my command: Love one another the way I loved you. This is the very best way to love. Put your life on the line for your friends. You are my friends when you do the things I command you. I'm no longer calling you servants because servants don't understand what their master is thinking and planning. No, I've named you friends because I've let you in on everything I've heard from the Father."

JOHN 15:11–15 MSG

As a friend of Jesus, you have every reason to rise with a smile on your face, say your prayers with gusto, and go about your day with the intention of feeling every bit of joy meant for you.

In fact, you become a joy ambassador. Everywhere you go, you share what you have. You think first of Jesus, then of others, and finally of yourself, and by definition, lead a life of joy, or at least a day of joy. All that joy can't help attracting others and causing your friendships to grow.

A desire for friendship comes from a place deep within you and is lit by the Spirit Himself. If your joy candle goes out, step back and ask for more light. You'll get it. It's your day to shine and to make friends with your whole heart!

A HEART FOR ALL THAT BRINGS JOY

Father, help me remember today that You have given me a light to share with the world around me. Help me to shine that light in the fullness of real joy and with a heart of love. Amen.

Taking a Joyride

Ask, using my name, and you will receive, and you will have abundant joy.
JOHN 16:24 NLT

Wouldn't it be nice to run away for a day? When you've been working too hard at the office, or you're overrun with chores at home, it starts to feel like just getting out of town would be a good idea. Of course, that "run-away" feeling doesn't happen just when you're in need of a vacation. It happens when you're in need of inspiration, affirmation, and love!

Take your heart on a joyride today. Slip over to the local park and walk until you start to actually feel the wind in your hair and hear the sound of the crickets over by the stream. Pick a favorite spot by the lake that's an hour or two from home and just give yourself the freedom to simply sit there and take in the glory it brings to your soul. Calm your spirit, and lift up your heart in prayer.

When you're driving in your car, it's a great time to pray because you can actually turn off the radio and quiet things down enough to hear God's voice. You can thank Him for all you have and rediscover the quiet joy that comes when you're sharing time with Him.

Ready? Go on and take a joyride! You'll be refreshed and renewed.

A HEART RIDE

Lord, please ride with me today and help me focus on You and the beauty around me. Help me to see all that You have given me so that I might have a heart of joy. Amen.

So Grateful for God's Guidance

*I will bless the LORD who guides me; even at night my heart instructs me. I know the
LORD is always with me. I will not be shaken, for he is right beside me.*
PSALM 16:7–8 NLT

Sometimes it feels like planet Earth is a school and we're just here to learn our lessons.
Perhaps there's some truth to that feeling because once God beamed us down to earth,
He started guiding us and helping us understand what He wanted from us. He has been
teaching us our whole lives and it feels good to know that we're getting divine guidance.

Think about all the things you have learned so far. It's truly amazing! Perhaps you
even remember dreams that helped to guide you, or moments you've shared in God's
presence that filled you with great confidence and joy. As you go through this day, ask
God what else He would like your heart to know. What else can you do to grow more
compassionate and giving, more generous and loving? Share your heart with God and
let Him mold you into the person He knows you can be.

It is always right to give God thanks and praise for what He has done in your life. Hug
Him to your heart everywhere you go today.

A HEART OF GRATITUDE

*Lord, let me be a child again in Your presence today. Let me sit at Your feet and learn
from You. Help my heart to grow in worthiness and in love for You and all others. Amen.*

Cheerfully Patient

God is the one who makes us patient and cheerful. I pray that he will help you live at peace with each other, as you follow Christ.
ROMANS 15:5 CEV

You're probably not a person who gets impatient in a traffic jam or blows a fuse when the kids track mud onto your freshly mopped kitchen floor. You may not even have to grit your teeth when the teens next door hold one more late-night band practice. More than likely, you do get a bit peeved every now and then because impatience just seems to happen.

When you find yourself momentarily losing it over the little things that come at you during the day, it's time to stop everything and seek God's peace. After all, you can only be stretched just so thin before you start to lose a willingness to have good judgment or offer grace to those around you. Lots of things can steal your peace and only a little heart to heart with Jesus can really bring you back to joy.

Ask God to help you when your patience is simply maxed out. Bask in His presence until you are truly restored and refreshed to continue on with the day. He'll quiet your jangled nerves and give you more ways to be cheerfully patient. He'll make your heart glad once again.

A PATIENT HEART

Lord, thanks for keeping Your banner of love over my head, even when my head is weary and my patience evaporates. Help me to be an example of cheerful patience in all that I do today. Amen.

He Knows Your Heart's Desire

May he grant your heart's desires and make all your plans succeed. May we shout for joy when we hear of your victory, and raise a victory banner in the name of our God. May the LORD answer all your prayers.

PSALM 20:4–5 NLT

The reason we long for a life that is heart-shaped is because we understand how important the things are that give us a sense of belonging, or of purpose, or of feeling loved. We know that the things that matter to our hearts are the most real and the most authentic parts of our existence. We want our hearts to lead because we trust the things God has already taught us about life; we have the experience of knowing what feels good to our souls.

God knows the desires of your heart. He put those desires there. He wants you to become a person who seeks His heart and then uses your heart in the ways that you treat others. He sees you as someone who can bring peace and comfort and joy to those around you. When you respond to the world with your heart, you are a child after the heart of the Creator.

As you seek His direction for your life today, may you discover that each step you take is one that is guided by His hand and that all your plans are fulfilled with gladness. May God be honored by all that you do today.

A HEART FULFILLED

Lord, guide me today to follow the desires of my heart according to Your will and purpose for me. Help me to see Your loving hand at work in my life. Amen.

Wholehearted Waiting

Wait patiently for the LORD. Be brave and courageous.
Yes, wait patiently for the LORD.
PSALM 27:14 NLT

We're used to instant everything. We don't have to chop wood to build a fire, or find some paper to write a letter and drop it in the mail. We don't have to plant a garden, grow the tomatoes, and harvest them before we can have a salad. We just have to turn on a switch, send an email, or go to the store and buy some produce. We like things to be convenient. Waiting is a burden and a waste of time. . .or so we think!

Having the heart to wait for something takes a fair amount of bravado. It means you have to stay positive, be upbeat, and keep busy while you wait. It means you have to trust that God is acting on your behalf even when you can't see or feel that anything is happening. Whether you're waiting in a line, waiting for some news, or waiting to find the person of your dreams, there's only one thing worth doing. You have to pray and wait with a heart focused on what God can do that you can't. Sometimes, it's in the waiting that you discover what is really important, what matters most to your heart and soul.

Today, pray for all the people you know who are waiting for something important in their lives. Pray that they too will be brave and courageous. Pray that God will reveal to their waiting hearts the blessings of what will yet come.

A HEART FOR WAITING

Lord, I am not very good at waiting for things. Help me to value the time that passes while I'm waiting for good to come. Help me to trust You with my whole heart. Amen.

An Honest Heart

Listen to my cry for help. Pay attention to my prayer, for it comes from honest lips.
PSALM 17:1 NLT

You have an honest heart. You do everything you can to live responsibly and to own your mistakes. You are willing to ask for forgiveness when it's necessary, and you're willing to forgive others. You hope, trust, listen, and learn, at least you try to do those things.

Sadly, we live in a worldwide culture that falls far short of the virtue of being honest. Honesty appears to be an outdated concept, one that doesn't hold as much weight as it did when Abraham Lincoln walked the earth. Our current generation doesn't look into the mirror to seek a reflection of a person with an honest heart.

Honest people actually stand out in our minds. God wants us to be honest with each other as well and to make an effort to see others as He sees them.

He wants each of us to seek Him with honest hearts for everything that matters to us.

Today, thank God that you have an honest heart. Thank Him for helping you know Him so you can build on a foundation of integrity in every area of your life. Be one more person that is known for your honesty.

A HEART OF PATIENCE

Lord, help me to be totally honest with You today. Keep me attentive to being as honest as possible with myself and with others in all I do. Amen.

Faith, Faithful, Faithfulness

It is good to proclaim your unfailing love in the morning, your faithfulness in the evening, accompanied by a ten-stringed instrument, a harp, and the melody of a lyre.
PSALM 92:2–3 NLT

The psalmist suggests that we proclaim, announce, and declare every morning the love God has for us and that we remember He is still with us as evening falls.

If we take that message to heart, then we will seek God's direction before our feet even hit the floor with the dawn. We will open our hearts and minds to His leading and His call and make Him a priority. We will walk with Him through the day, knowing that nothing we do really matters if He is not part of each detail.

We want to be steadfast about our faith. We want to live in complete faithfulness. When we do, we notice a difference in our attitudes, in our motivation for the work we do, and in our treatment of others. We see that God's love prevails; that our desire to share that love permeates every circumstance.

Then when evening comes, we can put on some nice background music and meditate on God's faithfulness as we prepare once again to proclaim it with every sunrise.

A HEART FOR FAITHFULNESS

Lord, thank You that Your love never ends. Thank You that each morning and each evening I can count on You, no matter what takes place in my life. Play Your music in my heart forever. Amen.

A Day of Fresh Mercy

The faithful love of the LORD never ends! His mercies never cease.
Great is his faithfulness; his mercies begin afresh each morning.
LAMENTATIONS 3:22–23 NLT

What an awesome promise it is that God's mercies are new and begin afresh every single day. That means you're not waking up to an old agenda. You're not relying on yesterday's quota for mercy and hoping with all your might that there's enough left for today. You've already got a fresh start.

You can pick a new bunch of mercies like grapes from a vine because you are indeed part of the real Vine. You can draw near to Him and allow Him to anoint your day, your family, and your work so that you can be at peace. You can start again with a clean slate.

This is not a small promise! If we look at our yesterdays and those things that we've done to mess up God's perfect plans for our lives, we might get downhearted and lose sight of the possibilities before us. We might even forget that God can do anything, including taking a big eraser and giving us a fresh start.

Let your heart rejoice and do a happy dance as you live today in the abundance of God's grace and mercy!

A HEART OF MERCY

Lord, I confess that I don't even understand Your kindness and faithfulness. I am in awe of Your tender mercies, and I'm grateful each day that I can trust in them again. Amen.

Well Done!

*"The master was full of praise. 'Well done, my good and faithful servant.
You have been faithful in handling this small amount, so now I will
give you many more responsibilities. Let's celebrate together!' "*
MATTHEW 25:21 NLT

You thrive when you get positive feedback. When someone starts to praise your work, your talent, or your gifts, it makes a difference in everything you do. You try harder, are willing to work longer, and you'll even take on more responsibility. You always feel better when you know someone appreciates your work, even if it's something as simple as the great job you did cleaning up the kitchen or framing a new piece of artwork for the den. "Well done!" is not a phrase that we take lightly.

As you think about that today, look for opportunities to offer praise to the people who are near and dear to you. Maybe you can salute a coworker who has gone beyond the call of duty to help you.

Maybe you can reward your son with a warm smile for picking up his clothes in his bedroom. Whatever you find noteworthy, positive, or affirming, be sure to offer that person a heartfelt bit of praise. Nothing brings joy to your heart like being told, "Well done!"

A HEART OF PRAISE

Lord, help me to be faithful in offering a word of praise or a kind comment to those around me today. Let me not hesitate to say, "Well done!" when it is richly deserved. Amen.

The One Who Made Your Heart

The LORD looks down from heaven and sees the whole human race. From his throne he observes all who live on the earth. He made their hearts, so he understands everything they do.

PSALM 33:13–15 NLT

Isn't it a wonderful thing to realize that someone you care about "gets" you? They understand who you are and why you do the things you do and no matter what, they come right back and love you just the same. For whatever their reasons, you can really do no wrong in their sight; you're simply someone they love.

If you're a parent, you may have feelings like that for your children. When you know that you're fully loved and accepted, it makes it a little easier to actually be yourself. You don't have to pretend to be something you're not because that close friend can see right through you.

This is literally the situation you have with God. He sees your heart before He sees anything else. He sees what motivates you and what causes you pain. He sees what sets you back and what moves you forward. He sees you, understands you, and loves you without reservation because He only has unconditional love to give.

As you meet others in the world today, see them as people God loves unconditionally. Seek to understand their hearts and offer them your kindness and affirmation. The One who made your heart will be pleased.

AN UNDERSTANDING HEART

Lord, open my heart and mind to Your tender care. Help me to grow in my desire to understand and truly "get" those who are part of my life today. Amen.

Sometimes Your Heart Hurts

I am exhausted and completely crushed.
My groans come from an anguished heart.
PSALM 38:8 NLT

One of the best parts of being a believer is that you have some place to go when life hurts. You don't have to take on the trials and the storms of life all alone. You have help; you have a God who sees you, knows you, wants to share in your heartache, and bring relief.

Sometimes the light goes out and you don't know which way to turn or what the clear path might be that is best for you or someone you love. You would like to help, but nothing you've done makes a difference. Some people turn to friends, drugs, or alcohol. You turn to God.

Today, you may not have a situation that hurts, but you may know someone else who does. Remind them, if you can, that they are not alone. Remind them of the Source of light and healing. As you do so, be God's hands and heart for that person. Your efforts will cause your own spirits to rise.

God sees what you do and will be proud of the way you share your heart even during difficult times with those around you. Rest in His love and healing power today. He knows what you need.

A HEART FOR GOD

Lord, thank You that You keep me close to You even when things are difficult for me. Help me to rest in Your care and offer hope to others when life causes them pain. Amen.

A Compassionate Heart

But when He saw the multitudes, He was moved with compassion for them,
because they were weary and scattered, like sheep having no shepherd.
MATTHEW 9:36 NKJV

Have you noticed that a lot of people around you are weary? They have to carry some heavy loads. Some of them bear personal burdens, coping with family issues, rebellious children, aging parents. Some of them are weighed down by financial issues, uncertain how to even begin to make things right again. They worry about whether they can pay the rent or manage all the responsibilities before them.

When we're weary, it's hard to make good decisions. It's hard to know where to turn or how to find meaningful solutions to our problems. Jesus had compassion on people because He could see that they were lost. They were overwhelmed by life and simply didn't have any sense that things could change.

You have a compassionate heart every time you pay attention to the needs of others. You see their needs and you want more than anything to help them. God wants to equip you to be part of their solution.

Today, seek God's help as you step into the world. Ask Him to draw near to you, providing what you need from His strength and love to make a difference in the lives of others. The blessings you share will fall back on you a hundredfold.

A HEART OF COMPASSION

Lord, draw near to Your weary children today, even to me when I am overwhelmed by life. Help us to come to You for strength and renewal as our Good Shepherd. Amen.

Peace Within

Search for peace, and work to maintain it.
PSALM 34:14 NLT

Practice peace. It seems like a simple concept to imagine living in peace with our neighbors and yet, we know how difficult it really is to do. Maintaining a sense of peace requires practice because it means our hearts must be engaged with the process. It means that we must choose wisely the attitudes we want to adopt and the choices we want to make. We have to let go more quickly and appreciate the differences between our thoughts and actions and those of others.

Our hearts must seek peace with great intention because it is so easily lost. One small criticism from a friend or coworker, one rejection when you expected approval, or one harsh thought to yourself, can stir you up and your peace evaporates.

When anything happens to you today that attempts to steal your peace, be ready in a positive way to deflect it and defend yourself. Take out your shield of faith and stand firm. You may find that the more you practice peace, the more contented you feel. The more contented you feel, the more joy comes into your spirit and into your household.

Open your heart to peace. Hold on to your peace, share your peace, and live in peace with each person you meet today. May the joy of the Lord be your strength.

A HEART OF PEACE

Lord, help me to live in Your peace today. Grant that I would do all that I can to bring harmony to the lives of others through Your grace and mercy. Amen.

We Belong to Each Other

So love truth and peace.
ZECHARIAH 8:19 NLT

Mother Teresa said, "If we have no peace, it is because we have forgotten that we belong to each other."

A lot of congregations practice "sharing the peace" on Sunday mornings. People move across the aisles to shake hands with each other and wish each other God's peace. It's a wonderful experience and one worth repeating as we leave the sanctuary and head out into the parking lot.

Sharing the peace with others means we understand that life is often difficult and uncertain. It means that we realize that we're all in this life together and what happens to any one of us actually affects the lives of all of us. When we offer each other this sacred wish for peace it is because we know from personal experience what happens when our peace is disrupted. We know that the stories we tell in our heads can be merciless and steal every moment of peace we might hope for on any given day.

Today, pray that you will be at peace with yourself and with God, and then step outside yourself to share that incredible sense of peace with someone else. It will do you both good, and your hearts will be glad.

LIVING IN LOVE AND PEACE

Lord, it isn't always easy for me to remember to share Your peace with others. Help me today to be an instrument of peace and Your love, according to Your will and purpose. Amen.

Written on Your Heart

"I take joy in doing your will, my God, for your instructions are written on my heart."
PSALM 40:8 NLT

When we put things in writing, we know we are free to go back to them any time we like. We read our favorite Scriptures over and over again. We pick up our novel where we left off, review some of the pages we already read, and get right back into it. When important things are in print, we tend to take them more seriously.

So what is written on your heart? God has given you His Word to refer to any time you are willing to do so. Some people are an open book and it's easy to understand where they are coming from because they lead with their hearts, showing genuine kindness. Others are more difficult to understand because they are less willing to share their feelings and thoughts. We even say that those people are hard to "read."

God reads your heart and He has impressed you with all the things that are important for your spirit to thrive and grow. He wants your soul to rejoice any time at all, and so He has written His law in your heart. He has put Jesus right in the center of your very being so that you can go back and remind yourself of what God wants you to know at any time. You don't have to guess. It's not a test that you can fail because He's written it in a place that makes it easy for you, a place the two of you can always share.

Let your heart find joy in knowing that your Savior is only a breath away. You have an eternal bookmark in the very center of your being. What matters most is already written on your heart.

A HEART OF KNOWLEDGE

Lord, thank You that You have made it so easy for me to find You. I don't have to search through volumes of books to get to the heart of what You want me to know. You have given me everything I need. Amen.

....

....

....

....

....

....

....

Signs of Love

How wonderful and pleasant it is when [people] live together in harmony!
PSALM 133:1 NLT

Living in harmony seems more like a fantasy notion than something that could actually happen. After all, there's one disaster after another brewing in the world and most of us don't have a clue how we could begin to fix the problems. In fact, we are pretty sure that we can't fix things because the world is out of control.

Living a heart-shaped life is about striving to achieve God's intended harmony. We may do this by making a slight correction in our attitudes toward others. We cease to see those who are different than we are as fearful or competitive and honor their right to be unique. We seek to bless all cultures and lifestyles. We simply let people live and breathe and seek to love them just as God made them. We can. . .if we choose to do so.

Perhaps what we need are a few more signs of love. Maybe one sign of love emerges each time you choose to be kind, or to bless someone you don't understand, or each time you strive to see through someone's stubborn exterior and look for the person God created. Your soul will be uplifted and your heart will carry you forward. You'll be the hands and feet of Christ because you chose to love, rather than to judge someone else. Your heart influences your thoughts and brings harmony and peace.

May this be a great day to bring harmony and show signs of God's love every place you go.

A HEART OF LOVE

Lord, I do pray that You would direct my thoughts to seeing others the way You see them. Help me to love first, to act kindly, and to share my heart with others according to Your will and purpose for me and for them. Amen.

Be Kind, Please!

Be kind to each other.
EPHESIANS 4:32 NLT

Albert Schweitzer said, "Constant kindness can accomplish much. As the sun makes ice melt, kindness causes misunderstanding, mistrust, and hostility to evaporate."

It's the time of year when ice is melting all around us. It's a good time to offer straight-from-the-heart kindness and forgiveness to those around you and usher in the warmth of springtime. If you've ever felt the sting of an icy relationship, you may be ready to let it go or make peace. Kindness makes a difference.

Think about how you feel when a total stranger offers you a helping hand. Maybe you needed a jumper cable to start your car or you were feeling frenzied by all you needed to accomplish in a day, and someone reached out and helped you without even needing to be asked. Maybe you simply needed a warm smile to refresh your spirits.

Today, if you can think of anyone who needs a tender touch of kindness, something you can provide in a generous dose, then send it their way. Be the ambassador of kindness wherever you go. Kindness won't cost you a thing, but it will enrich your life enormously and your heart will grow three times its size and bring you joy.

A HEART OF KINDNESS

Lord, I do try to be kind to those around me, but help me today to be especially aware of those that might not receive enough of the milk of human kindness. Amen.

Just a Gentle Word

Gentle words cause life and health.
PROVERBS 15:4 TLB

"You have the most beautiful eyes! In fact, your smile just lights up a room."

Compliments are awesome! Of course for most of us, receiving a compliment is harder to accept than paying a compliment to someone else. For some reason our own lack of self-esteem keeps us from appreciating the compliment, no matter how heartfelt it was. If no one ever remarks about the incredible dinner we made or the new car we just bought, we might get a little downhearted.

Think of the kindest person you know—the one who gives compliments from the heart. They warm your heart and make you glad to be in their presence. They have a way of doing good deeds without even noticing the great help they are to others. They just know what to say to make you smile. They make you feel confident, loved, and cared about.

Being a person of kind words is a gift. Most of us try to be kind in general, but the person who came to mind in the paragraph above would be labeled as truly kind and be viewed in a different category. Maybe there's room for more of us to join them. Let's use gentle words all day, making heartfelt and affirming compliments to those around us. It will cause our hearts to be glad.

A HEART OF GENTLE WORDS

Lord, thank You for the example of my friend who is so kind. Remind me that You can work within me to help me share more gifts of kindness with others. Amen.

Patience and Self-Control

[It is] better to be patient than powerful; [it is]
better to have self-control than to conquer a city.
PROVERBS 16:32 NLT

Power is a key that unlocks a lot of odd behaviors in people. A variety of situations allow for one person to be in a position of power, and someone else to be subordinate. It's true of kids on the playground, spouses, or people in a boardroom. Someone seems to hold all the power.

People in any role of power are only in the position they hold because God allows them to be there. God places people in positions of authority. He seeks to see if they will rule with kindness and wisdom. He wants the same exchange of kindness between spouses or kids at play. He wants us to be controlled by love.

Real power only exists in God Himself. Others, at best, imitate Him. Some, at worst, deny Him. The ones who truly aspire to greatness, the ones who attain any measure of actual power, are plugged in to the main Source of the universe, into God's power. The measure of power for any of us then is in what we do with the power God gives us. Our goal is to use any power we have wisely and well. Our opportunity is to have our hearts shaped by the power of love.

THE POWER OF LOVE

Lord, help me to keep a balance of power within me. Leaning on Your power, trusting in what You have given me, help me to patiently grow in Your name. Let me always be wise in any position of authority that I may have at home or at work. Amen.

Love and Fruitfulness

You did not choose me. I chose you and sent you out to produce fruit, the kind of fruit that will last. Then my Father will give you whatever you ask for in my name. So I command you to love each other.

JOHN 15:16–17 CEV

Being part of the Vine carries a responsibility. You're expected to grow and blossom and produce fruit. One form of fruit is love. We all want and need love that will last. How do we create that kind of love, the kind that doesn't require any sort of preservative? How can we squeeze more genuine love out of our daily actions, giving and sharing and doing the best we can to love each other?

If we look at the varieties of love shown on television or on movie screens, we seldom see anything that reflects even a shadow of real love. In fact, the word *love* is bandied about in so many forms, with so little meaning, that we may lose a sense of what it means to actually love others.

Whatever your experience is with love, you need to always go back to the genuine Source of all love when doubts arise. You may need to go back to the Vine. God chose you to bear fruit, to be part of the divine branch offering peace and love wherever you are. He will teach you the truth of love. He will shape your heart to produce the kind of fruit that truly lasts.

The Vinedresser knows exactly what you need and sends you out today to share His love.

A HEART OF LOVE

Lord, let me bear the fruit of Your love and share it with those I meet today. Teach me how to love bigger and better. Let me keep learning from You so that I have a genuine heart for others everywhere I am today. Amen.

Being Good or Being Better!

Remember that the Lord will reward each one of us for the good we do.
EPHESIANS 6:8 NLT

Do you ever stop to think about the things that you would like to do better? Maybe you'd like to be a better dancer, a better planner, or even a better friend. When you set a new goal like that, you go after it. You work on it. You take dance lessons, or get organized, or join the hospitality committee at church. You do all you can because you'd like to go from being good at something to being better at it. God applauds your thinking, especially when you apply it to the things you do for Him.

It's likely you are pretty good at what you do for God. If you think you still have room for improvement in the work you do for the Lord, then take steps today like you might utilize when you're developing any skill. Take a class, read your Bible more, join a group that can give you guidance and teach you a few new tricks. You may just go from good to better; and from better to best. Now that would be a goal worth striving for, don't you think? After all, whenever you achieve a greater level of expertise or skill, it does your heart good.

God knows you're good, but He also knows you can be even better!

A HEART TO BE BETTER

Lord, I want to be better at sharing my heart and doing good things for the people in my life. Help me to desire to do more than I've been doing. Give me a few lessons where I need them. Amen.

Writing a Little Love Note

Beautiful words stir my heart. I will recite a lovely poem about the king,
for my tongue is like the pen of a skillful poet.
PSALM 45:1 NLT

It appears to be no longer fashionable to send handwritten letters to the people we care about. We are all so used to the instant gratification of sending emails or text messages that we've lost the significance of sending love notes or friendly letters written in our own hand.

Those handwritten notes may have given you something a typed text can never achieve. You remember Dad's handwriting or the way your friend slants her words in a backward direction. Your imagination begins to work and you think of them sitting at the table or at their desk composing this note to you. You may even remember what fun it was to go out and purchase a box of elegant stationery. Yes, those handwritten notes were a special form of love.

Imagine today that your heart overflows with joy about someone dear. You could send them a quick text and suggest that you're thinking of them, but maybe seeing your handwriting on some nice stationery will be even more important; a gift they can keep and read over and over again.

God sent us His love letter in the form of the Bible, written down so that every day we can go back and read some of it; or reread portions that hold the most meaning for us. This is your day to write a little love note to someone you love. Take the time to share your heart and your handwriting, and add to the joy of the whole experience.

A HEART TO WRITE

Lord, thank You for inspiring my thoughts to send a note to someone special today.
I pray that I will try more often to make my communication with the people who
are dear to me even more personal by writing to them in my own hand. Amen.

Joy Is an Action Word

Ask and you will receive, and your joy will be complete.
JOHN 16:24 NIV

A famous quote by Edward Everett Hale says this:

I am only one, but still I am one.
I cannot do everything, but still I can do something;
And because I cannot do everything
I will not refuse to do the something that I can do.

If we want to experience the real spirit of joy that God meant for us to have, we have to be willing to do something. We have to step outside ourselves and reach out to others. We have to stop passing by the needs of others and react to those needs with a heart of compassion and love.

It's true that we can't do everything, but we can do something. We can pick one cause, one charity, one family, one friend, one something that will become the object of our help and our kindness. We can answer the call of our own hearts to contribute to being a solution for someone else's concerns.

Ask God to guide you today to where He most wants you to share your gifts and your talents and your kindness. You can offer a bit of hope by a generous gesture, or suggest a new path of possibility for someone to consider. God will use your smallest effort so it becomes someone else's greatest good.

A HEART OF JOY

It does make me feel better when I help someone else, Lord. Deepen my desire to reach out in a new direction to offer Your joy to others. Help me to always be willing to share what I can as a matter of heart. Amen.

When Your Heart Is Broken

The sacrifice you desire is a broken spirit.
You will not reject a broken and repentant heart, O God.
PSALM 51:17 NLT

When you're living a heart-shaped life it means that you approach everything you do heart-first. That is, that you strive to see others with the eyes of love. You work to understand the needs of those around you, even when you're disappointed by life. You recognize that God is working within you to create an even better version of the person you are yet becoming.

Sometimes no matter what you do, you experience a kind of grief in your spirit. You may have a child who is rebellious and still seeking truth, or you may have a friend who deceived you. One way or another, the experience is the same, your heart is wounded and perhaps even broken.

When that happens, take your broken heart to your Father. Seek His help in understanding if there is any other sacrifice you need to consider, some other aspect of your will that needs to be surrendered. Whatever you do, just know that God can help when you speak to Him heart to heart. He can mend your brokenness in any of its unhappy forms and make you whole again.

Whenever you sense a need to seek healing for yourself or others, put your concerns before the Lord and share them with all your heart. He alone has the answers.

A HEART THAT BREAKS

Father, You know that I sometimes do things that cause me great sorrow. I recognize that I need to bring those things to You for healing and deliverance. I pray today for anyone I know who has a broken spirit or an aching heart. Amen.

Ambassadors Forever

We are Christ's ambassadors; God is making his appeal through us.
2 CORINTHIANS 5:20 NLT

We usually think of ambassadors as emissaries of goodwill who seek to connect people wherever disparity looms and help them understand each other better. These ambassadors are masters of communication and can build bridges to love. They help people think and feel and react to life in more generous and giving ways. As someone with the gift of God's Spirit, you too serve as an ambassador for Christ.

As an ambassador of the heart, you open the way for greater understanding, conversation, and opportunity for those around you. You help bridge the gap about things they may misunderstand about God, themselves, or others. You are the messenger to bring them hope, and you deliver your message for their sake even more than for your own.

When you signed up to be a Christian, you took this role for life. Whatever you do from here reflects God's heart working within you. It is through your heart and hands that many others will be blessed. May God bless you with opportunities to shine for Him and keep you always in His favor.

AN AMBASSADOR'S HEART

Lord, I don't always remember that I have a full-time job with You, so I'll never be unemployed. You always have work for me to do, and I thank You. Help me to do it with Your heart and Your Spirit. Amen.

Be the Salt

"You are the salt of the earth. But what good is salt if it has lost its flavor?"
MATTHEW 5:13 NLT

We often put things in buckets of some sort, prioritizing them according to value or interest or commitment levels. We might put small things that happen to us in one bucket, big things in another, looking to determine the impact of each. Sometimes it's the small things that serve as examples to safeguard or nurture your spirit.

Being the salt for God is a good example. Salt is a small white particle of sodium chloride that we put on our food to enhance flavors. It's a small thing with a lot of power! It makes a difference to your food and to your body. The salt brings out the best in what you're eating.

You are the salt of the earth, perhaps the only salt in the lives of others. You are important to their well-being, and you can flavor their lives in such a way that they are blessed with God's favor. Your saltiness flavors their faith and causes them to act on it. Your "salt" changes their hearts to want more of what God has to offer.

It's no small thing to be the salt. You may want to pass the salt even more today.

BEING THE SALT WITH HEART

Lord, help me be the salt in gracious and positive ways. Help me to add flavor and richness and desire in the hearts of those around me to know You better. Let me shake up their lives with Your Spirit. Amen.

Don't Bug Me!

We give great honor to those who endure under suffering. . . .
You know about Job, a man of great endurance.

JAMES 5:11 NLT

Most of us don't want to have the patience of Job, because we don't want to be tested in the same way that he was. We don't want to endure every hardship known to man just to see if we can remain right with God. We're just plain grateful that we don't have Job's troubles. Or are we?

Even when our troubles are small, we often give them the same power as a mosquito that flies around our head when we're trying to sleep. It's a small thing, but you know that any minute it might swoop down in search of blood, and you're not interested in giving any. Before long, you can't sleep because you've got to conquer the source of your trouble.

Sometimes every problem you have feels like a mosquito hovering just over your head. As a person after God's own heart, how can you stop letting the little things become big things? Perhaps you can start by pouring your heart out before God, one to one. Thank Him for the things you *don't* have to endure. Thank Him for all that He has done in your life. Commit your steps and your heart to Him one more time. When you do, the chances are good that the humming of the mosquito will stop.

A HEART THAT ENDURES

Lord, I really don't like having all the little things in my life become so annoying. I'm sorry that I've given them more power than they deserve. Help me to patiently rest in You. I give You my commitment and my heart to seek Your good in all I do. Amen.

The Love of God

Understand, therefore, that the LORD your God is indeed God. He is the faithful God who keeps his covenant for a thousand generations and lavishes his unfailing love on those who love him and obey his commands.

DEUTERONOMY 7:9 NLT

You are loved by the God of the universe, the Creator of all things, the one who is indeed God. His love remains with you constantly. His love asks only one thing. . .a response. . .a genuine heartfelt response to His love.

What might it mean to us to show love and obedience and understanding to God? Oswald Chambers said, "The tiniest fragment of obedience, and heaven opens up and the profoundest truths of God are yours straight away. God will never reveal more truth about Himself till you obey what you know already."

Getting to understand the will of God in your life, and growing in His truth and love has everything to do with your desire to love Him, love others, and love yourself. It's not always easy to do, but you are called every day to obey God and offer His hand of grace and divine love to others. He created the whole world and He created you. His heart is for everyone to come to know Him.

Spread His love wherever you go today.

A HEART OF LOVE

Dear Lord, help me to be faithful to Your love by sharing what I know of You to others. Let the desires of my heart be about pleasing You in all I do. Amen.

At the Heart of Anger

People with understanding control their anger; a hot temper shows great foolishness.
PROVERBS 14:29 NLT

One of the things about walking with God is that we have to strive to be more like Him. Sometimes that means that we too have to be more forbearing, slow to anger, and willing to turn the other cheek. We have to be willing to see that we may not have the whole picture when it comes to someone else's actions. We may not have any idea about what drives them and what is at the heart of their anger.

The fact is that we don't have to know. We simply have to choose our own attitude and our own response with as much love as we can muster. The time that we need this approach the most though is when we feel anger taking root within us as well. Giving in to anger may only escalate the problem, causing needless and harmful gaps to develop in our relationships. All anger gives us is a stomachache.

Next time you find yourself seething under the skin because someone has spoken harshly to you, misunderstood you, or was simply mean to you, then stop, think, pray, and give it to God. Ask Him to create a response in you that is worthy of the issue. A hasty temper makes mistakes. A willing heart of love heals.

A HEART TO UNDERSTAND

Lord, help me to remember that reacting in a negative way never helps solve the problem. Help me to listen to Your voice when I have feelings of anger, and keep my heart connected to You until I find my way to peace again. Amen.

The Heart of a Family

Father to the fatherless, defender of widows—this is God, whose dwelling is holy.
God places the lonely in families; he sets the prisoners free and gives them joy.
PSALM 68:5–6 NLT

Your relatives are everywhere. Some of them are seated around your dinner table. Some of them are still seeking shelter from the cold. A few of them are imprisoned by attitudes and an overwhelming sense of defeat because life has not been easy for them. God knows that being human is no easy task.

Because He knows that sometimes we're alone, often when it isn't even our choice to be so, He rallies around us. He strives to be there in ways that can touch our spirits and remind us of His presence. He acts as a father and as a husband. He acts as a friend and as family. He offers light to those who are in literal prisons or those that simply keep us stuck in our hearts and minds.

God serves as a living example of why He works so hard to shape our hearts, minds, and attitudes. He goes before us so that we can see His light and follow in His way. This is part of our calling, to embrace others and include them in the context of what it means to be family. We are all related in one way or another. We all have only one Father, and He embraces His own children with great and powerful love.

It serves Him well when we follow in His footsteps.

A HEART LIKE HIS

Lord, I don't always see those around me as family, but I understand that all of us who love You and call on Your name are indeed related. Help me to see others with the eyes of love today. Amen.

The Good Earth

Then God saw everything that He had made, and indeed it was very good.
GENESIS 1:31 NKJV

Imagine God's love as personal and full of joy. As an example of the kind of love we're talking about, imagine too that you've worked all night, maybe even six nights to put together a beautiful dollhouse for your daughter for her birthday. You anticipate the smile on her face, the screams of delight as she sees your handiwork for the first time. The new dollhouse is the best birthday gift ever, and you settle back to watch your child play with delight at your creation.

After a month or so, you discover that the dollhouse is falling apart; the roof has fallen in. The house looks neglected. Your good work, so carefully and skillfully put together, is destroyed. You feel so badly about it you even wonder if your child did this on purpose or if she even really cares about the house. You're not even sure you really want to fix it if she's just going to be ungrateful and perhaps break it again. Your joy in creating this dollhouse, a total gesture of your love, simply diminishes!

Lucky for us, when the roof fell in at the Garden of Eden, God, in His goodness, started to make repairs. He was surely disappointed, but He didn't assume our misconduct caused permanent damage. He found a carpenter with incredible skill, one that could hold the door open through any storm. He didn't rely on our goodness at all. He just relied on the heart of His Carpenter!

HIS HEART-SHAPED GOODNESS

Lord, bless the things I do today, so that I am ready with my toolbox to repair any needs I find at home or in the neighborhood, as I offer the hand of friendship and Your goodness to others. Amen.

Stolen Peace

*Don't worry about anything; instead, pray about everything. Tell God what you need,
and thank him for all he has done. Then you will experience God's peace,
which exceeds anything we can understand.*

PHILIPPIANS 4:6–7 NLT

How much does it cost you to worry? Maybe it only costs you a good night's sleep. Maybe it takes away from the joy you should be having at your best friend's birthday party because your mind is somewhere else. Perhaps it even steals your vacation in the sun and the sand right out from under your feet. We have an intellectual understanding that worry never helps, but for some reason, it's nearly the first thing we do when things are not going our way.

At the very least, worry is expensive. It can bring poor health to your body and your mind. It can require medication to get you through the challenges it manufactures in your head, the stories that simply won't stop spinning there.

Today, stop worrying. That's right, just stop! It won't be easy, but you have other choices. You can pray about everything and put your anxieties in God's hand. You can put the burdens down and place your troubles at the foot of the cross. If you do, God's promise is that you can experience His peace and give your heart and mind a rest.

A HEART AT PEACE

*Lord, I surrender my worries to You and place them at the cross. I know You've
already paid my debt and You're willing to carry my burdens. Thank You for loving me
so much. Amen.*

A Heart-Shaped Life That Frees!

Every way of a man is right in his own eyes, but the LORD weighs the hearts.
PROVERBS 21:2 NKJV

When your goal in life is to perceive the world with your heart and to be open to God's leading with your mind, you are blessed with a sort of divine motivation. You see more clearly what God intends for you and for those around you. You sync your plans with His, and your actions become more honorable.

God is always seeking our hearts. He weighs what we do by the intention of our hearts. When you give with a generous and loving heart, it's very different than when you give, even the same amount of time, money, or effort, with a heart that simply feels obligated. Your heart is either shaped by God's desire for you to draw closer to Him and understand His ways, or it is shaped by the world, which has no guidance at all.

Whatever is right for you, pray that God will direct your steps so much that you will know exactly what He has in mind. Pray that He will see your generous and loving intentions and bless the direction you take. This is the joy of a heart-shaped life; one that frees you to be exactly who you are in the eyes of your Creator.

May all you do be twice blessed today.

A HEART-SHAPED LIFE

Lord, help me to stay so close to You that all I do has Your stamp on it; and that You can bless my efforts because my motives are connected to Your plans for me. Amen.

Renewing Your Mind

Let the Spirit change your way of thinking and make you into a new person.
You were created to be like God, and so you must please him and be truly holy.
EPHESIANS 4:23–24 CEV

It is safe to say that you may never embrace all the rules. Oh, you'll have the basic foundation under your feet, but even simple changes may suddenly stretch you into a new shape when the Spirit leads. Life will put you in situations that cause you to have to reconsider the ways you reacted to a similar experience in the past. Learning to love others may take on new dimension. After all, to love your neighbor is an incredible task in a world like ours, where literally everyone on the globe is your neighbor. Only God can shape your heart to give you the eyes to see all of His children as He does. Only God can change the way you think and make you a new person.

You can renew your mind with the help of the Spirit of God. He'll help you be intentional about what you desire so you can draw closer to Him. Ask Him what else you can do to please Him and show that you desire to love others more.

God will bless the work of your hands as He blesses your heart, renews your spirit, and puts your mind at peace.

A NEW HEART AND MIND

Lord, every time I think I understand what it means to love my neighbor, I discover a new neighbor I'm not so sure I like, much less love. Create in me the desire to be a more loving person in faithful service to You. Amen.

The Golden Rule

Treat others just as you want to be treated.

LUKE 6:31 CEV

By now, you've probably learned that most people are apt to treat you the same way you treat them. Most people! There are some though who persist in their efforts to keep people at a distance. It is all about attitude.

As someone striving to live a heart-shaped life, your call is to look past those who do not seem to respond equally to your kindness. You look past them on one level, and remind them who they are on another. If you treat them with respect based on the premise that you believe God wants you to see through their crankiness and into their hearts, then you'll be at peace. You won't look to create an "eye for an eye" moment. You will look to create a relationship with the eyes of your heart.

If you have a strong, positive attitude, your mind and heart will align more quickly to what God is calling you to be. When you treat others with a heart of kindness, they will respond in more positive ways. If they don't, you will have still made the best choice and God will bless you. He'll work things out with people who don't play by the "golden" rule in His own time.

A HEART TO TREAT OTHERS WELL

Lord, help me to have a more positive attitude about people, about life, and about the work I do. Create a deep desire within me to treat everyone well and to love them as You love them. Amen.

Peacekeepers

God blesses those who work for peace, for they will be called the children of God.
MATTHEW 5:9 NLT

Perhaps you've never been at a peace rally or marched on Washington, DC to try to get the attention of the decision makers. Maybe you've donated to peace campaigns or prayed for world peace. What you've done may not seem significant at all to you, but if you've contributed to the idea of peace and demonstrated a desire for peace, then you're a child of God. Peace is a desire within your heart to be aligned with God in all ways; feeling content in all circumstances, and accepting His divine grace and love.

Beyond the task of helping to keep peace in the world, you are a peacekeeper in your own home. You may also be the peacekeeper at work. Your spirit and the sense of calm that you bring to any situation shape and mold those around you, often changing attitudes and causing more harmony.

Blessed are you if you're a peacemaker. Make it your business wherever you are to be about the business of creating peace. Help bring chaos to its knees. God will take it from there.

WITH A PEACEFUL HEART

Lord, I may not be able to make a difference in an assembly of peace marchers today, but I can make a difference in my own home and my own neighborhood. Bless my efforts to share Your peace and Your love today. Amen.

Doing Good Deeds

Our people must learn to do good by meeting the urgent needs of others; then they will not be unproductive.

TITUS 3:14 NLT

At every age and stage of our lives, we have opportunities to do good things that will benefit others. We can aspire to have "productive" lives our whole life through. It's just a matter of seeing the work we do as good and knowing it is the work God called us to do.

Sometimes we hesitate to be a "do-gooder." When we're young, we may think we're excused from doing good deeds because we're just kids. As we grow older and have the responsibility of young children, we may think we don't have time to do good. If we're in the process of working our way up the ladder, then our jobs are in control of our lives and we feel too busy to do good. When we retire we're not certain we have the resources of time and energy to do good.

At one time or another we may find ourselves in a place of urgent need. We either need financial help, emotional support, or physical help to get from one place to another. We're called to remember the help that was given to us when we were in need, and then to reach out to others in any way we can. It's okay to be a "do-gooder." Do something good for someone else today. Your heart will rejoice in your effort.

A HEART TO DO GOOD THINGS ───────────────

Lord, remind me of all the ways that others have done good things for me, and help me look for ways to do good for others whenever I can, or wherever You guide me to do so. Amen.

An Attitude of Joy

Let every created thing give praise to the LORD, for he issued his command, and they came into being. He set them in place forever and ever.
PSALM 148:5–6 NLT

When you praise the Lord with all your heart and mind and soul, you are instantly lifted into the heavenly realms of grace and joy. He transports your spirit and brings it closer to Him with every echo of praise that falls from your lips.

He draws near to you and brings you comfort and a chance to feel His very presence. In joy, you can then thank Him directly for everything you have and everything you are. You can remind God that you recognize that without Him you are an empty vessel and that you are only filled with real joy when He pours His spirit into yours.

An attitude of praise is an attitude of prayer. You need to surrender to it, release the day's concerns, the circumstances that are out of your control and the weariness of your heart, and let God meet you in the praise circle. Reach up to Him, bask in the glory of His goodness and His intentions for your life. Remind Him once again how much you love Him for all He has done for you. Let your praise produce an attitude of joy.

Sing your loud hosannas!

PRAISE FROM THE HEART

Lord, I don't always remember to thank You for the wonderful things You have done for me, especially the gift of Your Son, Jesus. I praise You, Lord, with all my heart for all I am and all I'll ever be. Amen.

Searching with the Heart

Search for the LORD and for his strength; continually seek him.
Remember the wonders he has performed.

PSALM 105:4–5 NLT

Your day-to-day existence is complicated. You have a lot of responsibilities and a lot of people who depend on you. It can feel like you're surrounded by need, and the sheer effort it takes to support everyone else can leave you exhausted. Your success then is all about how you think and where you look for strength. It's about the trust you place in God.

Edward Everett Hale reminded us,

> *To look up and not down,*
> *To look forward and not back,*
> *To look out and not in,*
> *And to lend a hand.*

When faith looks up, it is inspired to search for God. When faith looks forward, it is trusting in His promises. When faith looks outward, it sees God's love everywhere; and when faith lends a hand, it moves to take care of God's own.

As you search for renewed strength and continued faithfulness, remember to look up and think of the wonderful things God has already done for you. It will cause your heart to rejoice.

A HEART OF FAITHFULNESS

Lord, remind me always that You are with me in all that I do. Help me to look for opportunities to strengthen my faith in You by serving those around me with love. Amen.

Being the Gatekeeper

*I would rather be a gatekeeper in the house of my God than live
the good life in the homes of the wicked. For the LORD God
is our sun and our shield. He gives us grace and glory.*

PSALM 84:10–11 NLT

A gatekeeper may be the person who decides who gets in and out of a particular door, or a gatekeeper may set things in order. The point of the psalm is faithfulness and your priorities. Your faith determines where you stand on any given day. You decide in your heart what it means to have "the good life."

For a person of faith, "the good life" is often about service to God. That service means sharing in His presence and His goodness, His light and His protection every day. As one of God's gatekeepers, it's important for you to determine exactly where you want to stand. You want to open the door so that others can also stand. It's your heart that determines the "good life" and your heart that seeks God's light and protection.

Being a loving servant, tending the gate, and welcoming those around you into God's presence can be the calling of your life. As you keep the gate open, honor God by bringing others closer to His side.

A WELCOMING HEART

Lord, it's hard to recognize the "good life" as the world defines it. The gates to temptation are everywhere and I know they do not lead me closer to You. Help me to be a more vigilant gatekeeper. Amen.

Have No Fear

"All who listen to me will live in peace, untroubled by fear of harm."
PROVERBS 1:33 NLT

It's not easy to keep peace within your soul these days. Five minutes of watching CNN or reading the paper and you feel anxious. If you're not worrying about the environment and having nagging concerns about the welfare of people all over the world, then you're given pause by terrorists who have no regard at all for human life. It's no wonder the makers of antidepressants are building a mega-billion-dollar industry. You simply don't know what to think from one day to the next.

You may not have choices about the forces of nature, or even about people who would continually try to wrap you in blankets of fear, but you do have choices about how long you allow your mind to dwell on those things. You can make yourself ill with the thinking, or you can give your fears to God. He will listen!

God does not want you to live in fear. He wants you to know that He is bigger than all of these issues. He sees you right where you are. He wants you to lean on Him for protection and strength. Ask Him to keep you safe and help you maintain peace in your heart. His peace is yours for the asking.

A LESS-FEARFUL HEART

It is so hard, Father, to understand all the things that go on in the world today. Please protect me, and those I love, and keep us safe from harm. Help us to count on You, no matter what we see in the news of the day. Amen.

Separating the Good from the Bad

A good tree can't produce bad fruit, and a bad tree can't produce good fruit.... Yes, just as you can identify a tree by its fruit, so you can identify people by their actions.

MATTHEW 7:18, 20 NLT

It isn't always easy to tell the good people from the bad ones. In our culture, we're often drawn to the beautiful people because we make the assumption that they would just naturally be good. We even profile people and make assumptions about who they are and what they do by the way they dress, by their ethnicity, or family of origin. We're always trying to separate the good guys from the bad ones. The problem is that we're wrong a good share of the time.

At some point, we discover that beauty and goodness do not necessarily go hand in hand. Perhaps we just don't understand beauty. If we understood God's definitions of beauty a bit more clearly we would see that the good person is always a beautiful person. Goodness and beauty do go together when they emanate from the Spirit of God.

Whatever your definition of beauty might be, remember that God searches for beauty from the inside out. You can too. Being good has nothing to do with your wardrobe or your wallet. It has everything to do with your heart.

A HEART OF GOODNESS

Lord, help me to seek what is beautiful in others based on their love for You and their love for other people. Shape my heart to be a better person in Your eyes. Amen.

Sometimes, It's Not about You

No one should seek their own good, but the good of others.
1 CORINTHIANS 10:24 NIV

Have you ever felt slightly depressed and, before you know it, found yourself curled up in a little ball? Everything is suddenly about you and what is or isn't happening to you, and you don't know what direction to walk or what steps to take to help yourself. You're sure that there's a plot in the world to just try to make you miserable.

When you feel like that though, the answer is quite simple. Get away from yourself. Step away from your own reflection. For your own good, let go of thinking about yourself and start to think about others.

If you step out of your world for a few minutes and reach out to help someone else, you might discover that things look different than they did before. Lending a helping hand takes away your focus on your own troubles and helps you begin to feel better. Helping others is a sure cure for what ails you.

Giving your heart and your help to those outside your four walls may not take away the things that led you to wanting to curl up in a blanket, but you'll recognize that it's not all about you and that you're not alone. There's a world out there and everyone needs a little help sometimes. Seek the good of others and God will bless you tenfold.

A SOFT HEART

Lord, help me remember that I'm not the only one with problems to solve. Help me do what I can for others, regardless of my own situation. Grant me Your strength to step away from my own worries and help at least one other person today. Amen.

Who Lives within You?

Those who are dominated by the sinful nature think about sinful things, but those who are controlled by the Holy Spirit think about things that please the Spirit.

ROMANS 8:5 NLT

We often talk about the things that we carry in our minds and hearts. We think about them as concerns, ideas, and dreams. As Christians though, we can also look at who's within us, not just what is within us.

When we are of a mind to please the Holy Spirit, we have surrendered that day to the Lord Himself. When we wander in confusion, not quite certain what to think about ourselves or the things going on around us, then we have given over our very center to the world. When we're lost in the center of the world, we can't see what God has for us, we can't see His hand at work in our lives.

As you approach a new day, be sure to call upon your Lord, Jesus Christ to be at the center of your very being. Ask Him to shape your heart in ways that allow you to see His love everywhere you go. When you do that, the Holy Spirit will guide you into all things that please Him.

A CENTERED HEART

Lord, it's not always easy to keep You at the center of my heart and mind. I get caught up in all the things I have to accomplish and the work I have to do, and I lose sight of You. Be near me today, and be the center of my universe. Amen.

A Cheerful Heart

A cheerful look brings joy to the heart; good news makes for good health.
PROVERBS 15:30 NLT

Why is it that some of the people you know seem to walk around with a perpetual frown on their faces? They aren't in a particularly bad mood, but they're just not willing to go all the way to a smile. What a difference it is when you run into a friend who always has a big smile for you, embraces you with a hug, and lets you know what a joy it is just to be around you.

God wants you to have a cheerful heart because that means you understand that He is in control of your life and of the rest of the planet. That means you are not trying to take on all the troubles of the world yourself and you're not simply dwelling on negative things.

The person with a cheerful look brings joy too. They make life feel good. Whatever you're going to do today, take a look in the mirror before you walk out the door. You may need to adjust the most important part of your wardrobe. . .your smile. See if your face is ready to meet the world, and then share that radiant smile with everyone you see.

A HEART THAT BRINGS CHEER

Lord, it makes a big difference to me when I spend time with the people who greet me with joy in their faces. Help me to be the face of cheerfulness to those I meet today. Amen.

The Oil of Joy

"You love justice and hate evil. Therefore, O God, your God has anointed you, pouring out the oil of joy on you more than on anyone else."

HEBREWS 1:9 NLT

Did you wake up bathed in the oil of joy this morning? What a wonderful image that is! When we belong to Christ, we're already washed, cleaned, and pressed into His service. We're anointed with His Spirit and able to do more than we ever knew was possible. The best part of that is God can work with your heart when it's warm and pliable. He can help shape your thinking and reshape your plans. He can help give you a vision of joy and purpose like you've never felt before because love is what drives you and His love is what sustains you.

As you look to all that you hope to accomplish today, believe that all things are possible and that you are prepared, protected, and ready to deliver on the promises of God's love for you. The beauty of oils is that they work quickly, are absorbed by your skin, and gently make their way through your system. Imagine that you've been liberally sprinkled with the oil of joy today and go out and share some of your blessing. Perhaps it will rub off on others in your path.

A WARM AND PLIABLE HEART

Lord, thank You for filling me with the oil of Your loving Spirit. Help me to share the joy and the blessing You've given me today to make a positive difference to others. Amen.

Soften Your Heart

*"Today when you hear his voice, don't harden your hearts
as Israel did when they rebelled."*
HEBREWS 3:15 NLT

Do you find that some days you're a great listener for God's voice, and other days you might as well be wearing earphones tuned into your favorite radio station, have the TV blaring, and the kids yelling, because nothing is getting through to you? The Bible often reminds us to keep our hearts soft.

In our culture, we sometimes think of softhearted people as weak and powerless. We make an erroneous assumption that we have to detach from sharing our emotions if we want to be effective in life; especially when we're in roles of leadership or authority. Yet, God seems to tell us to keep soft hearts, especially toward Him. That's how we can hear His voice, and that's how we can help others to want more of Him as well.

Open your heart to Him at every opportunity, having no fear of being softhearted, and you'll hear Him as He walks with you all throughout the day.

A HEART THAT LISTENS

Lord, I don't even realize that I have shut You out until I've done it awhile and I find myself wondering where You are. Then I discover I'm the one who walked away and closed the door. Help me to keep a soft heart and an open mind so that I can hear You drawing near to me. Amen.

Get a Grip

So take a new grip with your tired hands and strengthen your weak knees.
Mark out a straight path for your feet so that those who are
weak and lame will not fall but become strong.

HEBREWS 12:12–13 NLT

Did you ever watch one of those circus performers who steps into the arena and then another person jumps up on his shoulders? Then to your amazement about three other people jump up on the shoulders of each person, and now the guy at the bottom is standing there holding up four or five other people? You can't imagine how he doesn't just buckle under the weight of it all.

If you think of yourself as standing tall in the Lord, then you are like that person because all around you are people who are standing on your shoulders. They are weaker than you are and in need of connecting to someone who is strong and stable. When you are held in God's hand, you're able to hold some of His newcomers as well. His goal is to touch each person and lighten their load so that none will be lost. He's counting on you to remain in His grip. He knows that you will do all you can to share the true foundation of the world, the One who really holds them up all the time.

Commit to being strong in the Lord and helping others along the way as well.

A HEART OF STRENGTH

Lord, keep me in Your care, and help me to strengthen the way for others to know You. Help me to stand firm in You. Amen.

Living by the Spirit

Since we live by the Spirit, let us keep in step with the Spirit.
GALATIANS 5:25 NIV

What does it mean to you to live by the Spirit? How do you keep in step with the Spirit so that your heart can be guided by His grace and love each day?

Look at it this way. If you live by a certain work ethic, you demonstrate that by everything you do. You learn everything you can about your business, and you stay up to date on the newest information about it. You talk about it with others and probably even think about it when you're not working. You sometimes live, breathe, and sleep your work. That's living by your work ethic. You have some goals in front of you, and whether it takes training or shifting your direction, or even starting over, you're ready to do the work.

If you live by the Spirit, then you do the same thing. You faithfully read the Word so you can keep up with what God has to say, you pray and listen and wait for God's direction in your life. As one with a passion, you talk about it with those around you and think about it every chance you get. You live by the Spirit in all that you do, and you share your heart with others, hoping to draw them into God's kingdom.

Today, imagine that your work is simply to live in the Spirit in every possible way. Then step out into the world and let your light shine. You're sure to have an amazing day.

A HEART FIXED ON THE SPIRIT

Lord, as I try to fall into step with You today, lead me in the directions You would have me go, and help me to be mindful of You in all that I do. Amen.

Patience with Yourself and Others

Be completely humble and gentle; be patient, bearing with one another in love.

EPHESIANS 4:2 NIV

Your mother was probably the first person who gently told you to be patient. You may have been waiting for Christmas, your birthday, or for Dad to come home, and she would smile and say to "just be patient." You could hardly bear it, but you tried, and it took a lot of effort.

Now that you're all grown up, you might hear this message from your spouse or your boss at work, or even your friends. Waiting for something, waiting for anything, is just as hard now as it ever was.

Just be patient! You might bear the waiting in your head, but it's a little harder to do when the issue is a matter of the heart. When you're waiting for someone you care about to find a better life path, to trust God more, or to see that they are losing ground, then it's harder to wait. God gave you a heart that anticipates and grows excited with new ideas and opportunities. It rejoices when you see His hand at work in your life and in the lives of others. It even does some flip-flops of gratitude when things come together.

Your heart is not always practical and patient though. The more you recognize how often you have to be patient with others, the more you recognize the same principles apply to you. Be humble and gentle today, bearing with others and trusting in God to lead you. It will be worth any waiting you have to do.

A HEART OF HUMBLE PATIENCE

Lord, You know I'm not very good at being patient with others, much less with myself. Help me to be more of what You would have me be and wait with a humble and loving heart when I'm called to do so. Amen.

Love Is at the Heart of Everything

For this very reason, make every effort to add to your faith goodness; and to goodness, knowledge; and to knowledge, self-control; and to self-control, perseverance; and to perseverance, godliness; and to godliness, mutual affection; and to mutual affection, love.

2 PETER 1:5–7 NIV

If you were creating a recipe for right living, smart thinking, and faithful following, the verse above would do nicely. It reads like a list of ingredients. Add a little knowledge, a pinch of godliness, and a cup and a half of goodness and you'll be on the way to becoming the master chef of love. Well, maybe.

Adding goodness and self-control to your life always means you'll enjoy a little more of the good stuff life has to offer. After all, the more you give, share, and offer to others in the right spirit, the more will come back to you. Brotherly and sisterly kindness and love will reward you.

As someone living a heart-shaped life, God looks to you to lead the way. He wants you to shine your light on His people who have not yet seen Him clearly, and offer to help them do so. He wants you to give in ways that you may not have thought possible simply because of your love for Him. He knows you. He knows you have a lot to give, and He knows that love is at the heart of everything you do.

A HEART THAT SHINES

Lord, it seems like I'm always working on one of those special ingredients, hoping to do better, hoping to please You in the things I do. Whatever I do today, help me to do it with Your amazing love. Amen.

The Bigness of God

*This is what the LORD says—your Redeemer and Creator: "I am the
LORD, who made all things. I alone stretched out the heavens.
Who was with me when I made the earth?"*

ISAIAH 44:24 NLT

Do you ever stop to think about how "big" God really is? Do you sit in awe of the fact that He is your Redeemer and Creator and He did it all without a committee? He alone brought you into being and set your feet upon the earth. He alone is in control of the entire universe. He alone chose to love you simply because you asked Him to do so, and He did that before you knew to ask.

When you leave God in charge of everything, you set your priorities in order. You remind yourself that nothing exists because of you, but everything exists because of Him. You give up your own need to be in control, and you even stop asking why. You just let the divine greatness of God be the master of all things, including you. Let God be God and let Him be even bigger in your life.

One of the ways you know you're growing more "heart-shaped" is when you recognize that God is everything and that nothing else truly makes a difference. God working within you makes the whole difference to your life and what you share by His grace with others. He gave you a big heart because He is a big God!

A BIG HEART

Lord, I imagine that I need to "handle" things for You; that somehow You need my help to get things done. The fact is, You're big enough to handle everything. Thank You for allowing me to help You where I can, sharing in the joy of working with my Father. Amen.

No Anxiety

When anxiety was great within me, your consolation brought me joy.
PSALM 94:19 NIV

We usually think of Christmas when we put together words like "comfort and joy." They are words we so often express in songs and greeting cards.

Springtime gives us an opportunity to grasp what it really means to have God's comfort and joy. We need the promise that it brings because we miss God's presence in our daily lives. We get caught up with the sad news of the day; news that often shakes the foundation of the very core of human dignity and values. We feel its pressure and we need more light.

With God's help, we can be in the world, but we don't have to be "of" it. We can hold our hands up and out and grasp the Savior for comfort and relief. We can reach for His life preservers of faith to get us through the storms that hover nearby. We can seek Him with our whole heart and mind. When we do, He'll bring joy to our souls.

When the road of life gets too bumpy, head for the Rock of your salvation! Like a breath of fresh air, He'll bring peace to your heart.

A COMFORTED HEART

Lord, help me come closer to You whenever life makes me feel anxious and overwhelmed. Let me draw strength and peace and joy from Your hand and hold it closely to my heart. Amen.

Happy Circumstances!

Good planning and hard work lead to prosperity.
PROVERBS 21:5 NLT

We often have a tendency to blame our circumstances on other people when things don't go our way. We imagine we didn't have enough time, money, energy, support from friends, something. . .when things fail to come through. Those factors played into what did or didn't happen, but those things may not be the reason behind a lack of success.

George Bernard Shaw said, "People are always blaming their circumstances for what they are. The people who get on in the world are they who get up and look for the circumstances they want, and, if they can't find them, make them."

Part of our faithfulness to God is about not giving excuses when things don't go the way we hope they will. God is always available to help us create "happy circumstances" that will benefit our hearts and minds. He wants us to include Him in the planning and to be faithful in the asking.

If you don't see what you want for your life today, perhaps your first step in the planning is not to see what you can do, not to rely on your own strength, but to seek God's heart for the opportunity you have in mind. He'll be able to help you move toward your goal with joy. He'll shape your heart to seek Him first so you can discover His will for your life.

A HEART THAT PLANS

Lord, please be with me today and show me the places where I've gotten away from relying on You. Let me work with You to create the best circumstances for my life. My heart rejoices in You! Amen.

A Bigger Heart for Others

You see my shame and disgrace. You know all my enemies and what they have said. Insults have broken my heart and left me weak. I looked for sympathy, but there was none; I found no one to comfort me.

PSALM 69:19–20 NCV

Striving to have a heart shaped by God's mercy, grace, and compassion sometimes means that you have to get out of your comfort zone. It means you have to reach out and touch those who are unlovable, or at least feel unloved by the world.

You're surrounded by people who fit this description. They don't think anyone cares about them. They've lost any hope that someone will have sympathy on their situation and help them get to new and better circumstances. They have no one to comfort them. You may have felt these things in your own life as well. You may have had experiences that left you feeling weak and broken.

You know it's a dark place to be. Imagine the difference it could make if even one person held up a light for one other. Imagine that person is you. God will bless you with His presence and love. He will help you continue to grow a heart of sympathy and love.

A HEART TO HELP

Lord, help me be willing to notice at least one person who suffers in silence, feeling alone in the darkness. For anyone in distress, let me offer the comfort that only You can bring. Amen.

The Commandment to Love

Jesus said, " 'Love the Lord your God with all your passion and prayer and
intelligence.' This is the most important [of God's commands], the first on any list."
MATTHEW 22:37–38 MSG

When love commands you to seek God, you have lots of ways to do so. You can honor God with your passion. Look at the things that make your heart sing, give you renewed energy, and bring your spirit to life. When that feeling permeates your soul, you are better able to demonstrate your love for God.

You can honor God with your prayers. Take everything to Him. Put your sorrows and concerns and "what-ifs" at His feet. Put your joys, your excitement, and your hopes in His arms and embrace His love.

You can honor God with your intelligence. Give Him everything that goes on in your heart and mind. Surrender your goals and your ambitions and your dreams and trust Him to return to you those things that are truly yours.

Renew your commitment to love God and enjoy the pleasure of His company in even greater measure today. Express your heart and your love for Him by all you do.

A HEART FOR GOD'S LOVE

Dear God, help me to love You as You deserve to be loved. I surrender my passion,
my heart, my mind, and my spirit to Your care and keeping. I recommit my heart and
my life to You. Amen.

Love One Another

"But there is a second [command of God] to set alongside it:
'Love others as well as you love yourself.'"
MATTHEW 22:39 MSG

A command to love others as we love ourselves puts some of us in jeopardy. In part, it's because we've bought into the negative things others have said about us, or we have decided we're not very lovable. So we simply don't know how to love ourselves, and by extension, we're not good at loving others, either. In fact, we're not really sure what this command of Jesus really means.

If you've forgotten how to love yourself, take a moment and consider creating ways that might renew your understanding. Give yourself a gift of honoring YOU. Take note of each time you do, say, or understand something about yourself that allows you to see your heart the way God sees you. He loves you, imperfections and all. He doesn't love you for what you aren't. He loves you for what you are!

The more you learn to love yourself and appreciate your own gifts, the more you'll understand the service you bring to others through love. Once you get the big picture of that, you'll be ready to fill your favorite album with photos of all the new friends who are in your life; the ones you love even more than yourself. May you awaken today to the love God pours out from His heart to yours.

A HEART OF LOVE

Lord, I know I'm pretty stingy with myself. I often think that I'm not good enough to even be loved by You. Help me to understand what it means to have genuine self-love. Amen.

Encourage One Another

All of you should be of one mind. Sympathize with each other. Love each other as brothers and sisters. Be tenderhearted, and keep a humble attitude.

1 Peter 3:8 NLT

Compassion is not about emotion. It's not about how you feel about the woman down the street or the teenager next door. It's about being willing to help them when a need arises just because they are in need of human kindness. Compassion reminds you that your heart is in training, that it is still being shaped by your Creator. When your heart is willing to act simply because your desire is to make someone else feel better, then you have the kind of sympathy God is seeking. When you see a need in someone else's life, your hands will seek ways to help.

You can hardly read the daily paper of any city in the country without feeling compassion for people all over the globe. Your heart suffers with those who have undergone severe losses because of illness or natural disasters. You have a great desire to volunteer your time to help build a house with Habitat for Humanity or visit a shut-in and offer a word of encouragement. When you respond in a way that does your heart good, an interesting thing happens. You're given an instant gift. That gift is peace, and an even bigger heart.

May God continue to work with you, reminding you that you are His hands and feet in a world that is desperately in need of hope and tenderhearted encouragement.

A HEART TO ENCOURAGE OTHERS

Dear Lord, help me to reach out with a genuine sympathy to those in need around me. Remind me that anything I have comes to me from Your goodness and Your grace. Amen.

The Heart of Your Faith

You were saved by faith in God, who treats us much better than we deserve.
This is God's gift to you, and not anything you have done on your own.

EPHESIANS 2:8 CEV

Faith is God's gift to you. When you believe fully that you are saved by the grace of God, you understand that He treats you far better than you deserve. This is the meaning of grace. As a believer, you can have confidence in God's saving grace and equal confidence in your faith. Faith is a heart matter and grace is a God matter, and they are both enormous gifts to you from our Creator.

Martin Luther said, "Faith is a living, daring confidence in God's grace, so sure and certain that a person would stake his life on it a thousand times."

Would you stake your life on your faith?

Today, connect with God so fully that you don't close your eyes to rest this evening without knowing with certainty that you are loved and saved by your faith in Him. If you have any doubt at all about where you stand, then talk with God about it one to one and heart to heart. You are saved by your faith at this very moment. You are unconditionally and wholeheartedly loved!

A FAITHFUL HEART

Lord, help me to have more confidence in the fact of my salvation. Help me to live in such a way that I celebrate the joy of all that You have done for me each day. Grant me the faith that fills my heart with peace. Amen.

A Contented Heart

I have learned, in whatsoever state I am, therewith to be content.
PHILIPPIANS 4:11 KJV

You have a gift coming your way today. It's a wonderful gift and one that you might not always know is there. It's the gift of contentment, regardless of your circumstances. It's the gift that fills your whole body with peace. You're welcome to open your gift any time and use it as often as you'd like. It's pretty much up to you. You can be as content as you choose to be. You can be at peace in a moment's notice.

Restless hearts are not contented ones. They search everywhere for a way to calm their stretched nerves and quiet their spirits. They look for antidotes in pharmacies or liquor bottles, hoping for relief from whatever ails their hearts and minds. They exercise until their bodies are too tired to think anymore, or so they'll have enough stamina to carry the load again tomorrow.

You can have a contented heart. You can be content in whatever circumstances you have and be at peace with yourself. You can because your Father in heaven wants you to be at peace, and He gave you the gift of His peace through the Holy Spirit. Embrace Him. Open the gift of peace and don't leave home without it. Go on your way with a truly contented heart today.

A PEACEFUL HEART

Lord, it is not easy for me to find peace in the world and in my home and in my heart. I want to, but I'm not good at surrendering the things that make me so restless. Quiet my heart, and help me today to rest in You. Amen.

On Your Way Rejoicing

This is the day the LORD has made. We will rejoice and be glad in it.
PSALM 118:24 NLT

Smile! Okay, now try a really big smile! You can even clap your hands and laugh out loud! This is your day, and God made this day just for you. You can share it with the people in your family, your friends, your coworkers, or simply enjoy it all by yourself. Whatever you are doing today, remind yourself that God made this day for you and you can do with it whatever you want.

When you put on a happy face and let your feet dance a little, the world suddenly seems a bit brighter and a lot friendlier. It becomes a place where you can literally see the grace of God everywhere you go. It becomes the beautiful world God meant it to be.

Test this idea yourself. Go outside and offer a great big smile and a friendly hello to the first three strangers you meet and see if they smile back. Chances are good they will, even in spite of themselves, and you'll go on your way rejoicing. This is the day the Lord has made, and He made it just for you. That is something to sing about, offer a little praise, and discover even more reasons for your heart to be glad. Tap those feet! Come on!

AT THE HEART OF THE DAY

Lord, remind me of Your goodness in all I do today. You have given me all that I have and all that I need, and I praise You with all my heart. In Jesus' name, amen.

You're So Brave!

Be on guard. Stand firm in the faith. Be courageous.
Be strong. And do everything with love.

1 CORINTHIANS 16:13–14 NLT

Do you remember the most recent thing you did that took real courage? Perhaps you had to speak in front of a group of people and you're not very confident about speaking. Maybe you prepared a dinner for a group of guests you didn't know well and weren't sure what to serve. Or, maybe you stood up for a friend and others criticized you for doing so. Courage is what causes you to be strong and brave; it's a matter of the heart.

You may find it takes courage sometimes to even express your faith. You question if this is the right person, the right place, or the right time to witness. You think you're around people who probably don't want to hear what you have to say. You've tried to share your faith before and been made fun of in some way, and so it's not easy to open that door again.

But, look at you! You're so brave, you just go on standing up for friends, sharing what you believe, and being strong in the Lord. You're an example of what it really means to do everything in love. Do you know why? You do those things because God has given you a courageous heart. He has helped you to get past anything that may cause worry or concern and strengthened your heart and mind to do His will. Take a bow! Keep on doing what you do best because it's exactly what God wants you to do.

A HEART OF COURAGE

Dear Lord, grant me the courage to share those ideas that come straight from You. Remind me that You are near and that I don't have to be especially brave if I remember that You are my strength. Amen.

No Fear!

"Don't be troubled or afraid."
JOHN 14:27 NLT

You might think it's a rather ridiculous idea to face the world without some sense of fear. After all, it's pounded into your brain on a daily basis with every news report and newspaper. Things are not going well in much of the world, and you may feel you have good reason to be afraid.

Every generation from the past to our present time has experienced fear of something. It may have been fear of disease, fear of war, or fear of hurricanes, but it has been something. Today, with one touch of a computer screen, the whole world is brought into your home and your heart has to deal with it.

What can you do? You're told in John 14 to not be troubled or afraid. Can your faith truly help you overcome genuine fear?

Martin Luther King Jr. said, "Courage is an inner resolution to go forward in spite of obstacles and frightening situations; cowardice is a submissive surrender to circumstances. Courage faces fear and thereby masters it; cowardice represses fear and is thereby mastered by it."

Don't read the negative stories in the newspaper or on Facebook or listen to podcasts that don't serve you well. Turn off the news and get into the pews! You have the right to bask in the presence of the One who offers you His strength and courage to face every day. God does not want you to have a fearful heart and mind. Trust in Him!

A BRAVE HEART

Lord, help me to get past all the news that makes it hard for me to face any given day, and help me to keep peace in my soul and find my strength in You. Amen.

Picking the Fruit

*But what happens when we live God's way? He brings gifts into our lives, much
the same way that fruit appears in an orchard—things like affection for others,
exuberance about life, serenity. We develop a willingness to stick with things,
a sense of compassion in the heart, and a conviction that a basic holiness permeates
things and people. We find ourselves involved in loyal commitments, not needing
to force our way in life, able to marshal and direct our energies wisely.*

GALATIANS 5:22–23 MSG

This version of Galatians 5:22–23 is wonderful. It gives us a clear understanding of how the gifts of the Spirit really strengthen us and shape our hearts and minds. It even gives us a desire to start picking more fruit so that we can be filled with more and more of these wonderful things. The gifts of God's Spirit are available to us, and our heart's desire for them helps us to discover them.

Consider what you already have been given and see if there are yet some gifts that you would desire to experience more fully. If you discover a gift that is not yet clearly developed in you, then take today and focus your prayers there, and ask God to teach you more of His ways so that you can reflect Him in all you do. Allow God to be present in your heart and mind so that His gift to you feels natural and causes your love to overflow for those who do not yet know Him as you do.

Remember, the best peaches are always just slightly out of reach. The best of God's Spirit, though, is just a prayer away. May He bless you and keep you close to Him wherever you go.

A HEART TUNED IN TO THE SPIRIT ───────────

Lord, help me climb a little higher, work a little harder, and be ready to accept the gifts of Your Spirit. Open my heart and mind to all that You have for me. Amen.

You Were Appointed

*I appointed you to go and produce lasting fruit, so that the Father
will give you whatever you ask for, using my name.*

JOHN 15:16 NLT

When God appointed you to simply grow up with Him, allowing Him to shape you and help you become more than you would have ever been before, it was a gift to both of you. He knew that you would honor the gifts He gave you and that you would take your appointment seriously. For a good share of your life since your assignment began, you've been producing good fruit, helping others to see His face more clearly, and learning all you can about the work to be done.

John Blanchard asked, "How often do we need to see God's face, hear His voice, feel His touch, know His power? The answer to all these questions is the same: Every day!"

When your heart is tuned in to the Spirit, you see God's face more clearly, hear His voice more often, and feel His unlimited power in your life. You know you need His touch every day, and that means other people do as well. Your appointment will last a lifetime, and everything you do to bring even one more person closer to Christ will be added to your list of accomplishments. Ask for His help and He'll see that you get it. God wants you to produce the fruit that will last. Appointing you to do His work pleases Him.

SHAPED BY HIS SPIRIT

Lord, You have given me so many gifts, and I glorify Your name for all that You do for me. Help me to be wise and honor You always with the things I say and do. Amen.

Destiny Awaits!

When a potter makes jars out of clay, doesn't he have the right to use the same lump of clay to make one jar for decoration and another to throw garbage into?

ROMANS 9:21 NLT

It's not always easy to remember that you are not the Potter, but simply the clay. As the clay, you can be used by God in any way He chooses for the good of His whole human family. He clearly needs each of us to do different things to help usher in the Kingdom.

Your destiny is in His hands. If you give Him the right to mold you and hold you close, you'll discover that He has something beautiful in mind for you to become. He delights in you simply because you allow Him to utilize your skills and talents and ideas in whatever way pleases Him. He loves your willingness to give Him your whole heart, surrendering to His design for your life. Your future then is to be more beautiful in whatever use He has for your life.

Imagine a loving Potter who enjoys His craft more than you can know, shaping your life at this very moment. See Him looking at you with great interest, making certain that every detail is just right so that you will be perfectly set for the work He has in mind. Though He may have created many other such wonderful pieces for purposes all His own, you are unique, an original. You were designed with a heart to do great things. His purpose comes to fulfillment each time you seek His direction and thank Him for creating you exactly as you are.

A HEART SHAPED BY THE POTTER

Lord, help me to become all that You intended me to become by the works of Your hand. Let me be a labor of love, and a joy to Your Spirit. Amen.

Determined to Meet Your Goals

Take a lesson from the ants, you lazybones. Learn from their ways and become wise!
Though they have no prince, governor, or ruler to make them work,
they labor hard all summer, gathering food for the winter.

PROVERBS 6:6–8 NLT

It's easy to get sidetracked. We set up our plans and create our goals, and then life happens. Someone gets sick and needs our attention; the meeting you were waiting for falls through; the job doesn't happen; or a thousand other variables change your direction. While you're out taking care of those things that you didn't plan, other things aren't getting done.

Being intentional is a good thing, and it helps to guide your actions. If you know where you want to go, it's a lot easier to get there. Even if your boss isn't around, your partner isn't in view, or you're the only one there to keep yourself motivated, you've got to do it. You do it because your heart is fully engaged in the effort. You know that it is what you are meant to do.

You may have watched ants build their houses, lugging pieces of food, sand, or whatever else, in pieces three times their size, from one spot to another. They know the goal is to get ready for winter, and so they don't stop until nature shuts the door on their well-prepared nest. When you're determined to meet your goals, nothing can stop you, either. Getting sidetracked doesn't need to get you off track. Just keep at it. That's what the ants do. That's what God wants you to do as well.

A DETERMINED HEART

Lord, I get sidetracked sometimes about the things that are most important. Help me to stay on the path, working toward the goals we've set together. Grant me a heart that is determined to move forward with You. Amen.

Producing the Good Fruit

*"A good tree can't produce bad fruit, and a bad tree can't produce good fruit.
A tree is identified by its fruit. Figs are never gathered from thornbushes,
and grapes are not picked from bramble bushes. A good person
produces good things from the treasury of a good heart."*

LUKE 6:43–45 NLT

The Bible often makes the point that who and what we are has a lot to do with what goes on in the heart. We say that someone is good-hearted when they do kind deeds for others, or when they give selflessly to the well-being of those around them. Their work is a direct result of what they believe. In fact, everything they do is closely tied to the discipline of their hearts. You recognize those people by the fruit of their labors.

You often do good deeds. You give from the heart to those in need and to the people in your family. Challenge yourself today to produce even more of the great fruit. See if there is one person in your sphere of influence you may have overlooked. Keep growing, keep producing good fruit, and keep sharing your heart with others.

AT THE HEART OF GOOD DEEDS

Lord, let me share the good things You have given me today. Remind me of those people I have overlooked and who need my help, and give me an opportunity to plant new seeds of love. Amen.

Working for Peace

God blesses those who work for peace, for they will be called the children of God.
MATTHEW 5:9 NLT

As beautiful as it is to be blessed with a peaceful spirit and to feel God's peace in your heart, there is a greater blessing for those who work for peace in the world. Working for peace is a never-ending job. We live in a volatile society where many live in fear and anxiety. We've lost that small-town sense of innocence that seemed to protect us when we were young, and we wonder if true peace can actually be achieved.

You may not be a speaker, a writer, or a group leader, but you can still contribute to the peace in the world. How? You can be the keeper of peace in your own home or in your workplace. You can be the voice of reason when conflict arises. You can pray for the good of everyone you know so that their lives have greater peace. You can be a force for good simply by doing those things. You can remind people that they are connected neighbor to neighbor and heart to heart.

Open the door for peace in your heart, your home, and your community. You can shape the way people see each other, restore a sense of calm, and honor each one as a unique child of God.

A HEART THAT SEEKS PEACE

Lord, help me be a leader in the effort for peace wherever I am. Help me offer Your peace to all those I meet, remembering that each person is known by You, and each one is loved. Amen.

Be the Light

*"You are the light of the world—like a city on a hilltop that cannot be hidden.
No one lights a lamp and then puts it under a basket. Instead, a lamp is
placed on a stand, where it gives light to everyone in the house."*

MATTHEW 5:14–15 NLT

When you live a heart-shaped life, you discover that everything you do and say is affected by the Spirit of God living within you. You can be the light in many wonderful ways. Every time you offer a smile and a kind word to someone, you're the light. Every time you have compassion on your neighbor or even a stranger, you're the light. Every time you do something as the hands and feet of Christ, you're the light. In fact, unless you're sound asleep, you're actively engaged in being a shining star.

Your prayers are like the stars in heaven. They sparkle, shine, and illuminate the way for all those you offer up to God. You bring their needs to light and focus attention on them. Every time you pray, the light shines.

So much of the world seems to exist in the dark. It is starving for attention, for blessed illumination. The Spirit of God wants to shine on it and help it to thrive. The best way for that to happen is for us to reach out with joy, reach up with our whole hearts, and seek to shine wherever God has placed us. You are desperately needed to light a pathway for someone today. It doesn't need to be in some remote place miles from your home, it can be in the heart of where you live. Whatever you do today, make sure your light is strong and bright.

A HEART OF JOY

Lord, help me to shine Your light as brightly as I can today. Let me be the light of kindness, of friendship, and of compassion every chance I get. Amen.

Hold Fast to the Good

Prove all things; hold fast that which is good.
1 THESSALONIANS 5:21 KJV

Did you ever have something really good just slip right out of your hands? Maybe it was a job, a friend, or an idea, but without even realizing what was happening, you somehow lost this good thing. After it was gone, you fully understood what you lost. That belated understanding may have caused your heart to grieve.

In order to hold fast to good things, it may be good to take an inventory of all God has done for you so that you can truly thank Him with your mind and heart. You may lose something important simply because you never identified it and marked it as precious.

Your business today is to think about all the good things God has given you. Write them down and give Him praise for each thing on your list. Thank Him for the joy that you receive from these good things. Hold fast to His goodness to you so that you take nothing for granted. Your health, your home, your job, your family. . .thank Him for the amazing good He has done in your life. Thank Him too that you can come to Him with a heart of joy, knowing that you would have nothing without Him and that every good thing comes to you from His hand.

Give God thanks and praise.

A HEART FULL OF GOOD THINGS

Lord, I confess that I do not always deliberately take notice of the things that are going right in my life. I'm more apt to come to You when everything falls apart. Thank You for loving me so much. I am grateful for Your amazing provision and I cling to You with love. Amen.

Don't Drop Out!

*My dear child, don't shrug off God's discipline, but don't be crushed by it either.
It's the child he loves that he disciplines; the child he embraces, he also
corrects. God is educating you; that's why you must never drop out.*

HEBREWS 12:6 MSG

Have you ever felt like running away from your current life and starting over? Maybe
you've been trying to complete a goal, but it doesn't seem to come together. Maybe
you've been dreaming about the right job, the right person to love, or the right
place to live, but nothing you do quite happens as you hope. When nothing goes your
way, it makes you wonder if God thinks you're the only one who needs more discipline.
Doesn't anyone else need a little divine instruction?

Of course, the answer is that all of us who enrolled in God's school become part of
His education system. We get the perks and we get the discipline because it's all part
of the training. The good news is that the closer you get to graduation, the more He's
paying attention to see that you've gotten all the tools you need to move to the next
level. He cares so much about your well-being that He won't let you move ahead until
you're ready. This is part of His plan for shaping your heart to be more like His.

Don't give up or drop out! You're a great student, and God wants you to be everything He intended you to be. He knows your heart, and He believes in all you can do and
all that you will be. Good things are coming your way.

A HEART FOR LEARNING

*Lord, shape my heart so that it is willing to learn and grow and accept the work in
front of me. Thanks for being such a Divine Teacher! Amen.*

Be Cheerful All the Time!

*Be cheerful no matter what; pray all the time, thank God no matter what happens.
This is the way God wants you who belong to Christ Jesus to live.*

1 THESSALONIANS 5:16 MSG

The idea of being cheerful all the time seems a bit daunting. Even if you're a person with a great disposition, it would be pretty incredible to be cheerful *all* the time. It's not only that you need to be cheerful all the time, but you need to be that way *NO MATTER WHAT HAPPENS*! Now, that sounds impossible!

There's a small loophole, though, that might help us keep this in perspective. It's the one that says being cheerful is the way God wants you to be because you belong to Christ Jesus. He may be trying to tell us that things are okay, that you don't have to concern yourself with every mess that comes up in the world because you have a heart that is connected to His and He has your back.

Whatever happens then in your everyday life, you are a child of God, a follower of Jesus, and that means you have good reason to be cheerful. Your situation may seem less than what you'd hope for, but if you keep your heart connected to your Savior, and stay focused on Him, then you have reason for joy.

You may not be happy about each detail of your life, but you can always be happy in Jesus. It may be harder to remember this some days when things are not going well, but start with today and trust God with your heart, soul, and mind, and it could make all the difference. You might even find yourself smiling.

A HEART OF TRUST

Lord, help me to find my joy in You no matter what is going on in my life. Help me to surrender the details of living on earth and embrace the joy of living in Jesus. Amen.

Keep Growing!

But good people will grow like palm trees; they will be tall like the cedars of Lebanon. Like trees planted in the Temple of the LORD, they will grow strong in the courtyards of our God. When they are old, they will still produce fruit; they will be healthy and fresh.

PSALM 92:12–14 NCV

Living a heart-shaped life means that you are always seeking to see God's hand at work in new ways. You see Him in places that others might miss. You praise Him for what He does because He is always present with you; always causing you to trust and surrender and remember His love for you.

You nourish yourself in the richness of the Word and replenish your faithfulness through prayer and thanksgiving. You can never truly grow old because your faith stays as young and as spirited as the cedars of Lebanon in their grandeur and glory.

It is important to be aware of what you plant, so that you can reap the good of what you sow. As long as you remain in the presence of the Spirit, you will be blessed with renewed strength in the work you do. You will grow in the awareness of what God can do for your heart, mind, and soul, and you will become an inspiration to people everywhere.

God loves you, nurtures you, and wants you to grow stronger each day. Feel His blessing on your life, and give thanks for the tender care you receive.

A HEART OF BLESSING

Dear Lord, thank You for nurturing me and reshaping my thoughts and my life. I ask that I might grow in Your love and draw strength from Your presence each day I live. Amen.

Love Forgives

Hatred stirs up trouble, but love forgives all wrongs.
PROVERBS 10:12 NCV

Forgiveness is sticky. It's one of those things that we're all grateful for when we seek God's forgiveness to us. We appreciate knowing that He has unconditional love for us. When we come to Him with a contrite heart and a desire to change, He forgives us and blesses our efforts to do better the next time.

It's not so much fun when we have to forgive someone else, though. It's even less fun when we don't feel we need to ask for forgiveness. Often, we come to the humbling roadblock of pride, and we find ourselves walking around with a great big log in our own eye as we try to pick out splinters from the eye of someone else.

Saying I'm sorry can be difficult. Meaning it deep within the heart can be even more challenging. We can't say we're sorry and then remind the person of the wrong deed every time we get a chance. How would we feel if God did that to us? He puts our sins far from Him and remembers it no more. That's what a forgiving heart does. That's what He wants us to do too. We haven't forgiven what we truly haven't forgotten.

Love forgives all wrongs. Sometimes love forgives even without apologies. Love puts all wrongs at the cross of Christ and leaves them there.

That's loving and forgiving at its best. Go on, you can do it.

AT THE HEART OF FORGIVENESS

Lord, let me learn to be truly forgiving out of love for You. Help me to surrender any need to forgive or be forgiven to You and move on in Your grace and mercy. Amen.

....

....

....

....

....

....

....

....

Dare to Dream. . .Dare to Ask!

"You can ask for anything in my name, and I will do it, so that the Son can bring glory to the Father. Yes, ask me for anything in my name, and I will do it!"

JOHN 14:13–14 NLT

James M. Barrie said, "Dreams do come true, if we only wish hard enough. You can have anything in life if you will sacrifice everything else for it." "What will you have?" says God. "Pray for it and take it."

What will you have? What do you dream and hope for and fear all at the same time? It is important to be a lover of dreams for that is what fills the heart with joy and expectation. It is important to be a lover of prayer for the same reason. Prayer puts a foundation under your dreams and lifts them to a place of fulfillment and opportunity. Prayer puts your dreams in direct alignment with God. Ask Him to line your heart up with the dreams He's given you so that you can work together to create the vision. Give God the glory and ask Him to fulfill the desires of your heart.

Sometimes we dream, sometimes we pray, but often we forget to put our dreams in the Creator's hands so He can help us manifest them according to His will and purpose for us. Ask! Ask for your heart's desires in Jesus' name!

A HEARTFELT PRAYER

Lord, sometimes I forget to put my dreams in front of You. Help me to embrace the ways You shape the direction of my life, and help me to seek Your wisdom in all that I do. Amen.

Prudent Pruning; Beautiful Shaping

*"I am the true grapevine, and my Father is the gardener. He cuts off every branch
of mine that doesn't produce fruit, and he prunes the branches that do
bear fruit so they will produce even more. You have already been
pruned and purified by the message I have given you."*

JOHN 15:1–3 NLT

If you've ever tried pruning the bushes by your back door or trimming the hedges around the yard, you know that it's not easy work. You usually come back worn out from the experience, and your newly trimmed shrubs may still not look divine when you're done. With time, they grow more beautiful and you see the fruit of your labors. You start to think it actually was a good idea to get rid of those old branches. You realize that you've been a good gardener.

Our heavenly Gardener knows that you might not like it if He pulls you from some of the things that you've always liked doing, or He weeds out some old friends and directs you to find some new ones. He knows you might sulk a bit and not be your best for a while, but with time, He also knows that you'll come back and be more beautiful and more fruitful than ever. This is the way He brings you to fullness and joy; the way He shapes your heart to be more beautiful. Since you're already plugged into the vine of Jesus, it's a lot easier for God to work with you to enhance your life and the blessing you are to others.

With a little of His prudent pruning, you'll be amazed at your own growth and even awed to see how beautiful you really are under His care.

A HEART-SHAPED LIFE

*Lord, it's not easy for me to understand when You cut off some of the directions
I thought I'd go. Help me trust my life to Your care in every way and in all I do.
Thank You for making me more beautiful in You! Amen.*

Live in Harmony

Be happy with those who are happy, and weep with those
who weep. Live in harmony with each other.
ROMANS 12:15–16 NLT

Empathy is a matter of the heart. It is the desire and the willingness you have to be there in the crisis moments of others. You feel their pain in your heart and in your mind, much the way that God feels pain when you are sad. Knowing what God's grace and love do for you shapes your efforts and your tenderness toward those around you.

When you feel their joy, then you increase their happiness and bring even greater beauty to the moment. People with deep empathy for others may cry at movies, smile at speakers, or nod their heads in agreement with the pastor as he shares his Sunday morning sermon. Those with little empathy rarely let the feelings of those around them permeate their space. They prefer to hide behind their own walls and insulate themselves from either tears or laughter.

When you willingly share your heart and your spirit with others, you create greater harmony in the process. You remind your friends that embracing life heart-first makes a difference. God wants you to live in harmony with all your brothers and sisters. When you reach out to show His kindness, your heart reaches out as well, and everyone is blessed.

A LITTLE MORE EMPATHY

Lord, it is truly an honor to share in the joy and the sorrows of others. Bless those times in my life when I strive to bring harmony and love to any situation. Amen.

Enjoy Yourself!

*The best that people can do is eat, drink, and enjoy their work. I saw that even
this comes from God, because no one can eat or enjoy life without him.*

ECCLESIASTES 2:24–25 NCV

Imagine that you have cleaned all day, cooked a glorious meal for your family, added fresh flowers to the table, set out the good dishes, and prepared everyone's favorite dessert. You're totally pleased with your work and you're looking forward to your family coming home and enjoying the fruits of your labors. It feels good and you're happy.

Now suppose that your family comes home and no one seems to notice the beautifully polished woodwork or the lovely vase of flowers. Then, everyone sits down to dinner, eats it, and runs off even before the gourmet dessert, and you're sitting there dumbfounded. All your efforts have gone unnoticed. No one thanked you for trying, for giving, or simply for being there.

In similar ways, God has great joy in what He's done for you. He's provided for you and blessed your life. Suppose He anticipated special things that would give you great joy and spread them before you, then you came to dinner, hardly ate, and walked off without so much as a nod in His direction. His joy and yours would be diminished.

Today, make it clear to God, in as many ways as your heart can imagine, how much you enjoy the many treasures He's created for you. Give Him your heartfelt thanks and praise!

A JOYFUL HEART

*Lord, thank You for all You've given me. I am so grateful for all the gifts of
friendship, provision, and love You've provided throughout my life. Amen.*

Wealth or Riches?

Command those who are rich with things of this world not to be proud.
Tell them to hope in God, not in their uncertain riches. God richly gives us
everything to enjoy. Tell the rich people to do good, to be rich
in doing good deeds, to be generous and ready to share.

1 TIMOTHY 6:17–18 NCV

In God's sight, there's a big difference between wealthy people and rich people. Wealthy people have accumulated more toys and more of this world's goods. Rich people have accumulated more authentic friendships and relationships because of the ways they treat others. Wealthy people and rich people can both be generous and do great deeds with loving hearts. Heart-rich people are always the first to lend a hand when a crisis happens. Some wealthy people first check to see if they'll get a tax write-off before they do a good deed. The difference is not about money. The difference is a matter of the heart.

All of us are rich. We can be rich beyond our wildest dreams, and that has nothing to do with the size of our bank accounts. It has to do with the size of our spirits and our hearts. It has to do with how big a hand we are willing to extend to those near us and how much good we're willing to do. Only those good deeds bring true richness to our life experience.

Regardless of your income level, you can be rich any time you choose to be. God will multiply your good deeds with His grace and favor.

Give God the glory!

A HEART-RICH LIFE

Lord, open my heart to new experiences, help me to give generously wherever I can, and cause me to pray continually for those in need. Amen.

A New Wrinkle

*Whatever you do, work at it with all your heart, as working for
the Lord, not for human masters.*

COLOSSIANS 3:23 NIV

What a difference a little enthusiasm makes! When you work with someone who really loves their job, they make everything about it seem interesting and exciting. They bring a spirit of joy to the work that has nothing to do with how much they are being paid or what their title might be. They simply love their work and they work as though God Himself was their boss.

Sometimes as we get older, we lose youthful enthusiasm, and with every wrinkle comes another reason to give up trying or to give in to cynicism. Giving up enthusiasm does more than wrinkle the skin, it wrinkles the soul. It becomes harder and harder for us to bring back the joy we once knew.

Make this an enthusiastic day! Work with all your heart for the living Lord, and honor Him in all that you do. Laugh out loud today, and find reasons for genuine joy. Clap your hands and offer praise to God for the great work He has given you to do. Your enthusiasm will light up your heart and keep your spirit soaring.

You may be getting older, but you don't have to get new wrinkles!

AN ENTHUSIASTIC HEART

Lord, renew my spirit for the work I do, and help me to do it in joy for You and in harmony with those around me. Bless this day according to Your will and purpose, and help me put my heart into everything I do. Amen.

Take Care of the Earth!

God created human beings; he created them godlike, reflecting God's nature.
He created them male and female. God blessed them: "Prosper! Reproduce!
Fill Earth! Take charge! Be responsible for fish in the sea and birds in
the air, for every living thing that moves on the face of Earth."

GENESIS 1:27 MSG

In a world that is ever-shrinking, we often note the deterioration of our planet. Sometimes we express concern, other times we assume someone else will take care of our depleted rain forests or our poisoned rivers. We see it as someone else's job. After all, we can't be responsible for everything!

Yet, God commanded us in the very beginning to take care of the earth. To take care of His creation. He made all of it to sustain us and our children's children, and yet, today we face the stark reality of things going wrong. Global warming, major earth traumas, earthquakes, and devastating hurricanes have become the order of things. What can we do to take care of the planet God designed for us to live on? After all, this is home.

As Christians, we signed on to be caretakers. Caretaking is a matter of the heart. We have to put love into all we do even when it's about taking care of the very ground we walk on. We are called to protect the planet our Creator gave us. Take a moment today and thank God for the clean water you bathed in, the clean air you get to breathe, and the other things that make your life joyful and sustainable. Whatever else you do today, pray for your homeland. Pray for planet Earth!

A HEART FOR THE GOOD EARTH

Lord, help me be faithful to take care of my own little corner of the earth. Help me to see how I can be of service in the task of trying to heal our planet. Amen.

A Grateful Heart

Devote yourselves to prayer, being watchful and thankful.
COLOSSIANS 4:2 NIV

One of the ways you might recognize that your heart is being shaped by God's hand is when you find yourself simply being more grateful for everything. You take a walk on a bright sunny day and feel your heart swell up with the beauty that surrounds you.

You enjoy a visit with a good friend and walk away from the experience ready to praise God for His gift of giving you a friend like that. Wherever you go, you see His marvelous handiwork and you know that He is in control.

A thankful heart is a loving heart. It is a heart that knows that human beings exist, move, and breathe because of all that God has done. It is a heart that understands that it can never truly give God enough praise for this incredible home called earth.

May this be a day when your heart is truly aligned with God's goodness. May you give back to Him an alert mind and a grateful heart, ready to share all that you have with others. Let His love and light shine into your life today.

A HEART OF PRAISE

Lord, thank You for the blessings You have given to my life. I praise You for Your infinite and unconditional love. Amen.

Follow the Leader

Follow my example, as I follow the example of Christ.
1 CORINTHIANS 11:1 NIV

Do you remember when you were little and you played a game called follow the leader? You got in a line and whatever the first person did, you did too. If he put his foot in the air, you put your foot in the air; if he laughed out loud, you laughed out loud. It was a fun game and usually everyone had a chance to be the leader for a few moments.

Today you are still at the head of the line. You are the leader. If you follow Christ, you serve as an example to those who come after you. You inspire their thinking by the way that you talk and the words that you speak of comfort and love. You encourage their hearts each time you lend a hand to someone in need or reach out to heal a broken soul.

You're the leader, and for some people, you're the only Bible they'll ever read. You're the only example of Christ they'll ever see. The reason you live a heart-shaped life is because you want to be more like Christ. You want to show His love to everyone you meet, leading them in the direction that will cause their spirits to rejoice. This is the day the Lord has made, and He wants you to help others learn of His love, His saving grace, and His forgiveness. Lead with your heart and others will follow His light. Everyone is watching you today.

A LEADER'S HEART

Dear Lord, help me to be a good example to those around me. Let me share the hope of Jesus Christ so that others will want to line up right behind me and become the next leader. Amen.

The Exercise of Faith

Let us run with endurance the race God has set before us. We do this by keeping our eyes on Jesus, the champion who initiates and perfects our faith.
HEBREWS 12:1–2 NLT

More of us have become health- and diet-conscious in the past decade in the hope that we will live longer. We want to run the race as best we can, but to do this we have to remember the goal. The goal is to strengthen our faith so that we can endure to the end. The goal is to keep our eyes on Jesus.

Sometimes we confine our exercise to jumping to conclusions, running up bills, stretching the truth, or bending over backward. Some exercise their right to sidestep responsibility or lie down on the job. Others prefer pushing their luck or running late. These are spiritless exercises. They fall down in the face of obstacles and have trouble getting up again. They leave you winded and wounded.

Your faith asks you to exercise the joy you have in Jesus. Faith suggests you let God run beside you, and step up the pace a little when He calls you to do something. Exercise is good for you because it strengthens your heart in every way. Exercising your faith in Jesus is even better. Why? Because it strengthens your mind, body, and soul. So go on, get moving! With His Spirit, everything will work out and you'll be ready to take on the world.

WORKOUT FOR THE HEART

Lord, help me to run with You, not around You or ahead of You. Help me to get in shape so that I can win the race that You have set before me. Amen.

Stop Asking Why

Trust in the LORD with all your heart; do not depend on your own understanding.
Seek his will in all you do, and he will show you which path to take.

PROVERBS 3:5–6 NLT

When you were first learning to talk and attempting to make sense of the world as a child, you probably began by imitating sounds, then saying familiar words that pleased your parents enormously. After that, you started exploring the world for yourself, and pretty soon you had a head full of questions. Then one day you started asking, "Why?"

When you're in discovery mode, asking why can be a good thing and help you find the answers you're seeking. It can also bring you to a place of confusion as the results of your search take you into new territory and only serve to bring more questions to the table. The road to discovery can lead you on a winding pathway. Sometimes, you'll find the truth waiting for you, and sometimes you'll get off the path entirely.

Part of the learning process is about being able to ask questions, about seeking truth, and discovering what works and what doesn't. Part of shaping your heart has to do with your response to that learning. God is shaping each step you take, guarding your heart as you walk the path that He has set.

Keep your eyes on Jesus and He will direct you anywhere you need to go. Why? Because He loves you and paved the way for your salvation.

THE PATH OF THE HEART

Lord, help me to seek Your will with each step I take. Forgive me when I begin to smugly feel that I have all the answers. Keep me always on the path You want me to take. Amen.

Stand for Something so You Don't Fall for Anything

"If you do not stand firm in your faith, you will not stand at all."
ISAIAH 7:9 NIV

Somewhere along the way in our growing up, we begin to see the needs of others that are all around us. We become conscious of humanitarian causes and we do our best to support those we can. We're willing to stand up and be counted because it seems right to our hearts and minds to do so. God has built His compassion into our spirits, and we want to honor it.

We don't always know which causes to stand up for because so many of them are urgent and mean life and death, or at least a decent standard of living for the recipients of our aid. We try to stand on the side of good, and God blesses our efforts.

Fortunately, we can stand up for God without any confusion. He presents you with the case for Christ and simply asks you to believe. When you trust God and know what you believe, you can stand firm in your faith. When you don't, you're vulnerable and likely to fall for anything.

God wants to protect your soul, give you a safe ride and a ticket home. He's already done the hard work, you simply have to agree to come along with Him and get on the bus. You don't even have to pay for the ticket, because it's free. Jesus paid the price for you to climb aboard way back on Calvary.

Stand up for your faith and enjoy the ride. Your heart will rejoice and you'll be able to sing His praises at the top of your lungs.

A HEART TO BELIEVE

Lord, thank You for changing my heart and setting me free in the truth of Jesus. Help me stand up for You in all the things I do today. Amen.

The Gift of Jesus

Thank God for this gift too wonderful for words!
2 CORINTHIANS 9:15 NLT

Gifts you receive are interesting because you can choose just how often you'll use them. You can adore a particular gift and use it all the time, or you can put it on a shelf in a spare room and let it collect dust. You may even decide it's not for you and hand it off to someone else, or simply pack it in a box.

You can choose to do these things with the gift of Jesus. You may adore Him and make Him an important part of your daily life. You might keep Him somewhere near but be unable to actually say the last time you talked with Him or nurtured the relationship. You may even receive Him into your heart and then put Him away until you have time to consider more about His gifts to you.

You have a gift in God's Son that is too wonderful for words. It is shiny and new for you every day. It can bring you peace and help you at a moment's notice. Today, look around and see if Jesus is near, if you've thanked Him for all He does to give you a more abundant life. The good news is that you can actually decide to share Him with your friends and let others know of His love, and He'll be closer to you still. He's a gift that is just beyond words because He fills your heart with enormous love. Embrace His love in every way today.

A HEART GIFT

Lord, thank You for Your Son and the gift of His grace and love and salvation. Draw me closer to You in all that I do today. Amen.

It's All Possible

Jesus looked at them intently and said, "Humanly speaking,
it is impossible. But with God everything is possible!"
MATTHEW 19:26 NLT

Do you ever find yourself just running out of possibility-thinking? Your hopes are deflated, your joy balloons are out of air, and you're just not sure anymore what to expect or whether anything is going to happen that you've been praying for.

We're not always good at embracing all that God can do in our lives. We don't see His possibilities first because we're often too busy reviewing those past experiences that didn't come together as we had hoped. We aren't sure that anything can really change. . .even with Jesus by our side.

Yesterday is gone though. What's possible for you today depends on your attitude, your gratitude, and your willingness to connect with God and all that you trust Him to do.

If you're not walking closely enough to God to see His hand at work in your life, today might be a good time to step up to the Source of all possibility and plug in to what He really wants for you. You aren't equipped to do all things; only God can do that. Offer Him a heartfelt desire to be close to Him right now and He'll lead you into more joys and options than you ever imagined. He wants only your good!

A HEART OF POSSIBILITY

Lord, I admit that I run out of patience when I am waiting for something good to happen in my life. Help me to be patient and to plug in to Your possibilities for me. Help me to believe You're right there beside me in all I do. Amen.

Soul Searching

"Search all of history, from the time God created people on the earth until now, and search from one end of the heavens to the other. Has anything as great as this ever been seen or heard before?"

DEUTERONOMY 4:32 NLT

Some of us spend our lives searching for God. We find Him, and then we get ahead of Him or we leave Him behind and we forget all that He has done. We don't even realize we've done it until life goes haywire and we remember that we haven't spent any time with Him lately. Each time we're in His presence though, we experience joy that words cannot describe.

When you seek God with your whole heart, He can be found. He is not hiding from you. He is not offended by you. He is not waiting to judge you. He is only waiting to have a relationship with you. He wants to share His heart with you and have you share yours. He wants to be your friend and your constant companion. He knows you already, and nothing would give Him more joy than to have you know Him in return. Perhaps the greatest joy to the soul is that fresh discovery of genuine love each time you make the connection with Him again.

Soul searching is a worthy way to spend your time. Open your heart to God every day. Give Him a part of you that you've withheld; seek His face and His forgiveness. He'll bless your life a thousandfold and give you the desires of your heart. Keep discovering the mystery, the passion, and the joy that comes from knowing God and of walking with Him in steadfast love.

A HEART REFRESHED

Lord, thank You for lifting my heart by Your grace and helping me to discover new joys in You and in the blessings my soul receives anew each time I draw close to You again. Amen.

A Little Bit of Heaven

Let heaven and earth praise him, the seas and all that move in them.
PSALM 69:34 NIV

Dwight L. Moody said, "A little faith will bring your soul to heaven, but a lot of faith will bring heaven to your soul."

You know those things that bring you just a "little bit of heaven." Sometimes it's a beautiful day with billowy clouds and calm winds, sitting in a lawn chair with a bowl of pistachio ice cream and cherishing the moment. Sometimes it's getting the whole family together and making your favorite feast of roasted potatoes and barbecued chicken and embracing everyone around you in a way that brings peace to your heart and joy to your soul. When you live life heart-first, everything matters to you. Everything inspires your imagination to determine what you can do for the good of others.

Whatever creates a touch of heaven in your life is a gentle reminder of the love God has for you and the joy He wants you to have for yourself and to share with others. Your faith brings you into alignment with His will, and your trust in Him makes moments of joy come around more often. You have the opportunity any time you please to bring a little bit of heaven into the lives of those you love.

Stop for a moment and offer up your heartfelt thanks and praise, for He brings heaven to your soul.

A HEART OF JOY

Lord, thank You for blessing me with so many wonderful moments to enjoy. Thank You for quiet times and fun times with family and friends. Help me to offer kindness every chance I get to those around me. Amen.

A Few Good Deeds

Just as a person's body that does not have a spirit is dead,
so faith that does nothing is dead!
JAMES 2:26 NCV

If you're a fine-art painter, you haul out your canvas and your brushes and you set up shop wherever you go because you simply have to paint. If you're a writer, you observe the world and take note of it in such a way that before long, a story weaves itself into being, simply because you have to write. If you're a Christian, you share your faith, you give generously from the heart, and you tell others of your love for God, simply because you feel compelled to share the grace of God.

Whenever we have a passion for something, we want to live it, breathe it, and touch it as often as possible. We think about it most of the time, we learn more about it every chance we get, and we try to perfect our response to it. When your spirits are low though, you run out of energy and you can't feel the passion that lives within you. You can't think of a reason to paint or to write.

What makes your passion come alive again? It's simple. It's a matter of doing something special for someone else, getting closely connected to the Spirit of the One who made you, and recognizing the gifts of the world around you. In Him is life, and that life is yours any time you call His name.

Don't let anything take away the spirit you always have when you connect to the God of the universe, the One who holds your heart tenderly to Himself.

A HEART TO SHARE

Lord, help me to connect to You today in ways that revitalize my spirit and renew my energy and strength in You. Let me share my love for You with those I meet. Amen.

Expressions of Love

The only thing that counts is faith expressing itself through love.

GALATIANS 5:6 NIV

You know how to show your love to those around you. You always come up with the special treats, the freshly baked brownies, the plan to take everyone to the movies or out for pizza. You're the one who sends everyone a thank-you card for each kind thing they do and who volunteers for the Sunshine Circle at church. You're even the one who is always there when a need arises and the last one to leave when you've been called to lend a helping hand.

You are that person as much of the time as possible because you have a heart shaped by your heavenly Father to do good things for others. You've learned to be His expression of love in any way you can. From greeting cards, to smiles and hugs, to saying prayers for those we care about, expressions of love are important to creating the kind of environment that makes life feel abundant and joyful.

Matters of faith must always express themselves in terms of love. God is love, and His intention is for us to share His love with each other however we can. God's intention is for the world to see Jesus through the ways we try to love others.

If God's grace has shaped you to love, you are called to be a lover every day. You're called to love yourself, to love humanity, and to love those God specifically placed in your care.

A HEART SHAPED BY LOVE

Lord, it's not always easy to show Your love to the world. Sometimes others challenge my desire to express love. Help me to step out in faith and love everyone I meet as You would have me do. Amen.

Cleaning Up Your Heart

Create in me a pure heart, O God, and renew a steadfast spirit within me.
PSALM 51:10 NIV

Every now and then it's a good idea to take a little personal inventory. You might want to check in with your heart and see how your life is going. Are you genuinely thinking positive, loving thoughts? Are you praising God with your whole heart? Are you available to teach and share, or offer a kind word when needed?

Most of us need to do some clean-up work inside our minds and hearts now and then. We need to go in and vacuum out the spiderwebs of doubt or unbelief that manage to build little nests in our heads. We need to toss out a few old ideas that don't serve us very well, and freshen up with the insights God has given us in more recent months. We need to be sure that our hearts are in the right place, that place that allows us to love God with our whole hearts, minds, and spirits. We need to check on what we have allowed to shape our thinking. We may need to make a clean sweep.

Today, take a little dusting and cleaning time. Let go of things that hold you back from loving as much as you know you can and make room for more of God's Spirit to live within you.

A CLEAN HEART

Lord, help me get rid of those thoughts and ideas that are not serving me or You today and replace them with Your gentle Spirit of love. Amen.

The Hungry Lion

Control yourselves and be careful! The devil, your enemy, goes around like a roaring lion looking for someone to eat. Refuse to give in to him, by standing strong in your faith.

1 PETER 5:8–9 NCV

The hungry lion is out there. He laughs when you don't notice how he's yanking your chain. He thrives on making you feel that God can't help you, or won't forgive you. He loves to make you think that your personal demons are unbearable. Personal demons afflict the best of us and only prayer and steadfast attention can actually drive them away. We may fight to keep our weight under control, to keep a positive bank balance, or to stop smoking. It's hard to keep up with the demands on our lives, but we can if we remember that God shapes our thoughts and influences our steps. Our faith can offer us immeasurable help, and God can offer us strength and peace to overcome great obstacles, even those we create ourselves.

One of the most insidious things that has happened in modern cultures is that the enemy has created a new group of believers. These are the ones who don't believe there is an enemy. These are the ones who believe troubles are created by humankind, but not a supernatural kind. Whatever you believe, it appears that a battle is raging. A hungry lion walks about searching for ways to claim your soul. Stand strong in your faith, and refuse to give in to his deceit. Your strength and your shield is your faith in Christ Jesus.

A STRONG HEART

Lord, I feel helpless sometimes in the midst of the battles that continue every day in big ways and small ways. Guard me and protect me through Your Son, Jesus Christ. Amen.

Seize the Day!

Seize life! Eat bread with gusto, drink wine with a robust heart. Oh yes—God takes pleasure in your pleasure! Dress festively every morning. Don't skimp on colors or scarves. Relish life with the spouse you love each and every day of your precarious life. Each day is God's gift.

ECCLESIASTES 9:7 MSG

We love to imagine that we live life to the fullest. We rise each morning with a sense of bravado, cheer the world on, and give it our all. We want to. We don't!

Why? Maybe we don't because we begin the day as a challenge to be overcome instead of an opportunity to grow and change and become more than we are now. We have to go to work, to school, raise little children, or visit sick friends in the hospital. We feel like life is more about what we have to do than what we embrace or seek out because we're called to do it. Our thinking simply doesn't fit with the idea of eating our bread with gusto!

The teacher of Ecclesiastes had all the same issues you and I may have. He had to face the realities of life as he knew it and keep going. He had to keep trusting in God's love, mercy, and grace. Yet, he came away from all of that reminding us that each day is God's gift and each day we need to dress with joy and challenge the world with a robust heart. We need to and we can because God is right there watching over each breath we take.

When you live a life that is heart-shaped, it means you're so connected to God's desires for you that even the mundane things take on a sense of calling and offer personal reward. Go for the joy today in all you do!

A HEART OF JOY

Lord, I know You meant for me to enjoy life and to live it in a way that makes it all worthwhile. Bless me today, and help me seize the day with gusto! Amen.

Honor and Service

"So fear the LORD and serve him wholeheartedly."
JOSHUA 24:14 NLT

Think of the things you like to do "wholeheartedly." Perhaps you like to swim, and when you're doing laps in the pool, nothing else interrupts your joy because you are totally committed to the task at hand. Perhaps you like to clean a room and see it come back to life with each dusting and straightening of shelves and end tables. Perhaps you like to tell stories and you tell them with such adorable gusto that everyone wants to be near to hear the tale. Whatever it is, there are surely things that you do with your whole heart. These are the things that make life inspiring and full.

When Jesus commanded us to love God with our whole heart, He meant that we should do so with every breath, every opportunity, every service we might render. He meant that we should be committed to living with all the energy, gusto, and goodness that we could muster.

We live wholeheartedly because we want to honor Him in every possible way. Look at the things you're doing today. See if you can discover the moments that you're truly aware of serving God with great energy and enthusiasm, rather than simply doing a mindless task with no thought of purpose or no particular joy.

Awaken your spirit to the gift of serving with a heart of joy. It'll make your whole day go better. . .and your heart will desire to serve from abundance and love.

A WHOLEHEARTED LIFE

Lord, help me to show You my love in all that I do. Whether I'm reading a book or going to a job, let me do it with the joy of knowing that anything I do is part of my commitment to You. Amen.

Matters of the Heart

You have looked deep into my heart, LORD, and you know all about me.
PSALM 139:1 CEV

The renowned theologian Charles Spurgeon said this: "Neither prayer, nor praise, nor the hearing of the word will be profitable to those who have left their hearts behind them."

The purpose of a book like this one is to remind you that nearly everything that matters in your life has something to do with the perceptions of your heart. That means you are better able to understand what God designed you to do when you stay connected to others and to Him in every way your heart can muster.

He knows you. He knows every detail of what you think and what motivates you to act. What He hopes for in your prayers and in your praise then, is that you would engage Him often and well from those hidden places that only He can see. He wants you to be a person with a great heart.

Knowledge is a good thing and wisdom is essential, but your connection to God, and to nearly everything else around you, is a matter of the heart. If you've erected walls around your heart to protect you from life, or you've managed to quiet the stirrings of your heart by letting your head rule the day, then perhaps it's time to start again. This may be the day the Lord has waited for, the one where He can truly enter your heart and embrace your life.

Whatever you do today, do it with your whole heart. God will surely be pleased with your reflection.

A HEART FOR ALL THINGS

Lord, keep close to me today, and open my heart to see You and others more clearly. Amen.

A Kindly Word

Timely advice is lovely, like golden apples in a silver basket.
PROVERBS 25:11 NLT

We shy away from sharing our hearts sometimes when it comes to giving advice to our friends. Why? We build up all kinds of reasons. We tell ourselves it's not our business, we shouldn't get involved, or they have a right to do what they want. We even use those rationalizations when it comes to our children. Perhaps the real fear is one of being rejected by someone that means a lot to us, and so we assume it's a better thing to keep quiet.

This proverb is a beautiful reminder that sometimes the most loving thing we can do is offer our advice. If we offer it in kindness, with a heart for good, with the intention that our thoughts may be helpful to the one we're sharing our thoughts with, then it is the right thing. Then, we have put beautiful golden apples in a silver basket. We've put beautiful golden thoughts into someone's possibility basket to be considered.

Sometimes the Spirit Himself is prompting you to offer a helpful message. Be prayerful. Be kind. Lovingly share your heart with others and your advice will bear fruit.

A HEART TO SHARE WITH OTHERS

Lord, help me know the difference between sharing a self-motivated opinion and giving loving advice. Help me to listen for Your direction in all my conversations today. Amen.

Seeing with the Heart

LORD, my heart is not proud; my eyes are not haughty. I don't concern myself with matters too great or too awesome for me to grasp. Instead I have calmed and quieted myself, like a weaned child who no longer cries for its mother's milk. Yes, like a weaned child is my soul within me.

PSALM 131:1–2 NLT

When your heart is still, sitting quietly with God, nothing else in the world really matters. You have a sense of peace that you cannot receive in any other way. You are secure in your Father's arms.

When you have this kind of heart, it helps you to see others more clearly and to discern the actions God would have you take in any situation. Your actions are a reflection of what God Himself has laid upon your heart.

Thomas à Kempis said, "If your heart were sincere and upright, every creature would be unto you a looking-glass of life and a book of holy doctrine." When we learn to see one another as holy, as a being that God created, we understand more fully what it means to love as God loves us. We do not assume we know each person's situation, nor do we judge how closely the actions of another are aligned with our own. Instead, we see God in the faces of His children. We see His hand at work in those we cannot understand through head knowledge.

As you engage with others today, may you see each one as a child of God, one that you may serve in some very real way. God will bless your efforts and your life when you rest safely in His arms.

A HEART FOR ALL THINGS HOLY

Lord, help me to see only what You see in those I encounter today. Help me to respond with Your grace and love. Amen.

Fix Your Thoughts

Fix your thoughts on what is true, and honorable, and right, and pure, and lovely, and admirable. Think about things that are excellent and worthy of praise.
PHILIPPIANS 4:8 NLT

What you think about makes a big difference in what you do each day. If you think about worries and troubles in the world, quarrels in your family, or something your boss said that didn't sit well with you, then your focus is on negative things. It's important to think about what you're thinking about.

In Philippians we are reminded to think about things that are true, and honorable, and right. You have many things in your life that are true, and honorable, and right. The work of your hands or the relationships you share with your family may well come to mind. Or think about things that are lovely and admirable. Perhaps now you can smile at the thoughts of people in your life who easily express love and kindness.

Give yourself a chance right now to feel the joy of knowing you are a child of God and live as a child of God. Fix your thoughts on things above, and things on earth will feel more glorious. Go on! Put a flower in your lapel and remind yourself that every good gift comes from above, and your Father wants you to receive His gifts with joy. Think about all the excellent things He has done, and give Him praise.

HEARTFELT THOUGHTS

Father, help me remember that You have generously lavished me with gifts of love and joy. Help me to think about them and share Your gifts with others today. Amen.

No Worries

Don't worry about anything; instead, pray about everything. Tell God what you need, and thank him for all he has done. Then you will experience God's peace, which exceeds anything we can understand. His peace will guard your hearts and minds as you live in Christ Jesus.

PHILIPPIANS 4:6–7 NLT

Want to try an experiment today? Don't worry! That's right. For one day only, give yourself permission to cease to worry. Don't let a worry come anywhere near you, and if one tries to get in, just slam the door on it and go right past it. Easier said than done?

Okay, what if you start by giving God a heads-up on what you need. You can put all your concerns before Him and spread them out on a blanket at His feet. The trick is that you have to leave them there. You can't pick them up and carry them with you. Once they're on the blanket, your job is done. Oh wait, you need to thank God for all He has done for you already.

After you do this for twenty-four worry-free hours, see how it feels. What did you put in your mind to replace all those worries and fears? If you were flooded with peace and your heart was full of love, wrap your arms around that feeling. Isn't it great? If you did it for one day, try it again tomorrow. If you didn't quite do it the whole day, practice. Put worry aside and let grace come in.

A HEART WITHOUT WORRY

Lord, I know I worry about things that I need to surrender to You. Help me to offer You my concerns, accept Your help, and replace those worries with words of praise. Thank You, Lord. Amen.

When You Can't See Clearly

But we live by faith, not by what we see.

2 CORINTHIANS 5:7 CEV

When you're in the habit of "faithing" things out in life, you don't always get to see what's ahead. You go along and thank God that today is in His hand. You leave tomorrow in God's hand. It's always been a part of the walk of faith to know that sometimes you have to keep walking, even in the dark.

When you're walking in the dark, remember that even though you can't see clearly, you can still hear clearly. You can listen for God's voice and seek His direction. If you stay attuned to His voice, you'll break through to the light again before you know it.

We sometimes say that people have blind faith. There is no such thing. Faith always lets in the light, and it always knows the right direction. It moves closer to God with each step. Faith knows that it follows after the heart of God. It dispels the darkness and lives in the light.

Helen Keller said, "If the blind put their hand in God's, they find their way more surely than those who see but have not faith or purpose." Continue in your faith and fulfill your life purpose.

A HEART THAT SEES

Lord, I am blinded sometimes by the trappings of the world. I set my faith aside and try too hard to trust my intellect. Help me walk closer to You even in the dark. Amen.

Keep Looking Up

Can all your worries add a single moment to your life?
MATTHEW 6:27 NLT

Regret looks back and plays the "what-if" game. Worry looks around and tries to solve everything on its own. Faith looks up because it knows the only source of hope is there.

When things don't make sense to you, you can probably smell a spiritual lesson cooking somewhere. It's only when we can't understand something that we start to really explore it and try to get a better grasp of it. We assume there's a logical angle that we missed, and with just a little investigation, we'll figure it out and everything will be all right again. If we're lucky, or perhaps even better, if we're blessed, the searching takes some time. In the course of searching, we'll find what God wanted us to know. The lesson will be right in front of us.

We rely on our mind to guide us and on our intellect to make good choices. We think we can direct our steps because we've mapped out a plan. We put all the right things together, and yet somehow worry still walks in and hope loiters far in the background. Before we know it, intellect isn't running things, Spirit isn't running things, but worry is!

Today, make it a point to not look back or around, but joyfully and definitely to look up with great faith.

A FOCUSED HEART

Lord, help me to walk in faith with You today letting all my worries slip behind me, so my heart stays focused on You. Amen.

Lifting Weights

*But without faith no one can please God. We must believe that God
is real and that he rewards everyone who searches for him.*
HEBREWS 11:6 CEV

Most of us want to stay healthy. We watch our diet, try to avoid too many desserts and too many visits to our favorite fast-food chain, and we work out. We run, we jog, we go to the gym, and sometimes we lift weights. Weights help us get good muscle tone, maintain good body weight, and build strength.

Faith is important for good health as well. It lifts you up, strengthens you, and gives you a greater opportunity to enjoy life. Your faith shouldn't be something you carry around though; it should be something that carries you. It should help you exercise all your connections to God in very real ways. It will strengthen your spirit.

If you want to lift weights at the gym, go ahead. If you want to lift weights off your life, go to God. He'll help you lift your burdens. All you have to do is believe He's there.

AN EXERCISE OF THE HEART

Lord, I raise my hands to You and invite You in today to lift my burdens and help me enjoy all the good things You want me to discover. Amen.

Family Ties

God sets the lonely in families.
PSALM 68:6 NIV

Summer is usually the time for big family reunions and gatherings for all kinds of reasons. Graduations and weddings bring families together in joyful ways. The definition of "family" has changed dramatically over the years though, and many of us find ourselves structuring a "family" out of friends and neighbors as well.

The globe continues to shrink, and we have all become more familiar with family life on other continents and within other cultures. We're becoming increasingly aware that we are truly much more alike than we are different from our neighbors. We all seek love, approval, and joy within our families. When we can't find those things there, we move beyond them and create new "families" out of those closest to us.

As children of God, we all have the same Father, and in a very real sense we're all related. We're family! We can learn to love one another and find common joys and gifts to share, or we can become estranged and dysfunctional forgetting that we're of royal blood.

As you celebrate with your family this summer, remember that your kinship is deeper than simply sharing some common last names. You share the same Father.

A HEART FOR FAMILY

Lord, help me to appreciate and love the family You have given me, honoring Your name in all my relationships there. Amen.

Getting a Piece of the Rock

Truly my soul finds rest in God; my salvation comes from him. Truly he is my rock and my salvation; he is my fortress, I will never be shaken.

PSALM 62:1–2 NIV

Do you have someone in your life that you think of as your "rock"? You know, the person you count on when life gets you down; the person you know will always come through when you're in trouble. You might even have trouble imagining this person ever really breaking down because he or she is always so strong.

A former TV commercial once told us that if we got a certain insurance, it would be like getting a piece of the rock. That idea was supposed to make us feel that once we were covered by that particular insurance, nothing could really shake us. Everything would be on solid ground.

We can't be certain about insurance, but we have assurance in our faith in the One true God. He is your rock and your salvation and on Him you can depend. His strength is sure and His victory in all things is certain. If you're looking for a person, a place, or a thing on earth that will keep you forever safe, stop looking. The only place this kind of hope exists is in Jesus Christ.

A HEART OF ASSURANCE

O Lord, my Rock and my salvation, thank You for loving me so much and keeping me forever in Your care! Amen.

Rivers of Hope

I pray that God, the source of hope, will fill you completely with joy and peace because you trust in him. Then you will overflow with confident hope through the power of the Holy Spirit.

ROMANS 15:13 NLT

Don't you love sitting by a peaceful riverbank on a warm, sunny day? Maybe there are just a few light clouds in the sky and you can close your eyes and hear the crickets chirping and the fish jumping. Maybe you've brought a picnic lunch and you don't have a care in the world. You're totally at peace. Hold on to that feeling.

Is anything keeping you from flowing over with peace even when you're not on the riverbank? Is your hope choked by weeds and your joy simply suffocating under layers upon layers of life's problems? Then sit back, close your eyes, and take five minutes to renew your spirit and walk along the riverbank. God is waiting there to refresh you and give you a sense of peace and power that can only come through the Holy Spirit.

It's your right as a child of God to experience rivers of peace and splashes of deep joy. All you have to do is rest quietly by the Source of living water.

A HAPPY HEART

Lord, help me today to rest in Your fountains of joy. Remind me that You are with me always, and grant me Your peace. Amen.

Piano Practice, Baseball Practice, Hope Practice

Work hard at whatever you do.
ECCLESIASTES 9:10 CEV

We all know that "practice makes perfect" and that it takes a lot of practice to be good at something special like playing the piano or learning to dance. If you struggled through piano lessons as a kid, your teacher probably encouraged you to practice, practice, practice! Later in high school you might have been in a play, in the choir at church, or maybe you played on a baseball team. Whatever it was, the rule was still there to practice, practice, practice! You might have thought that you would never get very good at your task, but over time and with lots of practice you actually did get better. You may not have been the star, but still, you were pretty good.

The same rule applies now to your adult life and your spiritual practice. You may be pretty good at prayer and okay at Bible reading, but how are you at "hope" practice? When you practice hope in a very conscious, daily way you discover an amazing thing. Your spirit gets happier and happier. Hope practice feeds your spiritual muscles, and that's important for your total well-being. Today, be sure to get in some hope practice. Come on now, practice, practice, practice!

A POSITIVE HEART

Lord, let Your Spirit wash over me today and bathe me in peace and hope. Help me to be more aware of the importance of keeping a hopeful and positive attitude. Amen.

Collecting Your Inheritance

I pray that your hearts will be flooded with light so that you can understand the confident hope he has given to those he called—his holy people who are his rich and glorious inheritance.

EPHESIANS 1:18 NLT

We usually think of an inheritance as something that someone who loves us leaves us in a will. It is set aside to be given to us at just the right time. An inheritance helps to sustain our future.

When Jesus left Earth and went back to heaven, He left us an inheritance. He left us with a future. He didn't just leave the milk money or the winning lottery ticket. He left the greatest future anyone could ever wish for. He left you with eternal life. He ensured that you would exist in your Father's house forever.

In order to help you enjoy your inheritance later on, He also left you with a gift for now. He gave you the Holy Spirit so that you could have power on earth over evil, and so that you could understand the inspiration of the Word. He left you hope, joy, and strength to keep going amid any earthly crisis. You might even say He left you the end of the rainbow.

A HEART OF GRATITUDE

Lord, I am so grateful for all that You've done to provide for me, not just today but in the future as well. Thank You for redeeming my soul. Amen.

From Gloom to Bloom

Some people brought to him [Jesus] a paralyzed man on a mat. Seeing their faith, Jesus said to the paralyzed man, "Be encouraged, my child! Your sins are forgiven."
MATTHEW 9:2 NLT

Have you been there? Gloomy, frightened, paralyzed by irrational fears, and unable to function anywhere near your usual capability? Have you struggled with depression, melancholy, and worry? You're not alone.

Friends played a big role in the life of the paralyzed man. They literally brought him to Jesus, mat and all. They knew in their hearts that Jesus could heal him and that their friend would be able to walk again. Sometimes it takes that kind of faith, the kind that comes from those around you believing for you until you can walk on your own.

Whatever is keeping you down today, the Lord says, "Be encouraged, my child! Your sins are forgiven." You are free now to celebrate, move around, jump up and down, and rejoice in the grace of God because the clouds are moving. The sun is coming out again, and it's time for you to bloom.

TAKE HEART

Lord, I thank You for the friends who hold me up in prayer and keep me in front of Your throne. I thank You for blessing me and bringing me great joy. Amen.

Make the World Brighter

"When you put on a luncheon or a banquet," he said, "don't invite your friends, brothers, relatives, and rich neighbors. For they will invite you back, and that will be your only reward. Instead, invite the poor, the crippled, the lame, and the blind. Then at the resurrection of the righteous, God will reward you for inviting those who could not repay you."

LUKE 14:12–14 NLT

Martin Luther King Jr. said this: "God is able to make a way out of no way and transform dark yesterdays into bright tomorrows. This is our hope for becoming better men and women. This is our mandate for seeking to make a better world."

You are a part of God's way for making the world a better place. You may do it by inviting the lost and the lame to sit at your table, or you might feed the hungry through your favorite charity group. Whatever you prefer to do, you do it with a heart of grace and kindness! You do it because you know that you can make a difference! God will always reward you for helping those who could not repay you.

In fact, He already has! Give Him thanks and praise that you are in a position even now to make the world a little bit brighter and better.

A HEART FOR OTHERS

Lord, sometimes I take for granted the warm bed I sleep in and the nutritious meal I eat at dinnertime. You lavish so much on me. Help me to share all that I have with others. Amen.

Mending a Broken Heart

Their insults have broken my heart, and I am in despair. If only one person would show some pity; if only one would turn and comfort me.
PSALM 69:20 NLT

It is said that God can do wonders with a broken heart, if we are willing to give Him all the pieces. Your heart is a matter of deep concern to God, and He seeks to protect it in any way possible. He does it best when you remain close to Him, no matter what your circumstances may be.

When your heart is broken, you feel sad and vulnerable. Being vulnerable does not mean you are weak, however. In God's hands, your vulnerability is an amazing strength. It is a witness to your deep connection to the Creator and a voice that soothes the wounds of others.

If your heart is broken by insults or rejection, go back to the Source of your strength. Go back to your Father and put your hand in His. Tell Him all that you feel; give Him all the pieces so that He can help you mend again.

When you do, you will be restored. A restored and renewed spirit can then take the challenges of the world head-on and heart-first. Thank God that He always mends a broken heart.

A MENDED HEART

Lord, thank You for being there for me, for protecting my heart and mending my spirit. Help me to heal and move on quickly. Amen.

God Wants First Place

Dear children, keep away from anything that might take God's place in your hearts.
1 JOHN 5:21 NLT

If you could rank the ten most important things in your life, where would you start? Would you name your children, your work, or your spouse? Of course you would, and they should all be on your list. However, the Bible reminds us that God not only wants to be on your list; He wants to be number one. He doesn't want anything to be more important to your heart than your relationship with Him.

Everything in your life demands your attention. Many things need your focus and deserve to have priority. However, God knows you far better than anyone else can ever know you. He knows what you need, oftentimes before you know. He gives you grace, mercy, and peace, and He always has your back. He doesn't want to be number one for His sake. He wants to be number one for your sake! No one else can provide for you, love you, or direct your steps like He can.

Today, as you share your love with your family and friends, take time to honor the One who gives all things to you in the first place and who seeks after your good in every way. Give God the first place in your heart.

A HEART FOR GOD

Lord, help me to love my family in all the ways You've given me to love them, and then let me love You and worship You like no other. Please be my number One! Amen.

Moral Excellence

*Supplement your faith with a generous provision of moral excellence, and moral
excellence with knowledge, and knowledge with self-control, and self-control with
patient endurance, and patient endurance with godliness, and godliness with
brotherly affection, and brotherly affection with love for everyone.*

2 PETER 1:5–7 NLT

Defining morality in a world without hard-and-fast rules has become increasingly difficult. We claim to believe in the Ten Commandments, yet find reasonable excuses to allow for the exceptions of those rules. We still go to war and we put people in prisons on death row, and we still hate or ignore people we simply don't understand. We remain hard-hearted, and morality becomes a word we no longer think necessary.

Peter says that moral excellence is one way that we grow to know God better, and we become more patient with ourselves and others. Perhaps, as we begin to understand what real love is and have more love for those in the body of Christ, we can come to terms with what it means to be a person who lives heart-first, simply because God created us all.

We may not be able to claim moral excellence, but we can claim Jesus Christ as our Savior, our shepherd of grace, and the lover of our souls. With that, we can continue to learn from Him and become better at all that it means to follow the rules toward a more heart-shaped life.

A HEART TO KNOW GOD

*Lord, it is so hard to even understand some of the moral dilemmas we face today.
Help me to show genuine love for people everywhere. Amen.*

The Hope of the Future

"So there is hope for you in the future," says the LORD.

JEREMIAH 31:17 NCV

Henri J. M. Nouwen said, "Those who keep speaking about the sun while walking under a cloudy sky are messengers of hope, the true saints of our day."

You know them, the ones who go around with some sunny cliché on their lips and a smile on their faces no matter what is going on. You appreciate their optimism most of the time, but you wonder when they'll ever really face reality and see the world for what it is. You wonder why they just can't see the chaos we live in. Don't they watch the news?

Still, something in you almost wishes you were more like them. It can't be a bad thing to be more hopeful, to be more certain that God is with you and have more faith that things will be okay. It can't be a bad thing to listen to your heart in most situations.

Today is your day to be one of them, one of those joy-filled, optimistic, over-the-top believers in the Lord who trust that He holds the future and that it will all come out okay. God knows there's hope for your future, and He wants you to know it too. Keep His hope close to your heart.

A HEART FOR THE FUTURE

Lord, it brings me joy to think about a future filled with hope because of Your love and mercy. Remind me to lift up my heart in that hope as I go about my day. Amen.

You Can Do It!

*When I was really hurting, I prayed to the LORD. He answered my
prayer, and took my worries away. The LORD is on my side,
and I am not afraid of what others can do to me.*

PSALM 118:5–6 CEV

Sometimes we struggle with believing that we have anyone on our side. We want to pursue a dream or a new goal, but we don't have support from our friends and family. When that happens, pray! You and God are a majority, and together you can accomplish the goals and the dreams of your heart.

Henry Ford once said, "One of the greatest discoveries a person makes, one of the great surprises, is to find out you can do what you were afraid you could not do."

If you're waiting for the approval of others, you may wait a long time. If you're waiting for all the right circumstances and conditions, you might never see them come together. If you're giving yourself any excuse at all, pray about it and ask God to help you move forward according to His will and purpose for your life. Do it for your heart's sake, and do it for God's sake too.

A HEART THAT TRUSTS

Lord, help me to trust You and follow my heart for direction in my life. Help me to move forward according to Your timing and Your mercy. Amen.

Every Time I Feel the Spirit

*Be filled with the Spirit. Speak to each other with psalms, hymns,
and spiritual songs, singing, and making music in your hearts to the Lord.*
EPHESIANS 5:18–19 NCV

Have you had any of those great moments lately where you just feel the Spirit of God in your heart and soul? You know, the sense that you are so overcome with the joy of knowing God's love is in you that you almost feel giddy and can do nothing else, but rejoice and sing and pray.

If that hasn't happened to you lately, maybe it's time to figure out why not. The Spirit is available to you *all* the time, so having His Spirit move yours, can be a fairly common occurrence. It just requires more focus and a slight change of your heart.

Don't wait for a feeling to come over you. Just start those prayers of thanksgiving, humming those great spiritual songs and singing your heart out to the Lord. When you do that, your heart will rejoice because your spirit is moving.

Go on! Sing a little, and let your spirit dance.

A DANCING HEART

Lord, dance with me today as I lift my voice in prayer and praise to You. Move within my being, so that my heart and mind can shine Your light of love. Amen.

Your Daily Requirements

And now, Israel, what does the LORD your God require of you? He requires only that you fear the LORD your God, and live in a way that pleases him, and love and serve him with all your heart and soul. And you must always obey the LORD's commands and decrees that I am giving you today for your own good.

DEUTERONOMY 10:12–13 NLT

If you take a vitamin every day, you do that so you'll get your full requirement of the right vitamins and minerals and stay healthy and strong.

This list from Deuteronomy reads a bit like a dose of good vitamins. It tells you what you need to do to stay strong and healthy in the Lord. It gives you this advice "for your own good."

Somehow the words, "for your own good" strike a little fear in the heart because usually they mean you're not going to like the process. Your mother probably said, "Take this medicine for your own good." Your doctor might say, "Exercise for your own good."

Perhaps the way to read this list then is to start by telling God that you really do want to do the things that are good for you. Surrender your pride, your stubbornness, your selfishness, and step aside from what you think is good, and see if you discover what God thinks is good for you. Search your heart and take a closer look at God's daily requirements.

A HEART FOR YOUR OWN GOOD

Lord, I don't always like the things that are meant to be for my good. Sometimes I downright resist them. Help me to seek Your will with my whole heart for my good today. Amen.

Holy Spirit Fellowship

May the grace of the Lord Jesus Christ, and the love of God,
and the fellowship of the Holy Spirit be with you all.
2 CORINTHIANS 13:14 NIV

When you signed on with Jesus, you did so with your heart, mind, and soul. You did so because you wanted to share His grace and love with others.

Signing up for grace means that you accept the undeserved forgiveness and mercy that Christ offers you. It means you then share that forgiveness and mercy with others too. After all, you know you have been given a gift you didn't earn.

When you respond to God's love, it's a matter of the heart. It's a little different than signing up for your spouse's love or your mother's love. It means you are ready to be loved for the person you are. It means you're thankful to God for His incredible ability to love you unconditionally. It means you're prepared to live a heart-shaped life.

Finally, when you seek fellowship with the Holy Spirit it means you invite Him to walk with you, spend the day with you, be your lunch buddy and your business partner. It means you embrace His friendship and His direction for each step you take today.

This is your day to sign up for great blessings!

A HEARTFELT COMMITMENT

Lord, I don't often stop to think about the grace and blessings You give me. Help me sign up to receive more of You with my whole heart. Amen.

The First to Forgive

*How great is God's love for all who worship him? Greater than the
distance between heaven and earth! How far has the LORD taken
our sins from us? Farther than the distance from east to west!*

PSALM 103:11–12 CEV

How much space or time or energy do you put into the idea surrounding forgiveness?
If you've been injured by someone, have you kept that injury as fresh as possible for
the past twenty years? Have you taken it out of the aging wrappers, letting it fuel some
long-forgotten memory simply because you wouldn't know quite what to do without it?

We're funny about forgiveness. If we need forgiveness, we want the instant kind that
makes all the bad stuff go away quickly. Drop in a forgiveness tablet, watch it fizz, presto
. . .no more problem. That's what we'd like when we're the ones needing forgiveness.

When we're the ones doing the forgiving, well, that's another matter. That's something that weighs on our hearts and causes us to make excuses. God wants you to recognize how often He forgives you and how far away from Himself He puts your offenses.
He wants us to follow His example, and there's no way to do that unless you get your
heart involved.

Be the first to forgive; it will do your heart good.

A HEART TO FORGIVE

*Lord, grant me the willingness to forgive, be forgiven, and let go of past injuries. Help
me move forward today with a more loving heart. Amen.*

Try a Little More Kindness

*You will be rewarded for saying something kind, but all some
people think about is how to be cruel and mean.*

PROVERBS 13:2 CEV

You know that people are not all the same. Some are a joy to be around and some are not. Some people have a lot of heart and some are bent on keeping their hearts safely walled away. The interesting thing is that either way, we are not often aware of how others perceive us.

Maybe the best way to understand your own opinions and perceptions of others is to look in the mirror and note how you see yourself. Does your face reflect a kind and loving heart? Do you instantly judge how you look, dress, or wear your hair? Do you only find fault with the face you see in the mirror?

Kindness doesn't take more time. It doesn't require a special circumstance, and it doesn't have limits. You can't use up your kindness quotient. You can't get in a position of having no more kindness left, unless you've truly forgotten whose you are. God's Spirit is working a heart of kindness, gentleness, and goodness within you. Receive it and share it with others.

Pretend that it's always National Kindness Day! Go out there and let your kindness light shine, and start with the person you saw in the mirror.

A HEART OF KINDNESS

Lord, it seems so simple to just be kind. Yet, it isn't always easy. Fill me with a spirit of kindness for those in my life, and let me see them with a loving heart. Amen.

Your Will, God's Will, Whose Will?

*Since we could not get Paul to change his mind, we gave up
and prayed, "Lord, please make us willing to do what you want."*

ACTS 21:14 CEV

You've probably been saying the Lord's Prayer for years. You say it, you believe it, and you end it with "Thy will be done." What does it mean to want God's will to be done? How can you pray that prayer with an honest heart?

The scripture reference from Acts shows us that even the ancients weren't always ready to act as they imagined God wanted them to act. They had to ask God to make them "willing" to do what God wanted them to do. We're no different today. We often have to step back and give up our own assumptions of what to do next and pray the same prayer. "Lord, please make us willing to do what You want."

When you question whether you're doing God's will or your own, you may want to put everything else aside and ask God directly. Make it a priority to find out. God will lead you forward as long as you're truly interested in where He wants you to go. You must seek His will with your whole heart, and if your heart is not ready, you must be willing for Him to shape it even more. Sometimes we need God's help to change our minds and live more heart-shaped lives.

A HEART AND A WILL

Lord, I know that I look to You to lead me in the big things in my life, and I strive to do Your will each day, but help me to be willing to do what You want in all things. . .big and small. Amen.

Putting on the Armor

Be strong in the Lord and in his mighty power. Put on the full armor
of God, so that you can take your stand against the devil's schemes.
EPHESIANS 6:10–11 NIV

When you go through your closet to find the stuff you've outgrown so you can give it away to a charity, be sure you don't throw out your armor. It's in there somewhere, perhaps not quite as shiny as when you first put it on, but still in good repair and capable of doing the job. It may be slightly out of fashion, but it's never out of style.

You were given that armor for just one reason. It's your protective coating against the prowler who often wears sheep's clothing, just to catch you off guard. It's Spirit ready, and no matter what, it will keep you standing in God's strength and direction. In fact, it's indestructible armor and it was designed with you in mind.

So, get rid of those old shirts from college that you're never going to really wear anyway, and let go of those old worn tennis shoes, but never give away your armor. It is one of God's ways of protecting your heart and your soul any time you need it. Stay strong in the Lord.

A PROTECTED HEART

Lord, protect me as I go into the world today. Keep me strong in Your mighty power.
Amen.

Becoming a Wise Old Soul

My child, listen to what I say, and treasure my commands. Tune your ears to wisdom, and concentrate on understanding. Cry out for insight, and ask for understanding. Search for them as you would for silver; seek them like hidden treasures.

PROVERBS 2:1–4 NLT

Wisdom is kind of an old-fashioned word, but it still packs a punch! We may not consciously go around thinking about how wise we are or whether we have enough wisdom today, but maybe we should.

How do we seek to be wise? Most of us are wise at some things and foolish at others. Many of us just go from one day to the next without giving much thought to whether or not we make wise choices. As we strive to live a more heart-shaped life, it is important that we seek God's guidance about things that will make us wiser—not necessarily smarter, but wiser. After all, things of this world will not give us greater intelligence or common sense. God alone is at the heart of all wisdom and is your greatest Source to becoming a wiser person.

It's a new day and a new chance to pay attention to your choices. Look at the reasons behind what you do, and pray for wisdom in making your decisions. Let your head analyze your choices, and let your heart clarify your motivations. When you do, you'll discover some great treasures and become a wise old soul in all the things that truly matter to the heart.

A HEART FOR GREATER WISDOM

Lord, grant me greater insight and understanding about the choices I make. Create in me a desire to be wise in all matters of the heart. Amen.

Living a Life of Perfect Love

God is love, and all who live in love live in God, and God lives in them.
And as we live in God, our love grows more perfect.

1 JOHN 4:16–17 NLT

No matter how old we are, we are always learning about what it means to love. Through the various ages and stages of our lives, we've seen love played out and we've reacted to it, embracing it or building walls to keep it away.

We grow wiser in the arenas of love as we get older, but we seldom get to the place of feeling that we now understand love or that we live a life of perfect love. Perfect love is elusive and keeps us chasing it, hoping to somehow capture it before it gets away.

Our desire is to live in love, to have hearts that are open to God's love. We want to be people who embrace His discipline and His efforts to help us grow up in Him. Today, remember that God's love lives within you and it will remain with you forever. You cannot put it out like a flaming candlewick or lose it by your own neglect. You can only seek to know more of it and strive to see it in each person you meet, each desire of your heart, and each fervent prayer. God's love prevails and you have every reason to trust it and to know that He will love you and live with you eternally.

May He continue to shape your heart to see the beauty in others and shape your spirit to want even more of all that He desires for you. Live in God and in His love from now to forever.

A HEART OF LOVE

Lord, thank You for living in my heart and soul. Help me to seek even more of You in everything I do today. Amen.

May All Go Well with Your Soul

Dear friend, I pray that you may enjoy good health and that all may go well with you, even as your soul is getting along well.

3 JOHN 2 NIV

John's greeting may seem somewhat out of date, but his intentions are as current today as ever. Well-wishers still send people good thoughts for everything from health to new relationships to work life. On some level, we really do want our lives to be heart-shaped and we want our neighbors to be well and live happy lives.

The fine ingredient in this wish for good things though, is the idea of praying that things will go well with your soul. You can have a healthy body, healthy mind, and healthy relationships but still struggle with the health of your soul. God wants to renew your spirit and affirm His love for you. He wants your heart to be at peace knowing you are fully in His care.

As you share greetings with your friends and neighbors, you might say, "I hope you're well. I hope things are good for you. I pray that God watches over you. May things be well with your soul." When things are well with your soul, you experience life in a way that is filled with appreciation and motivated by kindness and love. Those are the things that help you experience happier relationships. When you're happy in your relationships, you feel better. Your heart is free to embrace life in a much bigger way.

May things go well with your heart and soul today.

HEART AND SOUL

Lord, may Your peace flow through me like a river and bring total joy to my soul. May my heart overflow with Your kindness and blessing. Amen.

Graceful Oaks

For God has planted them like strong and graceful oaks for his own glory.
ISAIAH 61:3 TLB

Don't you just love the leaves of summer? The trees are so majestic and commanding, and they offer you their leafy green shade for free. They bend in the breezes without breaking and they shelter living things that are near them. They command a certain respect.

Like the mighty oaks, God planted us in His garden. He put us there to care for it and to care for all the living things that are part of it. He put us there for His glory. He gave us hearts that can bend but not break as we strive to shelter those we love.

Consider the part you play in the garden of Earth. You may be like the mighty oak offering strength, support, and shade for those who pass by. You may be more like the maple sapling that will grow and share your sweetness and kindness to everyone around. Perhaps you're simply the gardener who will weed out the things that don't belong there and spread more seeds of joy and love.

You've been placed in the garden for God's glory. Open your heart to His voice, and be a graceful oak for someone in your life today.

A STRONG HEART

Lord, help me to grow stronger in Your light and share Your goodness with those who come near me today. Help me to plant more seeds of joy and kindness wherever I may be. Amen.

Samaritan Stories

*"Then a despised Samaritan came along, and when he saw
the man, he felt compassion for him."*
LUKE 10:33 NLT

Compassion is such a wonderful gift. We observe it in others and find it noteworthy. Perhaps it is noteworthy because compassion for others is not as common as we'd like to think. Curiously, we may discover in life that the people who are most compassionate, who truly demonstrate lives that are heart-shaped, may well be people we would never have guessed to be so.

The story in Luke about the Samaritan is just such an example. Samaritans were despised and priests were considered good, and yet it was the Samaritan who bravely took care of the injured man who lay on the side of the road. It was the Samaritan who actually lived a heart-shaped life, even to the point of getting the victim to a doctor and paying for his care.

Today, we have our own opinions about those we would call good, or those we despise. We imagine we can identify those who are of the wrong religion, wrong race, wrong political bent, or who live on the wrong side of town. Whatever it is, some people still walk by those in need. Some stop to offer help.

Jesus is helping even now to shape you to have a Samaritan heart. Be thankful that God has given you this gift, and use it to the full. Through you, God can make the hearts of others glad.

A HELPFUL HEART ——————————————————

Lord, help me to have more compassion for all of Your children wherever I find them today. Amen.

The Friendship Factor

There was an immediate bond between them, for Jonathan loved David.
1 SAMUEL 18:1 NLT

Friendship comes about in a number of ways, and sometimes the best friendships happen almost instantly. You meet someone for the first time and they become part of your life from then on. You get a feeling that you've known each other forever. It's such a wonderful thing.

C. S. Lewis said, "Friendship is born at that moment when one person says to another, 'What? You too? I thought I was the only one.'" It's important to have people in our lives who relate to the life lessons we've learned or who understand our goals and our heart's desires. Those are the people who sustain us when the hard times come along, holding us up in prayer and keeping us firmly planted in their hearts. These are the people who make a difference in our everyday existence.

Today is a good day to honor your friendships. Thank God for each of the people in your life who have shaped your heart by their kindness and love. No doubt, they thank God for you as well.

AT THE HEART OF FRIENDSHIP

Lord, I thank You for my dear friends and even the acquaintances who support my spirit, give me a hand, and strengthen my dreams. Please bless each of their lives today. Amen.

When the Light Goes Out

"This is what the LORD All-Powerful says:
'Do what is right and true. Be kind and merciful to each other.'"
ZECHARIAH 7:9 NCV

Our life journey takes us along many winding roads, and we sometimes find ourselves sitting in momentary darkness, feeling uncertain which way to turn. When the light goes out, we aren't even sure if we can go one step farther.

Albert Schweitzer said, "Sometimes our light goes out but is blown into flame by another human being. Each of us owes deepest thanks to those who have rekindled this light."

When we're left in the dark, we look to God to sustain us and we look to our friends to help us find the light again. The important thing to remember is that wherever you are, you may run across someone in that uncertain place, just sitting in the dark, waiting for you to turn the light on again. You know you lead a heart-shaped life when you are aware of the needs of others and have a great desire to help those who are lost.

Ask God to go with you and show you where you can shed the light of kindness on another human being. After all, God knew you'd come along just when you did. He's counting on you to reach out to share your heart and to reach up to shine His light.

A LIGHT HEART

Lord, when my light goes out, I am grateful for others who help me find my way again. Fill my heart with a desire to do any kindness I can do today. Amen.

Love Is such a Good Thing!

Love each other with genuine affection, and take delight in honoring each other.
ROMANS 12:10 NLT

Jeremy Taylor said, "The more we love, the better we are, and the greater our friendships are, the dearer we are to God." Well, if that's the case, where do we start?

Sometimes our love shows up in our service to others. We're the friendly neighbor or the volunteer for the project at church. We're the ones who draw people in when there's a conversation at hand, or the ones who offer to help even before we're asked. We give from the heart in ways that open doors and honestly show our genuine affection for those around us.

Sometimes we become reclusive though. We hide out from those situations where we might have to put ourselves out in some way, or give time and attention to things that simply are not on our agendas for the day. Sometimes we close the door on relationships and refuse to honor them.

No matter what your feelings were yesterday about how you would show love to the world, start again. Be authentic and friendly. Be kind and gentle. When you serve others with your whole heart, you are definitely dearer to God. Ask Him to guide you into living a heart-shaped day.

A HEART OF LOVE

Lord, I know that I'm often reticent to show the love I feel for my friends and family. Set me free to share my heart and Your love with others today. Amen.

Your Plans Are Good, God's Plans Are Better!

Rejoice in our confident hope. Be patient in trouble, and keep on praying. When God's people are in need, be ready to help them. Always be eager to practice hospitality.

ROMANS 12:12–13 NLT

It's always a good thing to be a planner. When you plan ahead, you're usually better prepared for the things that come your way. You're ready to cope with unexpected setbacks and move on with more confidence. Some of us are excellent planners and some of us are not.

However skilled we are though, it's important to remember that our plans are good. God's plans are better! When we signed up to be on God's team, we said (albeit in the fine print) that we would be there and be willing to serve in whatever way He might need us to serve. That might mean inviting unexpected guests for dinner with a gracious and warm heart, or even giving them a place to sleep. It might mean giving more than you thought you'd have to in a crisis to offset the immediate needs of others.

Each day, we need to have plans. Then, we need to surrender those plans to the will of our heavenly Father who is the only One who can see the big picture. . .the only One who can see everyone's need. Surrender your plans to God today and He will mold you and shape you according to His will. As He does so, all your plans will get even better.

A HEART TO PLAN

Lord, sometimes I get frustrated when my plans don't come together. I wonder what You could be doing in my life. When I reach out to others, I see Your plans bring greater blessing. Amen.

Branching Out

"I am the vine, and you are the branches. If any remain in me and I remain in them, they produce much fruit."

JOHN 15:5 NCV

We are part of the divine vine. God is pruning us and shaping our hearts to be more fruitful, yet we may discover that we spend a lot of time in the weeds. Producing fruit or living a life of love toward others is a lofty goal. To help us toward that goal, God gives us great varieties of ways to grow and blossom. He asks us to be fruitful with our time, our money, or with our generosity. He gently shapes our prayers, our acts of kindness, or our spirit.

You're a branch of the True Vine. Whatever you do to produce fruit reflects your connection to Him. Every act of charity, every good deed, and every heartfelt prayer serve to produce fruit for the good of the Kingdom.

Today, seek the help of the Vinedresser. Ask Him to keep stretching you, pruning you, and giving you the right soil where you can make a difference for Him. God loves to see you branching out in new directions according to His will and purpose for your life.

A FRUITFUL HEART

Lord, I don't always stop to see if the things on my to-do list are producing any fruit for the Kingdom. Let me keep mindful of You in all I do today, and give me a heart to be more of what You called me to be. Amen.

A Garden of Goodness

Their life will be like a watered garden, and all their sorrows will be gone.

JEREMIAH 31:12 NLT

We love gardens. We imagine happy little plants coming up and producing mouthwatering tomatoes, corn on the cob, and herbs of all kinds. We like harvesting our own little crops, knowing they didn't get filtered through a ton of chemicals before we prepared them for the table. It connects us in some way with generations before us who cultivated amazing gardens. It all feels so wholesome.

In a world where everything is mass-produced, preserved, shipped, and distributed from one part of the globe to another, something as simple as a garden can have real value to our souls.

Jeremiah talks about life in a watered garden. Water is the life force, the nourisher of the soil, and the life giver of the garden. A mix of water and sunshine will ensure that the garden will produce great bounty and in one sense feed its caretakers.

Your heart is like a garden as well, for from it comes the wellspring of life, wisdom, and goodness. It is the place where simple joys have meaning; the place that welcomes what life brings, balancing the rains and the sunshine.

When your heart is a well-watered garden, it is nourishing and refreshing to your spirit. If it isn't, then see if there are things that need to be raked and cleaned up, so you can start growing again. God will bless all your efforts.

A NOURISHED HEART

Lord, help me to grow in You and nurture those in my care according to Your design for our lives. Amen.

A Giving Heart

You must each decide in your heart how much to give. And don't give reluctantly or in response to pressure. "For God loves a person who gives cheerfully." And God will generously provide all you need.

2 CORINTHIANS 9:7–8 NLT

Giving is a wonderful thing, and we each must define for ourselves what it means to be a giver. We give our time, our money, or whatever assets we have to share. We give whatever we want, but there's only one way the Lord wants to receive what we give. He wants us to give because we have the heart to do so.

When you give because your heart is tuned in to a cause or a particular work of your church or because you just want to, then it's truly a gift. However, if you find yourself in a position where the collection basket is being passed and you're not sure you even have enough money to buy your own food, you need to stop and think about whether this is the right time for you to give. It may be. It may be the perfect time, but only if your heart says so and you're not just feeling pressured by the moment.

Be honest with yourself about how, when, and what you give. When your heart speaks to you to do it, do it. When giving is simply increasing your burdens, don't do it. Giving is a matter of the heart and capability, and God wants you to be a generous and cheerful giver.

A GENEROUS HEART

Lord, I always want to give, but sometimes I truly don't feel I can. Please accept my heartfelt offers to give in ways that please You. Amen.

God at Work. . .in You!

For God is working in you, giving you the desire and
the power to do what pleases him.

PHILIPPIANS 2:13 NLT

Perhaps you wonder what it is you can really do for God. After all, He can't really need you since you're just one person and you're not a theologian, missionary, or even a good prayer warrior. You may rationalize that it's okay if you're not doing God's will because you are just not that important in the scheme of things. If you have any thoughts like these, it's time for a change of heart.

The fact is, you are important to God and your work for Him makes a difference. You're His hands, feet, voice, and heart, and He counts on you to get His job done. God walks beside you, listens to you, and stays close to you because together you're a force to be reckoned with.

One reason God "needs" you is because He enjoys being around you and seeing you delight in His continual blessings. He especially enjoys seeing you come to life when you're doing good deeds, helping others, and offering Him thanks for all you have. God's need of you then is about designing a relationship of love with Him so that you can then live a life of joy in all you do for others.

It's a new day. Give God a chance to work wonders in your heart!

A HEART TO PLEASE GOD

Lord, thank You for all the good things You do in my life, and help me to never doubt that You and I together can make a difference in the world. Amen.

Starting Over

For I can do everything through Christ, who gives me strength.
PHILIPPIANS 4:13 NLT

We're always starting over in one way or another. We're either beginning a new job, a new relationship, a new exercise program, or something. Whatever it is we're starting, God wants us to understand we're not starting alone. He is always with us, and He encourages us to keep trying new things. With His help, we have a chance to embrace our lives with a clean heart, a positive attitude, and a willingness to serve.

Whatever it is that you're starting to do, remember that you get your strength from Christ who will help you move forward. He sees you, knows your heart, and knows what you need to accomplish the course you have set. He respects your dreams and the desires of your heart. Remember what Goethe said:

> *What you can do, or dream you can, begin it.*
> *Boldness has genius, power and magic in it.*
> *Only engage, and then the mind grows heated;*
> *Begin it and the task will be completed.*

Begin the new day, the new job, the new life, however it is meant to be designed, and know that you are strengthened every step of the way by God's love for you because you are always in His heart.

A HEART TO START AGAIN

Lord, it isn't easy to feel totally at peace when I'm starting something new. Remind me today that whatever I do, You'll be right there with me. Amen.

When It's Time to Quiet Down

*"Be still, and know that I am God! I will be honored by every nation.
I will be honored throughout the world."*
PSALM 46:10 NLT

From the moment you awake to a new day until you close your eyes again at night, your world is full of noise. It all begins with your alarm clock, then pushes its way into your consciousness through television, radio, and newspapers, and keeps going. It's hard to simply breathe and let God in. . .unless you have learned to quiet things down.

If God's still, small voice is trying to communicate with you, it may be drowned out by the endless highway traffic outside or the traffic of yesterday's problems and concerns that are still loitering in your mind. Stop! Breathe deeply, shut down the outside world, and invite your Father into your heart and mind. Pull up a chair for God and He will honor you with His presence. He wants to spend time just with you and help you drown out the noise of the world.

Meister Eckhart said, "The very best and highest attainment in this life is to remain still and let God act and speak in you." Reach up. Reach out to God, and let Him speak to your heart. It will make all the difference in your day.

A HEART TO LISTEN

Lord, it is so easy for me to ignore You in the midst of the turmoil that works around and through me all the time. Help me find peace in You today. Amen.

Making the Impossible Happen

Jesus told them[,] "I tell you the truth, if you had faith even as small as a mustard seed, you could say to this mountain, 'Move from here to there,' and it would move. Nothing would be impossible."

MATTHEW 17:20 NLT

Some of us have tiny faith. We'd like to have BIG faith, but we don't seem to get there. Why? Maybe it's because we don't ask God to help us build our faith. When we truly believe He can help with little things, we come back to Him to ask for help with even bigger things.

In order to have more faith we need a change of heart. We need to trust that God is there in the dark days and will bring us to the light. We have to believe that there is always a new possibility because of who He is, and not because of anything we can do on our own.

Norman Vincent Peale said that it was good to become a possibilitarian. He said, "No matter how dark things seem to be or actually are, raise your sights and see possibilities—always see them, for they're always there."

It's a new day, and when you have faith in Christ, impossible things happen. Set your heart and mind on Him and you may be amazed at how different your day will be, because with Him nothing is impossible.

A HEART FOR THE POSSIBLE

Lord, I have to admit that I don't always have big faith. I trust You're with me in the daily things, but I know I need more faith. Help me to believe and to receive more of You. Amen.

The Perfect Day

When the clouds are heavy, the rains come down. Whether a tree falls, north or south, it stays where it falls. Farmers who wait for perfect weather never plant.
ECCLESIASTES 11:3–4 NLT

Do you ever persuade yourself that you can't look for a new job, take that adult education course, or consider moving to a new community because you have to wait for the perfect conditions? Or maybe you do it another way. Perhaps you tell yourself that when you get this project done, then you'll be able to start another one, even if the current one no longer serves your needs or interests.

Like the person looking for the perfect mate, you might miss the perfect-for-you mate simply because you didn't know where to look. When you look in the right direction, and the condition of your heart is ready for change, change happens. Waiting for perfect opportunities and perfect partners may just be a way of never getting the job done.

It's a new and perfect day to move your life forward. May God shape your heart in such a way that you can see the new direction He has in mind. Then this day will be one of joy and possibility.

A HEART TO SEE NEW DIRECTION

Lord, remind me that this is a perfect day for me to do what You have designed for me already. Help me to stop waiting for something else to happen, and instead to trust You and just get going. Amen.

Slightly Used Pots

And yet, O LORD, you are our Father. We are the clay,
and you are the potter. We are all formed by your hand.
ISAIAH 64:8 NLT

By now you may be feeling more like a slightly used pot than a brand-new one. Perhaps the material that makes you *you* isn't brand-new, but each day, your heart, mind, and attitude can be revived.

What do you see when you look in the mirror? Once you get past the idea that you're getting older and you're working harder than ever to stay in shape, then you need to look further. You need to wait there long enough to see the "you" that God sees. You need to see the one the Lord loves and nurtures. You are being molded, shaped, and smoothed a bit more every day by His almighty loving hands. You are becoming all that He meant for you to become. You are beautiful clay in the hands of a master Potter.

As you look again then, you should see one of the most beautiful creations on earth. You should see a unique person, with a heart shaped and molded to do wonderful things for your Father in heaven. The Potter is proud of you.

A HEART-SHAPED YOU

Lord, I admit that I'm not very patient with myself these days. Renew my heart in You, and shape me so I can see myself with Your eyes and be encouraged to try again to be all You've made me to be. Amen.

The Good You Can Do!

Love your enemies, do good to them, and lend to them without expecting to get anything back. Then your reward will be great, and you will be children of the Most High.
LUKE 6:35 NIV

Most of us enjoy doing good things for others. We especially like to do good things for the people we love and the friends that help make life more valuable. We put our hearts and minds into doing those good things.

This passage in Luke offers you a different point of view. It says that we need to love our enemies and be good to them. Let's think about that. First of all, you probably don't have any real enemies, but you may have people on the relationship fringe that you have decided not to embrace for one reason or another. Maybe they don't think exactly like you do, maybe they live in ways that aren't comfortable to your spirit, or maybe you just see them as strange. Whatever it is, something keeps you at a distance.

Luke suggests that you keep giving, keep lending, and keep nurturing others until you no longer have an enemy. . .but a friend. This can happen, but only if you also allow God to change your heart. You may be amazed at the good you can do when love leads the way.

A HEART OF GOODNESS

Lord, I know You said we should love our neighbors, but I'm not always able to love some of them. I figured just ignoring them was okay. Help me to find ways to be good to them for Your sake. Amen.

Carrying Burdens

Share each other's burdens, and in this way obey the law of Christ. If you think you are too important to help someone, you are only fooling yourself.
GALATIANS 6:2–3 NLT

What kind of heart does it take to be willing to carry the burdens of someone else? John Baillie wrote, "Give me a stout heart to bear my own burdens. Give me a willing heart to bear the burdens of others. Give me a believing heart to cast all burdens upon Thee, O Lord."

Living a heart-shaped life means we're willing to carry burdens because we know that God is with us—walking beside us and helping to carry the load. He gently keeps us on course and lightens our load. He makes it possible for us to keep going and to keep trying to move forward. He blesses our efforts.

He also shapes us so that we look at the needs of others and consider how we can help lighten someone else's load as well. He calls us to give where we can, encourage and bless those who are struggling, and help them resolve difficulties. When we do this and turn our hearts toward Him, He strengthens and renews us, and the burdens become easier to bear.

Love means we care about others wherever we are and offer to carry their load whenever we can. Thank you for your generous and loving heart.

A HEART TO CARRY THE LOAD

Lord, help me to seek Your direction when it comes to discovering ways that I can help lighten the load for others. Amen.

Discovering the Difference

Humble yourselves before the Lord, and he will lift you up in honor.

JAMES 4:10 NLT

Most of us are familiar with Reinhold Niebuhr's Serenity Prayer. We appreciate the wisdom and the peace we receive when we pray along with him: "God, grant me the serenity to accept the things I cannot change; the courage to change the things I can and the wisdom to know the difference."

Acceptance of things we cannot change takes courage. Often we spend countless hours trying to discover how to solve a problem or how to change a situation, only to finally arrive at the place that prayerfully understands we have to be at peace with some things as they are.

Working for change also takes courage because obstacles must be overcome and new paths must be discovered. It takes courage to stand up for a cause or to try to improve an otherwise difficult situation. It takes courage to live heart-first.

Knowing the difference takes wisdom, and wisdom means that you put your circumstances before the Lord and admit your dependence on Him. The God of peace, courage, and wisdom will change your heart and help you discover the difference He alone can make.

A HEART OF TRUST

Lord, I seek Your peace and guidance in all situations where I struggle to make a difference. Shape my heart to desire Your will in all things. Amen.

The Winds of Change

"May the LORD bless you and protect you. May the LORD smile on you and be gracious to you. May the LORD show you his favor and give you peace."
NUMBERS 6:24–26 NLT

"Be the change you want to see in the world," Gandhi said.

Do you take note almost daily of things that need to be changed in the world? Maybe you think there should be more lighting on your street, or there should be more shelters for abused women, or maybe your community needs a better playground for the kids. Do you wonder when someone will get around to taking care of those things?

If you do, the winds of change are stirring around you for a reason. They are blowing opportunities right into your path and hoping you'll gather them up and do something about them. Change cannot happen on its own. It needs a constant force behind it, and if you find that a passion is brewing within your heart to get something done, then God may well be appointing you to the task.

Being the change that helps shape new direction and new perspective isn't easy, but when you work for God He will open doors to help those changes take place. God will favor you with His peace and bless you with the necessary change of heart to embrace His work for the good of others.

AT THE HEART OF CHANGE

Lord, I see things that need to be done in my community, but I assume that somebody else will do them. Make it clear to my heart when I need to be an agent for change, and grant me Your peace. Amen.

A Humble Heart

Humble yourselves in the sight of the Lord, and he shall lift you up.
JAMES 4:10 KJV

John Newton said this: "I am persuaded that love and humility are the highest attainments in the school of Christ and the brightest evidences that he is indeed our Master."

One of the ways God shapes us is through the gift of humility. With genuine humility, we understand that without God we are nothing. Without Him we cannot grow, change, or become all that we were designed to be. Without Him we miss opportunities to give and receive love. Without Him, we have no real purpose or focus.

With God though, we discover the meaning of humility. We discover the joy of serving others, of giving more than we ever imagined we could give, of sharing life in every way with those around us. Humility is a matter of heart.

We're in God's classroom, trying to learn as quickly as we can so that we can move on to graduation. He teaches us to work hard and to share. He shapes our hearts to love and forgive. The more we understand that He alone is worthy, the more we are humbled by all that He does for us. He lifts us up and gives us a sense of value and worth.

In true humility then, we learn to see one another as God's works in progress, always striving to do our best. We learn to see one another with love, seeking more committed and more authentic relationships. God bless your humble heart today.

A HEART LIKE HIS

Lord, help me to have a humble heart that pleases You. Amen.

Weeds of Worry

Humble yourselves, therefore, under God's mighty hand, that he may lift you up in due time. Cast all your anxiety on him because he cares for you.

1 PETER 5:6–7 NIV

Worry is like having weeds in your garden. They pop up everywhere, and if there are too many of them, they choke out even the good and healthy plants. You have to keep pulling the weeds up by the roots to try to get rid of them.

Worries come at us from every direction, and if we uproot one, another comes from nowhere and plants itself firmly in its place. Before we know it, we feel suffocated by life and wonder why we aren't feeling the sunshine on our faces. We feel weak and overburdened. We need God's help to reshape our thinking and give us hearts of joy.

You may not be able to keep worry from sprouting or even from coming into full bloom, but you can decide what you'll do when it comes along. You can hand it over to the Master Gardener and let Him deal with it. Your job then is simply to keep growing right where you are and let Him handle the rest. Before long, you may not even notice a stray worry that comes in because the Gardener will take care of it before you even know it's there.

Grow in His light, and let your heart be free of anxiety.

A WORRIED HEART

Lord, I know that worry tends to steal my peace any chance it gets. Help me to weed it out of my life and hand it over to You as quickly as possible. Amen.

The Right Track

Be strong and immovable. Always work enthusiastically for the Lord,
for you know that nothing you do for the Lord is ever useless.
1 CORINTHIANS 15:58 NLT

You're probably already on the right track and have been for a while, but Will Rogers reminded us that "even if you're on the right track, you'll get run over if you just sit there."

In other words, it's always good to keep moving, keep growing, and getting on to the direction God would like you to go. If your enthusiasm has been waning a bit lately, it might be time to set a new course, inspire your heart, and check with the Conductor to see just what your options might be. If your heart is aligned with your Savior and you want to go someplace special, you've got a ticket to ride.

If you're not on the right track, turn around, start over, or try again. After all, the game isn't over so you still have time to move forward as many spaces as you dare to go. Everything you do for God counts, and He's proud of your work even today. If you want to do something new, He'll be glad to make sure your ticket is valid for a whole new ride. As long as your heart is in it, you'll be making progress.

If you don't care where you're going, you can get there anytime. If you do care where you're going, you want to get there!

A DIRECTED HEART

Lord, shape my heart to do the work You have for me to do. Keep me running in the direction of the dreams that are mine to complete for You. Amen.

Turnips and Peas

All a person's ways seem pure to them, but motives are weighed by the LORD.

PROVERBS 16:2 NIV

God checks our motives when we do things that are a bit off track. We have to remember that He knows everything about us and there's nothing we can hide. He looks into our hearts and knows what makes us tick.

When our hearts are in the right place, we turn up for the work that needs to be done. In a garden, we might describe different turnips. There are those who "turn up" for the hard work, or the fun work, and those who don't "turn up" at all.

Those garden peas are a little harder to cultivate than the turnips though. We find the procrastinators, who never seem to get into the work needed; the philosophers, who talk a lot about the work needed; and the picky p's who just make the job harder for everyone. We can rake around the p's a bit and go for the pleasant ones who always try to help.

Whether you feel more like the turnips or the peas, remember God always knows what work you did in the garden because He sees your heart wherever you are.

A HEART WITH GOOD MOTIVES

Lord, help me be more aware of my motivations for things I do. Remind me that only You can keep my garden nourished and growing. Amen.

Blindsided and Dumbfounded

Give your burdens to the LORD, and he will take care of you.
He will not permit the godly to slip and fall.
PSALM 55:22 NLT

Have you ever been totally blindsided by something? Maybe you were fired from a job and had no real idea why, or your relationship of several years suddenly nosedived and ended, or your kid admitted doing drugs in college. Whatever it was, it probably left you speechless, dumbfounded, totally amazed, and shaken by the whole thing.

When that happens to us, we have to make choices about how we will handle the event. We can suffer in silence and create ulcers and other diseases in our bodies, we can yell at the top of our lungs and discover that nothing actually changed after that, or we can pray fervently for God's help and put the whole thing at His feet. When it comes to these kinds of personal sorrows, we really have no choice but to pray.

You were not created to carry the unexpected heart-wrenching sides of life all by yourself. In fact, you weren't created to carry them at all. You have to put them down. . . down at the foot of the cross. Your Father will know what to do from there. Only then will your heart find peace.

A HEART OF PEACE

Lord, when a crisis comes into my life, I'm anything but peaceful. Help me to bring my burdens to You and seek Your help to heal my heart. Amen.

Success and Failure

*"For I know the plans I have for you," says the LORD. "They are plans
for good and not for disaster, to give you a future and a hope."*
JEREMIAH 29:11 NLT

If you've ever been rejected, had an amazing idea turned down by a committee, or even had a well-thought-out plan go awry, you know what it feels like to fail. You worked hard, but you ultimately realize you are just not in control. You're not in control, and though it may feel like it, the rejection you experienced is not necessarily all about you.

Failure can bring opportunity; it can be a good signal to try another route or reevaluate a goal. It can even be a great chance to surrender your heart to God and allow Him to take over, shaping your life direction, renewing your enthusiasm, and giving you a new sense of purpose. Rejection can actually give you a greater chance for things to come together.

Imagine being Thomas Edison on the one thousand nine hundred and ninety-ninth try. He could have gotten discouraged and stopped right there. Or, he could have believed God meant for his work to be successful and with a renewed spirit tried number two thousand.

Imagine being a great writer and debating whether to send out your incredible manuscript for the fiftieth time after forty-nine rejections. Success has everything to do with attitude, persistence, and faith. God wants you to win at the plans He has designed for you. Put your heart into it and try again.

He designed you to win!

A HEART TO TRY

Lord, please help me get the right perspective when things don't seem to be going my way. Let me see Your hand in all I do, and renew my heart to try again. Amen.

Ark Building

Be strong and brave. Don't be afraid or discouraged.
1 CHRONICLES 22:13 NCV

You probably know the basic story of Noah and the ark and the rain and the floods. Imagine yourself in Noah's shoes as the one who believed God, was a friend of God's, and therefore was determined to be obedient to what God wanted. If you can imagine Noah's response to God because you believe you would have done those things as well, take it to the next step.

Imagine now that you're on dry land, there's not a cloud in the sky, rain has never been an issue, and no one ever heard of a flood. Now, there you are, the person who believes that God gave you instructions to build a great big boat because the earth was going to be destroyed shortly and you were going to have the only getaway crew. What are you thinking? What are the neighbors thinking? Surely you might question whether you heard God correctly. You question, but you keep building.

As the boat gets finished, you get the next instruction, which is to gather up animals from everywhere in pairs so they can help you get things started as you begin the world anew. If your friends weren't laughing before, they're now pretty much in hysterics. But you keep going.

You know how the Noah story ends, but you don't know how your story ends. The question is not if you believe God, but rather, do you believe God so much you'd build an ark in the middle of the streets of Manhattan if He asked you to? Only your heart knows for sure.

A BRAVE HEART

Lord, I try to follow Your rules and Your plans for my life. Help me to have the kind of Noah-faith that means I will bravely follow You always. Amen.

Blushing Again!

Even fools are thought wise when they keep silent;
with their mouths shut, they seem intelligent.

PROVERBS 17:28 NLT

Do you ever feel slightly embarrassed by something that came out of your mouth before you could stop it? You made a comment that makes you blush from head to toe and you're not quite sure how to recover from it. Retreat seems the best option.

Mark Twain said, "Man is the only animal that blushes. Or needs to."

We probably have lots of reasons to point fingers at one another or even at ourselves in recognition of the embarrassing things we've done or said. The truth is, most of the things that make you blush aren't really worthy of the pink in your cheeks. When the wrong thing is said, the right thing is sure to find its way shortly. When the wrong thing is done, the work begins on how to repair the damage and create a difference so it doesn't happen again.

Let's not be embarrassed over the little human things we do. Let's be embarrassed over the things we choose to ignore in our hearts. Let's find a way to speak, or in obedience to God, be silent. When we do, our hearts and minds will be properly aligned and His will can be done.

A HEART OF WISDOM

Lord, help me be patient and not speak foolishly when I disagree with what someone else is saying. Direct my thoughts, and help me put quiet trust in You. Amen.

Round Pegs and Square Holes

This is the day that the LORD has made; let us rejoice and be glad in it.
PSALM 118:24 ESV

Are you the same person today that you were a year ago? How about last week or even yesterday? If you're blessed and you're growing, then you're constantly changing. You're becoming more of the person God designed you to be all the time. You may see that the new version of you doesn't exactly fit with your old attitudes toward life.

As God continues to give you a heart-shaped life, He inspires you to think in new ways. You see things from a perspective that you never understood before. You think with your head, but you move past that and check in with your heart. You simply live differently. You may feel like a round peg in a square hole, but that's okay.

You're on a path of discovery. Reach up and connect to the Source of your light and love and let Him show you where you'll fit the best. All the good things are getting better. Your heart will guide you to a place of true joy. Celebrate all that life brings you today, and give God the glory!

A HEART TO REJOICE

Lord, I'm growing and changing, and sometimes I'm afraid of what that means. Help me to move in the direction that will bring us both great joy! Amen.

Bend, Don't Break!

I love the LORD because he hears my voice and my prayer for mercy.
Because he bends down to listen, I will pray as long as I have breath!
PSALM 116:1–2 NLT

Physical exercise is about stretching and bending. It's about limbering up and becoming more flexible. Spiritual exercise is about stepping out and stepping up to follow Jesus. It's about surrendering your heart to the One who can really make a difference in your life. It's a heart exercise from the inside out.

Some of us are not very flexible. We cannot bend very far without serious consequences. We're comfortable, and getting nudged out of our comfort zone doesn't make us happy.

God wants you to reach a little further than your grasp today. Exercise some greater opportunities to serve His people. Lift someone from their suffering or hug someone with the spirit of warmth and caring if you want to do some bending exercises. It's so much easier to bend than it is to break.

The Lord listens to your heart, softens it, and makes it more flexible to handle the needs of others. If you bend with your heart, it won't get broken.

A FLEXIBLE HEART

Lord, I am still learning to give over the things I think and feel so that I can create more opportunities to love others as You would have me do. Help my heart become more flexible. Amen.

Time Is on Your Side

*And we know that God causes everything to work together for the good of those
who love God and are called according to his purpose for them.*

ROMANS 8:28 NLT

Time crawls along when you're waiting for something important like results from a lab test, a letter from your soldier husband, or Christmas. It has no respect at all for how anxious you are or what fears manifest in the waiting process.

On the other hand, when your birthday rolls around you wonder where the time went. You are awed at how quickly one day melts into the next and how the years are nearly spinning out of control. Suddenly, you're the age your mother was when you thought she was old. It just can't be. Somehow time has passed and taken you with it.

Sometimes you're waiting for God to work things out in your life. You've been praying and waiting and praying and waiting some more. You want to believe that good things are happening or that God is busy putting things in order, but you simply don't know what is going on. Let time be on your side. Know that God is on your side and that He is indeed aware of the things that matter to your heart. He's not only aware of those things, He knows exactly what you need to fulfill your purpose in Him.

Whatever you may struggle with today, trust that God has it in hand and that He holds you close to His heart all the time.

A PATIENT HEART

Lord, waiting is always hard, and yet, time spins out of control. I wonder where the days go. Help me to live the moments, fully aware of all You're doing right now, in the present. Amen.

The Clouds Are Gathering

Examine yourselves to see if your faith is genuine. Test yourselves. Surely you know that Jesus Christ is among you; if not, you have failed the test of genuine faith.

2 CORINTHIANS 13:5 NLT

God has a plan for you and He won't let go of it. It may seem that He's keeping a distance, or He's giving you time to work things out for yourself. Keep praying and keep checking to see if He's nearby, and you'll discover that He's been there all along, guiding you and shaping your direction.

If you've been walking through stormy times, just keep walking because God is already ahead of you waiting to help you, waiting to heal you. He is there standing in the light and will shine it on you to direct your path.

If your faith is in need of a heart transplant, ask God to help you. Ask Him to give you a heart like His, steadfast and genuine. He will sustain you no matter what life brings your way.

A STEADFAST HEART

Lord, please keep walking with me on this journey of life. I'm not always sure I can see which way to go, so I'm counting on You to lead me and shine a light on my path. Amen.

The Ideal Heart

I am fearfully and wonderfully made.
PSALM 139:14 KJV

Anne Frank recorded these words in her diary: "It's really a wonder that I haven't dropped all my ideals, because they seem so absurd and impossible to carry out. Yet I keep them, because in spite of everything, I still believe that people are really good at heart."

The world as we know it is far less than ideal. Many people live in uncertainty and fear and slip into the shadows. Some have totally lost their way, and yet, we might echo with Anne Frank that we still believe people are good at heart. Ultimately, we know we are fearfully and wonderfully made.

The ideal of living a heart-shaped life then is one of choice. We can choose to have our hearts changed so that our perceptions about others are kinder and gentler. We can look to be a solution to the things that cause darkness to prevail and help to bring the light into the lives of those closest to us. God has called you to carry the light, shining the light of His love everywhere you go.

As you go about your day, look up to God, seek His face, radiate His warmth and love to those around you. Why? Because you too believe that people are good at heart.

A GOOD HEART

Lord, I get discouraged trying to be a light to others, especially if they do not respond to that light. Remind me that I was designed by Your loving hand for this very purpose. I thank You and praise You for all You are and all You've done for me. Amen.

Why We Have Hope

*We also glory in our sufferings, because we know that suffering produces
perseverance; perseverance, character; and character, hope. And hope does
not put us to shame, because God's love has been poured out into
our hearts through the Holy Spirit, who has been given to us.*

ROMANS 5:3–5 NIV

Doesn't it cheer you up from the inside out to know "God's love has been poured out into our hearts through the Holy Spirit"? That image is breathtaking and gives you all kinds of reasons to rejoice. You have love continually pouring into your veins and into your heart and mind. You are never at a loss for the greatest love of your life.

God's love is the reason you have hope. When you face a trial and find your comfort in God's arms and your direction in His Word, then your hope rises again. You know that you are never alone and that nothing can happen to you that He does not know. He knows your grief and your sorrows. He grieves with you and helps you persevere.

When you keep going, keep trusting, keep believing in what He has planned, then your character is ever stronger and your hope is alive. You do not have the hope of those who wish on stars in the heavens. You have the hope of those who believe in the Son of God and the gifts that only the heavenly Father bestows. Rejoice in your sufferings and even more in your hope, and let your heart be glad. Receive His love today.

A HEART OF HOPE

Lord, we have walked a long way together by now and have had our share of ups and downs. Thank You for always being with me, my everlasting Hope and loving Heart. Amen.

Counting Your Blessings

*Let us draw near to God with a sincere heart and with
the full assurance that faith brings.*

HEBREWS 10:22 NIV

Living a life that is shaped by God's hand means that you have to stay ever close to Him. You have to approach Him with a sincere and honest heart that seeks to be more like Him and remembers all He has done.

Wake up and count your blessings! Before your feet touch the floor with the morning sunrise, thank God for a good night's rest and for the warm bed that kept you feeling safe and cozy.

Thank God for watching over you and for giving you the strength, energy, and presence of mind to begin a new day. Seek His will and His presence for each decision you have to make and each step you take.

This is your day to count it all joy when you see His face in others and when you reflect His grace to those around you. He sees you and knows you. He guides you and blesses you with a complete assurance that He has your back and that your prayers are heard.

When you live a heart-shaped life, it is always a good day to draw near to God in the full assurance of faith. He will sustain you all through the day and keep your heart in alignment with His own.

A BLESSED HEART

Lord, help me to always want to be close to You, learning from You and growing in faith because of You. Bless my heart and my efforts to bless others in return. Amen.

Heart Work Is Hard Work

And in every work that he began in the service of the house of God, in the law and in the commandment, to seek his God, he did it with all his heart. So he prospered.

2 CHRONICLES 31:21 NKJV

John Flavel, sixteenth-century theologian, declared, "Heart work is hard work indeed. Get your heart broken for sin while you are actually confessing it; melted with free grace even while you are blessing God for it; to be really ashamed and humbled through the awareness of God's infinite holiness, and to keep your heart in this state not only in, but after these duties, will surely cost you some groans and travailing pain of soul."

Being shaped and molded by God is not always easy. When we surrender our hearts to Him, to be guided and blessed by Him, then we know He will do two more things besides. He will love us into being the person He meant for us to become, and He will forgive us any of those things that fail to meet His standards.

As the ancient theologian reminded us, we may surely suffer some pangs of guilt over our own brokenness. We may indeed, but thankfully God does not leave us there. He lifts us up out of the muck and mire and puts us on solid ground. He cleans us off and gives us a chance to start again.

The best we can do on any day is to surrender our hearts into His safekeeping and He will see to it that we are able to stand, strengthened by His own loving hand, for He puts even more love into our hearts.

THE HEART WORK

Thank You, Lord, for loving me just as I am and for creating a clean heart within me. Let me do all that I can to live a heart-shaped life. Amen.

Stepping-Stones

You have made a wide path for my feet to keep them from slipping.

2 Samuel 22:37 NLT

Did you skip stones across the water when you were a kid? Sometimes you could get the rock to bounce five or six times before it finally started to sink. It was fun to see how far it would go, and it was a lesson in understanding the physical universe a bit more.

You may also remember trying to stand on slippery rocks as you crossed a creek bed, hoping you wouldn't fall into the water. Sometimes those stones were mossy though, so that made the balancing act a bit harder and you'd fall in the water anyway.

Now that you're an adult, it may seem like you're still trying to find the stones that are safe to stand on while you figure out what direction to take. When you stand on the Rock, stepping-stones may be slippery, but you'll always be certain of your next steps.

Today, God wants to remind you that He doesn't want you to slip out there in the world and fall beyond His grasp. He wants to hold you up and make a way for you to get safely to the place you're meant to go. As long as your heart is open to His guidance, He'll make sure you never fall.

THE HEART TO FOLLOW

Sometimes, Lord, I try to step out ahead of You as though I can just skip across the water like a stone that won't sink. Help me to take each step with You and stand firmly in Your care, not getting ahead of You but simply following in humble gratitude. Amen.

The Wings of Faith

But those who trust in the LORD will find new strength. They will soar high on wings like eagles. They will run and not grow weary. They will walk and not faint.

ISAIAH 40:31 NLT

When God gives you a new heart, He gives you wings to fly. Imagine yourself as a tiny bird that flies up high, seeking to touch the sky, and then looks back to the earth to see where to land. Soaring on your wings, you seek God's presence, and swooping back toward earth, you seek to do His will. This one flight of fancy helps you see the whole picture and understand things in a new way. You feel energized and strong enough to change the world.

God always knows the whole picture. He knows why it's important for you to go through what you're going through. He knows it's important for you to stay close to Him and seek His help with your life. He knows He can strengthen you and help your soul grow stronger when you are near Him. He also knows how much you can handle and when it will be best for you to simply rest in Him. He holds your heart and He has your back in whatever life brings your way.

Faith gives you wings when you're willing to fly high enough to get a new point of view and when you desire to know God's vision for your life any time you feel uncertain. Your wings are not clipped by adversity; they are strengthened. Get out there and fly higher today!

A HEART WITH WINGS

Lord, I embrace the wings of hope and faith that You have given me. Help me to always look to understand Your intention for my life and spirit. Amen.

When You're Smiling

A glad heart makes a happy face.
PROVERBS 15:13 NLT

Some people search all their lives for a definition of happiness. They believe that they will be happy when. . .they have the right job, they fall in love, they have kids, they learn to dance, or whatever else they might perceive as a shortcoming now that can only be fixed somewhere in the future. For them, happiness is always somewhere up ahead.

When you live a heart-shaped life though, the definition of happiness is always in the present. You are happy right now at this moment because your happiness is not built on some effort of your own. Your happiness rests on the fact that you know you are loved and you know that you have eternal life. You can put a smile on your face every day of the year.

Happiness then may not be the result of having more things, finding the perfect mate, or learning a new skill. Happiness may only be defined by something totally within your grasp, totally available to you at every moment. Happiness is an inward peace emanating from the heart and exploding outwardly to become a broad smile on your face. Yes, happiness comes from a glad heart.

God has loved you from the moment you were conceived and He will love you until the day you return to Him. He is always smiling when He thinks of you. Be sure to smile back today.

A HEART THAT SMILES

Lord, bless all those I love with plenty of reasons to smile today. Amen.

Family—Gotta Love 'Em!

If anyone does not provide for his relatives, and especially for members of his household, he has denied the faith and is worse than an unbeliever.

1 TIMOTHY 5:8 ESV

If you're lucky, you've got the perfect family. Everyone loves everyone else all the time, respects each one's boundaries, and agrees with each one's goals. Wait a second, that's not luck, that's some kind of TV sitcom from the '50s. There isn't a family anywhere quite like that.

Family structure and norms have changed. Traditional families have given way to blended families, single-parent families, and all kinds of other combinations of families. Regardless of the structure, it's still true that the people we call "family" are important, and we need to devote a lot of time and energy to one another's well-being.

Your family is your main support system. They are the ones who mold and shape you and push you to become more. As John Donne once wrote, "No man is an island." We're all part of other people's lives for a reason, and we weren't meant to go it alone in the world. Family is where you learn to open your heart to love and where you first learn about God's love for you.

Your family is your current culture, your root, your support, and your blessing. Thank God for each person in your family today.

A HEART FOR FAMILY

Lord, my family is important to me, and I know they are important to You. Please help us to love one another heart-first. Amen.

Are You My Mother, My Sister, My Brother?

Whenever we have the opportunity, we should do good to everyone—especially to those in the family of faith.
GALATIANS 6:10 NLT

Those you think of as family, whether they are biological or psychological family members, provide the essential ingredients you need of support, kindness, encouragement, and interest in your welfare and your life as a whole. They are your teachers, mentors, and sponsors. They are your sounding boards, helpers, and volunteers to get you through the ups and downs of daily living. They are God's tools in the effort to shape your life according to His plan and purpose. Together, they are the heart and center of all that brings meaning to your life.

These are the people who strive to do good in ways that help you become more than you would be otherwise. They pray for you and worry about you. They advise you and love you. They are God's hands and feet, and they respect you.

Give thanks today for the amazing family God has given you, to provide a place where you belong and to help you understand what love really means. Be sure to let your brothers, sisters, fathers, and mothers know how much you love them.

A HEART FOR FAMILY

Lord, You are so good to me. Thank You for blessing me with a multitude of wonderful brothers and sisters, people who will always feel like family to me. Amen.

Try to Be Helpful

*Don't get tired of helping others. You will be rewarded when the time is right,
if you don't give up. We should help people whenever we can,
especially if they are followers of the Lord.*

GALATIANS 6:9–10 CEV

Your life is full! Some days you're so tired you can hardly think. Your family needs your help, the kids are demanding, and the world outside is full of people with their hands out. You are overwhelmed and maybe even tired of helping everybody else.

The writer of Galatians reminds us that we may be tired, but we shouldn't give up. We have to remember the needs of others. We're God's heart and His hands in the world. William Penn wisely said, "If there is any kindness I can show, or any good thing I can do to any fellow being, let me do it now, and not deter or neglect it, as I shall not pass this way again."

When you offer a word of solace, give a gift of love, or lend a hand, people's lives are blessed and so is yours. Your kindness makes a difference, and your generous spirit shows you are a child of God.

Kindness opens doors, embraces weaker souls, and encourages those who may be downhearted. Think of how often someone else's kindness made a difference to you. Be helpful! Smile! Try to never grow weary of doing good things for others.

A HEART OF KINDNESS

Lord, bless those I meet today, and remind me to offer a little kindness wherever I can. Help me to share Your light and Your generous Spirit. Amen.

Embracing Forgiveness

The LORD is like a father to his children, tender and compassionate to those who fear him. For he knows how weak we are; he remembers we are only dust.

PSALM 103:13–14 NLT

Martin Luther King Jr. said that "forgiveness is not an occasional act: it is an attitude."

Acts of forgiveness may well be a matter of attitude, but they are also matters of the heart. The forgiveness attitude must be embraced, tutored, created, and educated just like any other attitude or opinion you hold. One reason it takes a lot of heart is because the first person you must be willing to forgive is yourself. You surrender to God those actions you're not proud of so that the weight of them does not hold you back from other important matters in your life.

Embrace God's gift of forgiveness. Once you've turned those concerns of your heart over to Him, leave them there and let Him help you become more of what you are meant to be. Allow God to grow in you in such a way that even your smile is more radiant. Your heart will be free in every way to pursue Him with gusto.

At this very moment, God offers you the right to be loved and the right to be forgiven. Embrace Him with your whole heart!

A FORGIVEN HEART

Lord, thank You for Your forgiveness, and help me to be more forgiving to others in my life. Amen.

Speaking from the Heart

But respect Christ as the holy Lord in your hearts. Always be ready to answer everyone who asks you to explain about the hope you have, but answer in a gentle way and with respect. Keep a clear conscience so that those who speak evil of your good life in Christ will be made ashamed. It is better to suffer for doing good than for doing wrong if that is what God wants.

1 PETER 3:15–17 NCV

As your love for Jesus grows, so your heart grows too. Your perceptions change from those that only human minds can muster to one that a divine mind shapes and molds. The changes in your heart and mind are noticeable, and people will gravitate to you without even being conscious of why they do so. It's all because you radiate a light that offers the peace of God's presence and you offer that light with great joy.

Your faith is not in a container that hides you away; it is a floodgate that opens your heart in such a way that others become attracted to Jesus, your Holy Lord and Savior. This is your cause, your purpose, the reason you celebrate and keep your heart focused on Christ. He is the assurance that you know and the peace that brings hope to everything.

Thank God today for His amazing presence in your heart and in your life. He is truly the answer to your every need.

A HEART FOR CHRIST

Lord, thank You for living within me and helping my spirit to grow strong in You. Bless those around me with Your light and love as well. Amen.

It Only Takes a Spark

"For God loves a person who gives cheerfully."
2 CORINTHIANS 9:7 NLT

Most of us appreciate the idea that "little things can mean a lot."

When the last match in your pocket lights a fire that keeps everyone around it warm, it means a lot. Your single match accomplished a great deed.

When you offer your sandwich to a hungry person, a smile lights up the face of a stranger, and that means a lot. When you help the needy, your efforts combined with everyone else's efforts make a difference.

The point is that we sometimes neglect doing the little things because we don't recognize how important they are. Your small gift, whether it's a smile, a sandwich, or the match that lights a fire, is the spark that changes lives. Your spark can light up the world. A single coal trying to burn on its own will ultimately burn out, but when it is placed together with other coals, fires of possibility warm everyone around.

God has given you a heart to make a difference and the opportunities, in big ways and small ways, to share His love with others. Be the match that lights someone else's way. Carry the torch of God's love for others, and pass it along wherever you are.

A HEART TO MAKE A DIFFERENCE

Lord, help me to share Your love with others today and make a difference in any way that I can. Bless my little efforts, and multiply the joys they bring. Amen.

Gifts of the Heart

"Do to others as you would like them to do to you."
LUKE 6:31 NLT

Give strength, give thought, give deeds, give wealth;
Give love, give tears, and give yourself.
Give, give, be always giving,
Who gives not, is not living;
The more you give, the more you live.

The writer of the above quotation may not be known, but the words live on. When you give from your heart, you never run out of the energy or opportunity to give even more.

When you stand for a cause, give to a friend, or add expertise that gets a job done, then it brings an opportunity for celebration. Giving makes you feel good. God blessed you with very specific gifts so that you could share them. He puts you in the exact right circumstances so your heart is touched by what you can contribute to bring joy to the situation.

You offer heartfelt prayers on behalf of others, words of encouragement, and do good deeds in the Lord's service. You show that God has indeed shaped your heart to love those around you. Thank God for giving you His love and a heart that is so willing to be a gift to others.

A GIVING HEART

Lord, You have given so much to me. Thank You for any opportunity I may have to give back to others in Your name. Amen.

The "Getting" Frenzy

"You should remember the words of the Lord Jesus:
'It is more blessed to give than to receive.' "

ACTS 20:35 NLT

Somewhere in the course of growing up, we got the impression that the person with the most toys wins. Though it may be a loosely motivating idea, it put us into a "getting" frenzy. We had to have the latest cell phone, the coolest technology, or the greatest surround-sound network. The problem is that the "getting frenzy" doesn't help you become more giving to your neighbor.

Winston Churchill said, "We make a living by what we get. We make a life by what we give." Most of us think more about the getting than the giving, and we may not even realize we have that focus. Remember that even if you don't have all the latest technical gadgets, if you sleep in a warm bed at night, eat dinner on a regular basis, and have clean water to drink, you're living in a state of wealth. You have more toys than a good share of the world enjoys.

Be grateful, and thank God with your whole heart for His mercy and provision. Then let God shape your heart and spur you on to greater giving on behalf of those in need. Let your giving become a lasting blessing wherever you are.

A HEART OF GIVING

Lord, I praise You for the provisions You have made in my life. Help me to share all that I have according to the direction of Your Spirit. Amen.

A Heart for All Seasons

There is a time for everything, and a season for every activity under the heavens.
ECCLESIASTES 3:1 NIV

Sometimes being a friend is mastering the art of timing. There is time for silence. A time to let go and allow people to hurl themselves into their own destiny. And a time to prepare to pick up the pieces when it's all over.

OCTAVIA BUTLER

Friendship requires an interesting set of heart skills to make it work well. You have to know when to jump in with your advice and your good intentions and when to back off and let your friend figure out things alone. You have to know when to share a laugh, a hug, a moment, or when to listen with your heart. Friends carry burdens together, and sometimes friends stand apart or step back.

The key is that friendship is all about love and about giving. You give love, energy, time, thoughtfulness, and strength. You give separation, silence, and prayer. You give from the heart because that's what God made you to do.

As you think about your close friends today, honor them before God, and give Him praise for the many joys you share.

THE HEART OF FRIENDSHIP

Lord, my friend is so important to me and I'm not always sure how to best take care of her needs. Help me to be as giving and tender as possible today. Amen.

Follow the Leader

You are my friends if you do what I command.

JOHN 15:14 NLT

Remember when you were a kid and you played a game called "Follow the Leader"? You were supposed to imitate whatever movement or action the leader did and see if you could keep up with the moves. The game was somewhat about focus and paying attention. You weren't supposed to do anything except follow the leader.

In your adult life, you still follow the leader. Your boss says to do something and you do it without question. Your child says they need something from the store and if you agree, you go get it. Your spouse wants to have you go somewhere and because it's your spouse, you go. You're good at following.

Jesus wants to know that you're following Him even more than all the other people in your life. He wants you to follow your heart in a way that leaves no room for anyone or anything else to come between you. By checking in with your heart, you get a clear understanding of what motivates you.

It's great to walk beside the others in your life, but it's important to remember there is only one leader, your Lord and Savior, Jesus Christ. Follow Him closely with every beat of your heart.

THE HEART OF A FOLLOWER

Lord, help me follow in Your footsteps today so that every action I take can receive Your blessing and be worthy of You, reflecting Your heart for others. Amen.

The Dimmer Switch

A friend is always loyal, and a brother is born to help in time of need.
PROVERBS 17:17 NLT

Close friends are essential for our well-being. Few of us survive the journey of life well if we have to walk alone in the world. Some friends assist us for a short time, walk part of the way with us and then move on. Others start the journey with us in grade school and stay connected to us forever. Real friends are with us through lessons we learn, memories we create, and opportunities that flourish and cause us to grow.

In any friendship, the roles are constantly being reversed. The heart of friendship is about offering strength in time of need, or simply being there to hold a hand. Friendship turns on the light, turns up the light, or turns out the light, depending on the situation. Friendship then, is like a dimmer switch, and when it's plugged into the Source of Light Himself, it can make an amazing difference. Friends with great hearts help each other see everything more clearly. When they stick together, God blesses them both with even more love and admiration.

Celebrate your friends. Enjoy the delightful fact that God loves you so much, He provided very special people to show you His love each day.

A FRIENDLY HEART

Lord, thank You for blessing me with friends who strengthen me, laugh with me, and help shape my life in worthwhile ways. Bless each of the friends You've given me today. Amen.

It's All Possible!

"All things are possible for one who believes."
MARK 9:23 ESV

Brother Lawrence said, "All things are possible to him who believes, yet more to him who hopes, more still to him who loves, and most of all to him who practices and perseveres in these three virtues." Forgiving the masculine pronoun, we'll assume this statement to be true regardless of gender.

Hope and love will get you on the right path, and with practice and perseverance you'll get where you were designed to go. All things are possible, but sometimes God makes you the catalyst. You have to find the way around the obstacles, have faith through setbacks, and continue on even when you've failed. You have to believe your objective is possible to achieve.

When you have put the desires of your heart before God and have waited with patience and trusted that things would come together, but nothing happens, you may be missing one ingredient. You may need to believe God will act on your behalf for one reason and one reason only. . .because He utterly adores you. Only with Him are all things possible.

A HEART OF POSSIBILITY

Lord, it is hard to pursue my dreams when they don't come together for a long time. Please help me to patiently hope and believe that they are yet to be, according to Your will and purpose. Amen.

Intentional Living

*For everything, absolutely everything, above and below, visible and invisible. . .
everything got started in him and finds its purpose in him.*

COLOSSIANS 1:16 MSG

When we believe that everything got its start from God and that everything finds its purpose in Him, it can't help but change our perception about the way life is supposed to work. When your heart is focused on the things that God has done and what God may yet be able to do through you, everything changes. There's only one God and there's only one you, and the two of you have great things to accomplish.

You may be wondering what your purpose is or whether there's any real difference you could make in the world. Here's the answer! You have a purpose, and there's no one who can accomplish the work you are meant to do, but you. You're on a mission, and everyone else you know is on a mission as well.

God searches the hearts of His children so He can create clear paths to helping each one fulfill His purposes. Your goals and your heart's desires are all ways God achieves success in meeting the needs of people everywhere. He works through you and shapes your heart to do that work with love and mercy. He knows every detail and what it will take, and so He wants you to draw near to Him for strength and for wisdom. His intention is for you to succeed in every good way. Work with Him and fulfill your purpose in Him.

A HEART OF PURPOSE

Lord, help me to be the purpose You meant me to be and to do my life work with joy. Amen.

You Are So Well Made!

I praise you because you made me in an amazing and wonderful way. What you have done is wonderful. I know this very well. You saw my bones being formed as I took shape in my mother's body. . . . All the days planned for me were written in your book before I was one day old.

PSALM 139:14–16 NCV

God created you, every inch of you, every thought, every joy, and every experience life brings are part of His design for you. There is never a moment that He does not care about you and have compassion concerning your life and well-being.

C. H. Spurgeon said, "He who counts the stars and calls them by their names, is in no danger of forgetting His own children. He knows your case as thoroughly as if you were the only creature He ever made, or the only saint He ever loved."

Take a moment to reflect on what it means to be so fully known and fully loved. Look at your choices and your life direction and know that you are perfect in the sight of the One who made you and desires the best for you at all times. Give Him your whole heart because your Creator wants to help you achieve all your plans.

A HEART FOR GOD'S DIRECTION

Lord, thank You for loving me so much and for blessing my life in so many ways. Give me joy in knowing that You direct my steps today. Amen.

Prayers of the Heart

In the same way, the Spirit helps us in our weakness. We do not know what we ought to pray for, but the Spirit himself intercedes for us through wordless groans. And he who searches our hearts knows the mind of the Spirit, because the Spirit intercedes for God's people in accordance with the will of God.

ROMANS 8:26–27 NIV

C. H. Spurgeon reminded us that "God always has an open ear and a ready hand, if you have an open and ready heart. Take your groanings and your sighs to God and he will answer you."

Sometimes we're not certain how to approach God because the concerns of our hearts are heavy and we don't know what words will get God's attention. When your heart is open to God and ready to seek His help, the words are not important. It's the condition of your heart and the willingness to be open and honest with God that truly makes the difference.

If you are a prayer person, God can easily hear your heart because He knows already what you are trying to say. He knows your needs even more than you may know them yourself. If you aren't certain that you know what to say when you come before God, you can be sure that He sees you coming and is ready to listen and respond.

The prayers of your heart let God know that you want Him to be part of your life under any circumstance. Open your heart to hear all He wants to share with you today.

A HEART AT PRAYER

Lord, I'm so grateful that you understand the complexities of my life and the concerns of my heart. Please receive my prayers with Your gracious love. Amen.

Do You Really Want It Your Way?

And this world is fading away, along with everything that people crave.
But anyone who does what pleases God will live forever.

1 JOHN 2:17 NLT

You may have grown up in a world where you learned that life was like a competitive sport and you had to learn to play or you'd be sitting on the sidelines. In the struggle to come out on top, you may have determined that things would have to happen your way or not at all. After all, you believed you always had to compete in the race.

In order to get things done, C. S. Lewis said there are two kinds of people. There are those who say to God, "Thy will be done," and those to whom God says, "All right, then, have it your way."

Every day we make a choice. We give God a passing nod on our way to work and tell Him we'll check back later after the work gets done. Or, we give the work to God and we say, "Be with me, and guide and direct my efforts according to Your will and purpose."

You may be able to "have it your way" at your favorite fast-food restaurant, but it's important most days to honor God with all your heart and remind Him that nothing means more to you than doing things His way.

A HEART TO DO GOD'S WILL

Lord, I try to stay on top of things and take care of everything You've given me to do. Please take away all the things on my to-do list, and only give me back the ones we can do together. Amen.

One Day at a Time

"So don't worry about tomorrow, for tomorrow will bring its own worries. Today's trouble is enough for today."
MATTHEW 6:34 NLT

You may have a habit that you've been trying to break for years. You're good at it for a while, you let things go quickly and turn them over to God in record time, but then, like most bad habits, it shows up again. Worry! It's one of those things that never really goes away. In fact, many of us will make up things to worry about if we don't have enough on our minds already.

Mark Twain made this comment near the end of his life. He said, "I am an old man and have known a great many troubles, but most of them never happened."

The same is probably true for us. Most of the things we run through the worry mill never happen. Worry may keep you up half the night or simply ruin your day. Maybe we should do what Mary C. Crowley did when she said, "Every evening I turn my worries over to God. He's going to be up all night anyway."

If you can, turn your worries over to God all the time, knowing that He cares about you and wants to help you live more fully and more joyfully. Take it one day at a time, and have confidence that God has even your worries in His hand.

A WORRY-FREE HEART

Lord, help me let go of worry and turn my troubles over to You. Help me believe with my whole heart that You are in every detail of my life. Amen.

Believe It or Not!

How great is our Lord! His power is absolute!
His understanding is beyond comprehension!
PSALM 147:5 NLT

Some of us aren't always sure what we believe. We have the God of our childhood who seemed to recognize us and be there for us, and we understood that He was our Savior as we enjoyed holidays like Christmas and Easter. But then, the adult in us took over and our childlike faith started questioning everything, and uncertainty became the order of the day.

Miguel de Unamuno tried to distinguish between a belief in the idea of God and a true belief in God Himself. He said this: "Those who believe that they believe in God, but without passion in their hearts, without anguish in mind, without uncertainty, without doubt, without an element of despair even in their consolation, believe in the God idea, not God himself."

In other words, your faith in God becomes more real as your passion for God comes through your heart first. Your heart is a guide, a protector, and the key to your life of faith. Believe it with all your heart and your faith will strengthen and renew you and answer all your questions.

A HEART TO BELIEVE

Lord, help me to trust You and to get to know more of You in every area of my life. Please hold my heart close to You and keep it safe. Amen.

Hey, Why Are You Hiding?

When the cool evening breezes were blowing, the man and his wife heard the LORD God walking about in the garden. So they hid from the LORD God among the trees. Then the LORD God called to the man, "Where are you?"

GENESIS 3:8–9 NLT

When Adam and Eve did something that they were pretty sure might not sit well with God, they hid in the bushes. It's interesting that they imagined even for a moment that they could hide from their Creator. The truth is, we're not much different.

When we are doing or thinking something that we don't want to share with the Lord, we try to find a place to hide. We might think that we can ignore God and simply hide out in the jungle of the world. Just like with Adam and Eve though, He knows exactly where we are. . .He knows exactly what we're doing. . .all the time. We can't hide.

Eventually we decide, as Adam and Eve did, that we may as well come clean with God and let Him know we're not so sure about what we're doing, and we'd like His help anyway. We have to come out of hiding and give Him a chance to restore us and give us a new heart. We want to be made whole once again in His sight. If there's anything you've been trying to hide from God, this may be a good day to surrender it and let Him guide you back to the place you're meant to be. Let your heart be your guide.

A HEART TO COME CLEAN

Lord, I ask You to be with me right now in all that I do today, and help me to make wise and loving choices according to Your will and purpose. Forgive those things I try to hide, and help me to stand firm with You by my side. Amen.

The Home Planet

*God made the earth by his power. He used his wisdom to build
the world and his understanding to stretch out the skies.*

JEREMIAH 10:12 NCV

Earth is your home. Every day and every night, it sustains you, nourishes you, and provides for you. Whether you live in the city or the country, by oceans or the deserts, you are a guest here. You reside on Planet Earth at God's bidding and by His design. Your home is not one to be taken for granted.

Rebecca Harding Davis wrote, "We are all of us from birth to death guests at a table which we did not spread. The sun, the earth, love, friends, our very breath are parts of the banquet. . . . Shall we think of the day as a chance to come nearer our Host, and to find out something of Him who has fed us for so long?"

As you stretch out to embrace the new day, see if you can discover more of what the Host of the banquet would like from you. Thank Him for providing such bounty on your behalf. Seek Him with your whole heart and mind, and thank Him for this place you call home.

A HEART FOR HOME

Lord, You have provided so richly for me that I sometimes forget to thank You for Your goodness. I praise and thank You, Divine Creator, for knowing me so well and taking care of my every need. Amen.

Abundant Living

Always be full of joy in the Lord. I say it again—rejoice!
Let everyone see that you are considerate in all you do.
PHILIPPIANS 4:4–5 NLT

Do you ever stop to think about what you are thinking? If you did, would you be surprised to find a host of negative thoughts filling up your mind, and probably your body, and cluttering your choices so that you can hardly know what step to take next? Many of us have minds that are full of clutter, and the best thing we can do is give them a clean sweep. We need to have a Shop-Vac handy so we can get the grime out of our systems on a daily basis.

When your thoughts are happy, positive, and full of grace, you're a different person. You're more productive, you're more fun to be around, and you give without even thinking, to provide for the needs of others. You live a heart-shaped life because all is well with your soul.

If you could learn to think better thoughts, you might learn to create better actions. God started the universe as a thought, then He spoke it into existence. His thoughts had enormous power. Your thoughts and your actions are powerful in a lot of ways too. Let joy fill your thoughts and offer you the best responses to life to make the grace of God possible.

A HEART OF JOY

Lord, I don't stop to thank You enough for the great joys in my life. I will think more about those things today and praise Your name. Amen.

Find It in Your Heart

No, the word is very near you; it is in your mouth and in your heart so you may obey it.
DEUTERONOMY 30:14 NIV

C. H. Spurgeon wrote this about King David: "David said, 'I found it in my heart to pray this prayer unto Thee, O Lord.' "

How many of us seem to begin to pray without really thinking about the prayer? We rush, without preparation or thought, into the presence of God. But David did not make that mistake; he found his prayer in his heart. Prayer is the product of a humble heart and a heart renewed by grace. I pray that the Lord will give us a "heart to pray."

When you're ready to pray then, check in with your heart. Look to see if it is indeed focused on the Lord Himself. Discover whether it is prepared to talk to the Creator of the whole universe. Set yourself apart with a time and a place where your heart can speak freely and your love can flow. Give yourself a place that is quiet and holy; a place for you and the Lord to truly communicate.

It's not difficult to understand the Word of God because He has already placed its very essence in your heart and He knows you by name. Call Him when you have prepared your heart to listen to His voice. It's the most important way to discover how to live a heart-shaped life.

A HEART TO PRAY

Lord, help me to prepare my heart to listen to You and to seek Your guidance in all that I do this day. Amen.

The Road Not Taken

"Be strong and courageous. Do not be afraid; do not be discouraged,
for the LORD your God will be with you wherever you go."
JOSHUA 1:9 NIV

Do you remember Robert Frost's famous poem about two roads that diverge in the woods and he has to choose which path to take? One path is well worn as many have taken it before, and the writer finds it tempting to go that way as well. The other path is riskier: it isn't as well mapped out or as convenient, and it may have more twists and turns and opportunities to be lost. The writer considers his steps and finally tells the reader that he decided to take the path "less traveled by."

We're often faced with divergent paths and have to take the risk of determining which way to go. The safe route is always tempting because we know what to expect. We know that we're apt to meet many others who are already on the path ahead of us. It feels certain and secure. The risky route is much more difficult to choose, and yet it has a certain appeal. It may not prove to be worth the risk, or it may offer more than we ever hoped.

Life is a divergent path and it keeps asking you to make choices. The gift of God and the blessing is that God will walk with you whatever your choice may be. If you're strong and courageous, you could choose to move in a new direction and take on a new adventure. Seek God with all your heart and He will help you choose the best path for you.

A HEART WITH CHOICES

Lord, thank You for giving me wonderful opportunities and for being with me in the choices I make. Help me be willing to step out in faith to take the road less traveled. Amen.

On Overload?

The LORD always keeps his promises; he is gracious in all he does.
The LORD helps the fallen and lifts those bent beneath their loads.
PSALM 145:13–14 NLT

Do you have days that simply overload your circuits and you wonder if you'll burn out, derail, or whatever the potential hazard of overloading yourself might be? We live in a fast-paced culture that seems to demand that everything had to be done yesterday.

We may have to complete a quota at work or manage a household and somehow find time to live, breathe, and pray. In addition to those things, we try to build in time to exercise, be social, and to be a gracious volunteer. We go to church and keep up with friends, and before we know it, we simply want to run away.

The Creator who set things up so that we could live in a garden, probably didn't have this scenario in mind. He probably hoped we'd live in peace and harmony and find ways to care for Him and one another that would be truly fulfilling.

Take some time today and get back to the garden. Bask in the coolness of the shade and enjoy God's peace. You don't need to be in a constant whirlwind. You need to carve out moments to let your heart rest in God's care.

A HEART AT PEACE

Lord, I am constantly on the run and I'd truly welcome some time to simply relax with You today. Help me to return to the garden of Your grace and glory. Amen.

The Best You and the Worst You

If part of a batch of dough is made holy by being offered to God, then all of the dough is holy. If the roots of a tree are holy, the rest of the tree is holy too.

ROMANS 11:16 CEV

Your worst days are never so bad that you are beyond the reach of God's grace. Your best days are never so good that you are beyond the need for God's grace, either. In fact, the best of you and the worst of you are always in need of God's divine intervention.

The scripture from Romans is a great thought because it helps us see that even though we may not be perfect, if we indeed are offering a part of ourselves to God, then the whole of us is actually offered to God. The parts we haven't intellectually turned over to Him are still in God's hands. He continually helps to move us in the right direction so that we can discover more of what He has for us.

As you consider where you are in life, your successes and your defeats, your good qualities and those you'd rather sweep under the rug, know that you are never out of God's mercy and His grace. He sees you as holy whenever He sees His Son in you. Let the Son guide your life into God's grace and bring you joy. Let Him reign in your heart forever.

A HEART OF FAITH

Lord, thank You for giving me the faith to know Your grace and mercy. Help me apply Your love to the matters of my heart. Amen.

Getting Unstuck

If you are wise and understand God's ways, prove it by living an honorable life,
doing good works with the humility that comes from wisdom.

JAMES 3:13 NLT

Sometimes we feel stuck! We're stuck in a career because we can't go back for more training, or we're stuck in a neighborhood because we can't afford to move, or we're stuck in a loveless marriage and we don't know how to fix it. Whatever it is, we are just plain stuck.

If you're stuck, you don't have to stay there, even if you can't find another job just now or a new home. One way to get unstuck is to shift your focus by simply doing good deeds for others.

Volunteer in a place that is totally different from anything else you do, or volunteer in an area where you'd like a new job opportunity. Learn a new skill or start a new hobby. Make small changes that will stimulate your thinking and help you create new ideas.

Doing good deeds not only shifts your focus, but it helps to shape your heart. It reminds you that a lot of people make life into a positive experience, and they may have far less than you do.

You're not stuck as long as you take your concerns to God, change things in whatever ways you can, and let your heart guide you to do good deeds. The rewards will be surprising.

A HEART TO CHANGE

Lord, I don't always know how to help others because I have so much trouble getting unstuck from my own thoughts. Help me to live with hope and expectation and share the bounty You have given me. Amen.

It's Us vs. Them

*Yet we hear that some of you are living idle lives, refusing to work
and meddling in other people's business. We command such
people and urge them in the name of the Lord Jesus Christ
to settle down and work to earn their own living.*

2 THESSALONIANS 3:11–12 NLT

When we set ourselves up as the judge and jury for our neighbors, coworkers, or anyone else, we come to some pretty amazing wrong conclusions. We may imagine that we're on one side of a fence and they are on the other; it's us versus them! They just don't work hard enough, they don't care as much as we do, or they don't understand what really needs to be done or what needs to change. If only they would get it right, everything for us would be much better.

When you think like that, it may be time to check in with God and seek His help in shaping your heart then and there. You may be the one who needs to get things right so that life can be much better. You may be in need of a heart transplant.

You've probably heard it said that it's not wise to get too involved in other people's business. This scripture seems to confirm that idea. Your heart has only one objective. It wants to be right with God. When your heart is right with God, He guides you into His will and purpose, and you can be sure He focuses on what *you* need to change, not what *they* need to change. Ask Him to direct your thoughts and your heart.

AT THE HEART OF TRUTH

Lord, I often expect others to take care of life the same way I would. Help me to see them and love them as You do and stop trying to judge the differences between us. Amen.

Bless the Loaves and Fish!

Jesus took the five loaves and two fish, looked up toward heaven, and blessed them.
MATTHEW 14:19 NLT

Some families say grace before every meal. Some say grace just at dinnertime, and some just eat with no thought of God. You probably grew up with one variation or another on mealtime prayers, and however you practiced it, you may not have given much thought as to why you actually did it.

The example of Jesus was to receive God's blessing or offer a prayer of thanks before every meal. His example showed us that we should thank God for providing the food we eat and the basic necessities of life. When Jesus blessed the bread, there seemed to always be more of it to share. Even five loaves and two fish could feed multitudes when he needed it to do so.

Before you consume one more bite of Mom's chicken Kiev or Dad's grilled salmon, turn your heart and mind to the Giver of all life and all nourishment and thank Him. After you do, you can be sure that everything you taste will have an especially inviting flavor, and the blessings will flow.

A HEART OF GRATITUDE

Lord, bless the food that I share with those around me today. Thank You for taking such good care of my basic needs. Amen.

Head and Shoulders above the Rest

Rather, you must grow in the grace and knowledge
of our Lord and Savior Jesus Christ.

2 PETER 3:18 NLT

We grow in knowledge by what we take in, but we grow in our capacity to give and love by what we give out. We're designed to grow. It's the main job we actually have here on earth, and God gave us all we need to do it very well. What you take into your mind and give out with your heart makes all the difference.

For example, you may have excellent head knowledge of the Bible. You may know every scripture and just when to say it in the right context, but you may not have a good grasp of God's Word. Knowing scripture changes the way your heart perceives others, the way you act, and the way you speak. God speaks to your heart and searches the motives of your heart. He cares more about the motivations behind what you do than about the actions you decide to take.

It's a good day to seek God's heart and stand tall with Him. You're already head and shoulders above the rest because you have been searching for Him with your mind. As you engage Him more fully with your heart, you will see more clearly and grow in the special favor of the Lord.

A HEART TO UNDERSTAND

Lord, I have been reading Your Word most of my life, but I'm not always good at giving and learning from the heart and I know You want me to do so. Help me to take my head knowledge and move it into heart knowledge. Amen.

No Longer a Child

When I was a child, I talked like a child, I thought like a child, I reasoned like a child. When I became a man, I put the ways of childhood behind me.

1 CORINTHIANS 13:11 NIV

No doubt, you were a great kid and you have the T-shirt to prove it. You can remember your dreams, the fun stuff, and the ways you thought about life then. A childlike perspective may still serve you in some good ways, especially in matters of the heart, but in other arenas of life, maturity is a blessing.

It's okay to grow up. In fact, it's a lifetime project. You may even be too adult in some ways, and still a kid in others. It's a process! Growing, changing, and learning are part of God's design to help us become more Christlike.

Augustine of Hippo put it this way: "If you are pleased with what you are, you have stopped already. If you say, 'It is enough,' you are lost. Keep on walking, moving forward, trying for the goal. Don't try to stop on the way, or to go back, or to deviate from it."

Because you're no longer a child, you have only one choice, and that is to keep walking and moving forward. Let your heart and mind lead you to Jesus and cause you to believe all that He makes possible.

A CHILDLIKE HEART

Dear Lord, help me walk forward to the place You would have me go with a heart that is mature in You and a faith that remains childlike. Amen.

Broken Pottery

*And yet, O Lord, you are our Father. We are the clay, and you
are the potter. We are all formed by your hand.*

ISAIAH 64:8 NLT

If you've ever worked with clay to create beautiful objects, you know that it can be both versatile and fragile. An inspired piece you really love may break apart in the firing process or in the glazing, and you have to start again. You may have to rework the clay until you come up with something that satisfies you or meets your objective. Isaiah's image of us as the clay and God as the potter is a great reminder of what we can become in God's hands.

Sometimes you may feel like a lump of clay, with no real form or special beauty. You don't know what your direction is and you feel like you're without purpose or motivation. You want God to shape you up.

When you surrender to being God's design, you may still have setbacks or feel utterly broken. Other times, you may also have a sense that you are functioning at a high level and are strengthened by the Potter's hand. Whether you feel broken or beautiful, remember that you are always lovingly being formed by the Master who sees your heart and knows exactly the beautiful vessel you need to be for His purpose.

A HEART SHAPED BY GOD

Lord, I pray that You would shape my mind, body, and spirit with Your loving hand today. Amen.

The Reality of Hope

*Faith shows the reality of what we hope for; it is the
evidence of things we cannot see.*
HEBREWS 11:1 NLT

Faith, belief, hope. . .these are all things that keep us going, keep us trying. When we were children, we hoped for things. . .a new bike, a puppy, a chance to go to Disney World. We hoped because we were all about getting a desired result.

Hope, coupled with the faith we have in Jesus Christ, changes our hearts and gives us strength. It helps us to see that we can trust and believe God in all we do. We can look to God to take care of the details of our lives, and so hope remains. The Hope of the Ages is with us every day, watching over us, and challenging us to be faithful and strong.

Today, think about the things you hoped for yesterday, and give God thanks and praise for honoring those hopes or pray again for the desires of your heart. Your hope will then carry the blessing and assurance of God's hand at work in you.

A HEART FILLED WITH HOPE

Father, there are many times when I fear I will lose hope. Then You come into my life in a powerful way and remind me that You are always with me. Thank You for Your steadfast love. Amen.

What You See Is What You Get!

*We know that God is always at work for the good of everyone who
loves him. They are the ones God has chosen for his purpose.*

ROMANS 8:28 CEV

It's great to create a vision about the things you want to accomplish, the direction of your dreams and heart. It helps to set that vision before God and walk with Him toward the goal. If you know where you want to get to, it's a lot easier to get there. What you see even in your imagination, is what you can achieve. Seeing is believing!

At times, the disappointments of life make it hard to maintain a vision and to keep surrendering the goal to God. This is the point where you ask God to shape your heart and mind to trust that He alone holds your ultimate purpose and plan in His hands. Nothing will make you happier than achieving the goals He has set. See it! Believe it!

Today, hold on to your visions and dreams, hope in God's grace and desire to fulfill the joys of your heart, and move forward. God will bring everything together for your good at the right time. Trust that He has a plan and is working it out for you even now.

A HEART OF FAITHFULNESS

Lord, help me to continue in hope and faith in You to accomplish all the things that are mine to do. Thank You for Your endless blessings! Amen.

Guarding Your Heart

Above all else, guard your heart, for everything you do flows from it.
PROVERBS 4:23 NIV

If you've suffered a broken heart, you don't take the idea of protecting your heart for granted. You know what it feels like when matters of the heart go awry. All the valentines and greeting cards in the world can't cure you when love has wounded you. No matter how old you are, it's not easy to protect your heart.

Romance aside, a lot of things can happen that will cause your heart to ache. You might experience the death of a friend, the anger of a child, the loss of a job that you really enjoyed, or the defeat of something that you strived for with your heart and soul. Life is full of things that can damage your heart, and the best you can do is try to protect yourself.

You need to pray for God's protection as well. Ask Him when you feel uncertain about a situation, to be with you, strengthen and renew you, and help you to move on. Stay totally connected to the One Source who wants your heart to be blessed always.

BLESS YOUR HEART

Lord, I have trouble protecting my heart. I pray today that You will refresh and renew my spirit and keep me safe in Your care. Amen.

Heartspeak

The mouth speaks what the heart is full of.
MATTHEW 12:34 NIV

Have you noticed the profound difference of when you're speaking from the heart and when you're just talking? Granted, sometimes you have no particular passion about the topic of a conversation and so your heart remains somewhat detached.

When you do feel passionate about the topic, however, it's a whole different conversation. Now, you're involved, you're listening attentively, your body is poised, and your feet are on the ground because you don't want to miss a beat, or perhaps a heartbeat, of what is going on. You are ready to make your point or cast your vision in a voice that expects to be heard.

That kind of fervor is part of having a heart full of compassion. When you speak from the heart with kindness and love toward those around you, you make an impression and you light up your listeners. Heartspeak is about you. It's about sharing the deeper faith of your heart and mind and getting others to pay attention. It's about letting God's light shine.

Today, listen to what your heart has to say.

A TALKING HEART

Lord, I am grateful that You have blessed me with a loving heart. Grant that I might find ways to share the joy of knowing You with others today. Amen.

Creating the Right Heart

You must love the LORD your God with all your heart,
all your soul, all your mind, and all your strength.

MARK 12:30 NLT

One writer said, "To put the world in order, we must first put the nation in order; to put the nation in order, we must put the family in order; to put the family in order, we must cultivate our personal life; and to cultivate our personal life, we must first set our hearts right."

We're in the business then of setting our hearts right. Jesus stated it another way when he said that we should seek God with all of our heart, mind, and soul. Perhaps in seeking God, we may cultivate our personal life in a way that pleases God and sets our hearts right.

Today is a great day to do some housecleaning. Give yourself a chance to sweep out cobwebs of doubt and worry. Ask God to help you create a more loving heart so that you can improve the future by creating a present that serves God and others. Set your heart on God the Father and He will continue to shape it with love.

SETTING YOUR HEART RIGHT

Lord, create a clean heart in me today, and renew a right spirit within me so that I can love You and serve You more fully. Amen.

Don't Lose Heart!

*"Look! I stand at the door and knock. If you hear my voice and open the door,
I will come in, and we will share a meal together as friends."*

REVELATION 3:20 NLT

There are times when we simply lose heart in the things going on around us. We don't care as much about others, and we can't really hear God's voice, no matter how loudly He may be knocking at the door. We're simply not home and we're not able to serve the needs of anyone, especially ourselves.

Charles Spurgeon said, "Neither prayer, nor praise, nor the hearing of the word will be profitable to those who have left their hearts behind them."

If the door to your heart is closed for repairs, you might want to see what you can do to heal it and move on. There are a lot of good things that you need to know about and a lot of good people waiting to connect with you. More than that, the Spirit of your heavenly Father is waiting to come in for lunch and remind you that He is always home with you. He will help you in any way He can to mend your heart and help you breathe more easily. Don't lose heart, your Lord is there for you.

A HEART TO HEAR GOD

Lord, help me to lean on You when I'm not sure where else to turn, and give my heart Your peace and Your strength. Amen.

Follow Your Heart

*For the LORD sees every heart and knows every plan
and thought. If you seek him, you will find him.*
1 CHRONICLES 28:9 NLT

The wisest of us don't have all the answers. We conceive of plans and ideas, sometimes we go after them and sometimes we let them sit and imagine they simply weren't plans that were meant to be. Though it could be true that some of your childhood dreams are long gone, some few are still important because they are dreams that God instilled in you, gave you the talents to achieve, and still strives to help you bring to fruition. He knows you so well and He wants you to follow your heart, especially if you let Him lead you along the way.

If you seek Him, you will find Him. He will turn toward you and meet you halfway. He will never leave you in an uncertain path, for as soon as you call out to Him, He's there. If there's a longing in your heart today to do something you've never done, or go someplace you've never been, or simply to change a habit or your life direction, then it's a good day to follow your heart.

Ask God to go before you, to guide your steps, and to bring you to the place that only He can to give you your heartfelt desires. Offer Him thanks and praise for all the ways He will meet you to make your dreams come true. Go ahead and follow your heart!

YOUR HEART'S DESIRES

Lord, it isn't always easy to figure out the next steps or the wisest course of action. Help me to follow my heart to You to create each step according to Your wisdom for me. Amen.

The Heart of Honesty

"As for you, if you walk before me faithfully with integrity of heart and uprightness. . .and do all I command and observe my decrees and laws, I will establish your royal throne over Israel forever."
1 KINGS 9:4–5 NIV

Whatever happened to integrity? Do you remember when you were growing up and your mom insisted that you had to tell the truth even when you knew it might get you into trouble? Well, you told the truth anyway, because getting into trouble over what you had done was better than Mom finding out you lied and then getting into even bigger trouble.

Somewhere along the way, a lot of people have forgotten the values they learned in childhood. They've forgotten that it's still important to tell the truth and to be honest with others.

Sure, you can get away with those little untruths where you pretend to like your boss's funky tie or your mom's new haircut. You can even refrain from speaking out when you're struggling with honest emotions. Your heart knows when it is being honest and when it is unwilling to seek the truth.

If honesty is to remain a virtue, then we've got to give it a chance and deliver it ourselves. You'll be glad when you work harder to authentically share your heart. . .honest!

A HEART FOR HONESTY

Lord, let honesty come from my heart and my lips in all my actions and interactions with others. . .and especially with You. Amen.

God Forms Your Heart

From heaven the LORD looks down and sees all mankind; from his dwelling place he watches all who live on earth—he who forms the hearts of all, who considers everything they do.

PSALM 33:13–15 NIV

From your first crying breath, God has held you in His arms. He has nurtured you, nourished you, and stood beside you from the first moment He laid eyes on you. He's your Redeemer and your Father. He holds you closely to protect your heart and mind.

Because of His great love for you, He watches over you all the time. He knows you better than any human being could know you, and that is why He is fully capable of helping to form the things that cause your heart to grow.

He wants you to grow in love for others. He wants you to grow in praise, admiration, and worship of Him. He wants your heart to grow so big that it can hardly be contained in your body. He considers everything you do.

As you seek His guidance today, ask Him to help you develop a greater heart for those things you've overlooked before; be kinder, be wiser, be conscious of all you say and do. Let your heart lead you into all joy and bring you possibilities only God can give you as you walk with Him today.

A HEART TO GROW

Dear Lord, please help me to be aware of the way that I look at life; help me to strive to walk heart-first into my day, and open my eyes to see Your love everywhere. Amen.

A Mirror Image

May God give you more and more mercy, peace, and love.
JUDE 2 NLT

Let's try an experiment. Stand in front of a mirror and say three nice things to yourself. What did you say? Could you really compliment yourself in a positive and affirming way?

If you couldn't think of three nice things to say to yourself, you might want to take a look at why. Being honest with yourself is a good thing, and in truth, it also means that you're being honest with God. No one knows you better than God. He always sees your heart, so you can't hide from Him.

The idea here is not to get you to just talk tenderly to yourself, although most of us need to do more of that, it's about getting your heart straight about who you are and what you believe about yourself. How you see yourself greatly affects the way you treat others. When you believe in your goodness, you believe in the goodness of others as well.

Go back to the mirror and take three deep breaths. Get acquainted with the person staring back at you and have an honest talk. This could make the rest of your day more authentic and bring great joy to your heart.

A HEART TO KNOW YOURSELF

Lord, help me to honestly reflect the things that I believe and the choices I make. Then let me be honest with You. Amen.

Keep Smiling!

A cheerful look brings joy to the heart.
PROVERBS 15:30 NLT

Did you ever walk by a perfect stranger who gave you the gift of a smile that just warmed up your spirit like sunshine? When you offer the world your smile without reservation, your day feels lighter and brighter too.

On the contrary, the Eeyores of the world, who choose to always see the gloomy side of life, remind us that a positive and cheerful disposition is indeed a gift, and an exquisite one at that. In case, you're trying to remember who Eeyore is, he's the adorable donkey in *Winnie the Pooh* who just thinks every day is gray and every obstacle was only placed there for him. He just assumes life is hard. You may know people like that.

When we assume life is hard, more often than not, we experience the difficulties life has to offer. When we assume it is positive and joyful, we receive much more joy and delight. It's all about the attitude of your heart and mind.

Today, put on an attitude that says there is nothing but sunshine in front of you, and let it all show in your face. You're bound to cheer up perfect strangers—and yourself as well.

A HEART OF JOY

Lord, thanks for giving me so many wonderful things to experience in the world and for helping me create a day of delight. Help me to remember to keep smiling for You. Amen.

Heart and Soul

For you were like sheep going astray, but have now returned to the Shepherd and Overseer of your souls.

1 PETER 2:25 NKJV

You know one thing for sure. The God of your heart is also the God of your soul and your mind. He aspires to be with you in every circumstance and aspect of your life—the quiet moments, the disappointments, the soul-searching cries—for He knows you and loves you.

When your heart goes astray, you both feel the loss. God misses you but loves you still. God awaits your return because He holds you in His hand. When you choose to live a heart-shaped life you do it with your whole soul, you do it with everything you've got. You recognize that there is nothing else in the world that offers you assurance the way that His love, mercy, and peace do. You know that only inside His love and grace can you live fully and well.

It's a new day and God's mercies are fresh every morning. He wants your whole heart because He has His whole heart to share with you. He wants to see your face turned toward the Son so He can embrace you with joy. Spend the day intentionally open to His love and it will be a refreshing day for your heart and soul.

A SEEKING HEART

Lord, You love me more than I understand and I'm more grateful than I can ever express. Thank You, thank You! Amen.

The Living Expression of God's Kindness

Dear children, let's not merely say that we love each other; let us show the truth by our actions. Our actions will show that we belong to the truth, so we will be confident when we stand before God.

1 JOHN 3:18–19 NLT

Mother Teresa had an enormous heart for God and for people. She shared her love and her faith every day. Her actions spoke volumes, and the blessings of her life will be with us forever. She was devoted to caring for others and selflessly and tirelessly provided inspiration to those around her. The following quote from her is worth reading every single day:

"Spread love everywhere you go; First of all in your own house. Let no one ever come to you without leaving better and happier. Be the living expression of God's kindness; kindness in your face, kindness in your eyes, kindness in your smile, kindness in your warm greeting."

Can you imagine being the "living expression of God's kindness"? What a beautiful picture this creates! Today, be God's kindness. Show your compassion in your home, in your heart, and in your face. Let the kindness of your actions speak volumes.

A HEART OF KINDNESS

Lord, it is awesome to think about Your lovingkindness to me, and I thank You and praise You for such great love. Help me to share Your kind of love with others today. Amen.

The Tender Heart Business

Finally, all of you should be of one mind. Sympathize with each other. Love each other as brothers and sisters. Be tenderhearted, and keep a humble attitude.

1 PETER 3:8 NLT

Business books today often speak not only about getting a job done well but about treating people well who do a job. It's more about heart and not just the bottom line. In the business of life there is really one bottom line. Showing kindness and a tender heart is always our business.

As the character Scrooge says in Dickens's *A Christmas Carol,* "Mankind is my business." Mankind, humankind, womankind, people-kind. . .that's our business! What we are after is the Christlike heart that is needed when dealing with people we love, and even those who may be strangers.

Samuel Johnson said, "Getting money is not all a man's business: to cultivate kindness is a valuable part of the business of life."

The job today and every day is to cultivate kindness and make it your business to share a heart of sympathy and love for those at home and those God brings into our lives.

A HEART FOR OTHERS

Lord, since I enjoy my life so much more when others are kind to me, remind me that I can return the favor today. Amen.

The Heart of Forgiveness

Be kind to each other, tenderhearted, forgiving one another,
just as God through Christ has forgiven you.
EPHESIANS 4:32 NLT

Forgiveness is a matter of the heart that is unlike any other. It brings change and acceptance to both the giver and the receiver. It refreshes your view of the world, widens your perspective of those you consider to be in your neighborhood, and brings mercy to every situation. You see more clearly that what the world needs now is a genuine spirit of forgiveness.

Rude and crude and mean and nasty have all been out there for some time and are having a field day at our expense. Isn't it time to combat them with big doses of kindness, generous amounts of forgiveness, and love whenever you have the chance? As one writer put it, "To understand is not only to pardon, but in the end to love."

If you want to be part of the change you'd like to see in the world, then let the grace of God rule in your heart in such a way that you can share His forgiveness for all human beings with great joy. Forgiving yourself and others lightens your steps like nothing else can do.

A HEART VIEW OF FORGIVENESS

Lord, I know You have forgiven me over and over again. Help me to be more tenderhearted toward others and seek to follow Your forgiving example. Amen.

Glory to God

*Our faces, then, are not covered. We all show the Lord's glory, and we are being
changed to be like him. This change in us brings ever greater glory,
which comes from the Lord, who is the Spirit.*

2 CORINTHIANS 3:18 NCV

When you have a heart for the Lord and you strive to live a heart-shaped life, you are changed. Your body language is different, the light in your eyes is different, even the way you talk is a reflection of the person you are becoming with God's help. You're looking more and more like Him as you turn to Him, come to know Him better, and respond to life with His help.

You look a lot like your Father! Now that's the most beautiful thing that can ever be said about you when you acknowledge and know your Father in heaven. You let your light radiate in ways that you could never have believed possible. You want to do this because God has turned His face to shine upon you and you have opened your heart to see Him.

Remember always that you are walking in greater joy each day as you walk in the Spirit, for God covers you with His glory and gives you His eyes to see the world. May God light your way wherever you go today.

A HEART FOR GLORY

Lord, thank You for shining the light of Your love on me. Help me to share in Your glory and offer that same radiance and joy to those around me. Amen.

See Your Neighbor

"Love your neighbor as yourself."
MATTHEW 19:19 NIV

Do you ever feel slightly invisible? You wonder if anyone really knows who you are or how you actually feel about things. You even wonder those same things when it comes to your family and friends. Likewise, you may live in a neighborhood for years and scarcely know the people in the houses all around you. You remain largely invisible, but God did not intend for you to live that way.

Your challenge today is to "see your neighbor." That's right, see if you can actually get to know someone new. Be intentional about meeting people you have barely known and show them what God has done in your life. Ask them to share the ways God has shown up in their lives. Encourage each other's hearts and minds.

Find out the name of your mail carrier, your dry cleaner, or the paperboy. The older man who walks by your house every day has a name. The grocer and the guy who picks up the trash do too. Practice making yourself and your neighbors more visible.

If you sincerely get to know those around you, your heart will grow and no one will be invisible. Today, share your love and your joy in Jesus.

A HEART TO BE NEIGHBORLY

Lord, I confess I don't know my neighbors very well, but I know how loneliness feels, and I ask You to help me be better at getting to know the people in my neighborhood. Amen.

Good-Hearted You

*Do not withhold good from those who deserve it when it's in your power
to help them. If you can help your neighbor now, don't say,
"Come back tomorrow, and then I'll help you."*

PROVERBS 3:27–28 NLT

We may imagine that the powerful people in the world are the civic leaders, the judges, rulers, and the ones with great wealth. What if we have the idea of power all wrong?

Perhaps the most powerful person you know is the neighbor who welcomes family, friends, and even strangers to her table. Perhaps it's the woman who loves with her whole heart, or the man who generously gives his time, money, or labor without ever asking for anything in return.

Real power, then, may be the strength that comes from a good heart, the impact of a kind word or bit of advice, or the hand that reaches out when tragedy strikes. Real power is what you have inside your heart and mind because Jesus lives within you. Real power is made entirely of love. Rekindle your own power today. The more love you give away, the more you have. Funny, but you could have the strength of ten people just by showing love to others.

A POWERFUL HEART

*Lord, help me understand what real power is within me, and help me go after that
power in the spirit of love. Amen.*

Quiet Desperation

*Every good and perfect gift comes down from the Father
who created all the lights in the heavens.*

JAMES 1:17 CEV

Henry David Thoreau said that "the mass of men lead lives of quiet desperation."

Somehow that thought pales in comparison to the lives we were meant to live. Jesus promised in John 10:10 that He had come to give us life in abundance. What makes the difference between getting a life of quiet desperation and a life of abundance?

Desperation focuses on all that we lack, and worry fixes our minds on ourselves and not on the Lord. When we strive to live a heart-shaped life, then we have to trust and believe in possibility. With your heart open to abundance, you can see the good and perfect gifts coming to you from your Father in heaven.

Since you're the child of a King, abundance is all around you, and God wants to lavish you with love and all good things. He has a lot of gifts to give you, and if you don't feel that you're receiving them, it may be that you need to sit a little closer to His throne.

AN ABUNDANT HEART

Lord, help me to believe that You have an intention for good things for my life. Create a life of abundance all around me, and strengthen my heart to accept Your gifts of love and kindness. Amen.

What Your Heart Knows

*I have discovered this principle of life—that when I want to do
what is right, I inevitably do what is wrong.*

ROMANS 7:21 NLT

Probably nothing grieves our heart more than knowing the right thing to do from the wrong one and yet for some odd reason, doing the wrong thing anyway. How can you break that kind of habit, or simply remain true to your own decision to make better choices?

One way is to start with a simple action, prayer! If you align your heart's intentions with God right away, you're more likely to do the thing you really meant to do. Prayer gives you the opportunity to invite God into your situation. It helps you to take the time to think twice about what you'll do. It gives God a chance to create a bigger space in your heart to receive the blessings He has for you.

Make prayer part of your heart's intentions every day. You'll find that more of your plans will succeed because you'll take the actions you really meant to take. You won't be disappointed by what you do because you'll truly succeed at doing the right thing.

A HEART TO PLEASE GOD

Lord, help me to take the time to talk with You about my choices and intentions. I want to please You in the things I do today. Amen.

Every Beat of Your Heart

Teach us to use wisely all the time we have.
PSALM 90:12 CEV

St. Augustine made a great list that is helpful when we want to live a heart-shaped life and use our time wisely. He said that in order to grow in faith, and therefore for our hearts to grow in love, we need to do the following: "Order your soul; reduce your wants; live in charity; associate in Christian community; obey the laws; trust in Providence."

Let's look at these and define them from a heart perspective:

- Order your soul—give priority to the things that will help your heart and soul to grow. . .namely, prayer and meditation, and Bible reading.
- Reduce your wants—learn to be content with what you have, and recognize the gifts God has already given you.
- Live in charity—share all that you have with those in need, and do it with a heart of genuine love and compassion.
- Associate in Christian community—attend Bible study with your friends, volunteer for activities at church, and help your neighbors.
- Obey the laws—see the laws of your community and country, and even more the laws of God, as being designed for your good.
- Trust in Providence—trust, believe, and honor the God of your heart in all things.

When you put these things into practice, you'll renew and refresh your faith each day and your heart will benefit in every way.

A HEART OF WISDOM

Lord, help me to practice my faith in ways that will strengthen and renew my spirit and give me a heart that is truly a reflection of Your love. Amen.

Sometimes You Win!

If you love your life, you will lose it.
If you give it up in this world, you will be given eternal life.
JOHN 12:25 CEV

This scripture sets up life as a winning and losing proposition. As a believer, you've already made the choice to surrender your life to Christ so that you are with Him from this point on.

When you look at the events of your day though, you may not always set them up as a win for yourself. Here are a few ways that winners have discovered make a difference:

- Winners are part of the answer; they don't add to the problem.
- Winners find solutions; they don't find excuses.
- Winners get things done; they don't wait for someone else to do it.
- Winners say "yes" first.
- Winners make the difficult, possible; they don't make the possible, difficult.
- Winners start every task by surrendering it to God; they don't carry it all themselves.
- Winners are the clay; they let God be the Potter and mold and shape them to live with kind and compassionate hearts.

It's your day to win! Embrace the ways that God would shape your heart to do His will. You'll always come out ahead.

A HEART TO WIN

Lord, help me be a winner with heart today, according to Your grace and mercy. Amen.

Check the Guidebook!

"For the Spirit of God has made me, and the breath of the Almighty gives me life."
JOB 33:4 NLT

Do you ever wish you were given a guidebook at birth? You know, the kind of guidebook that would truly give you answers when things get tough! Or one that would give your heart a boost when it's a bit weary?

Well, in a way, you did. The manual might not have your name engraved in the right-hand corner, but your name is actually in a heavenly book somewhere. We call the manual God gave us the scriptures or the Holy Bible, and we can find help on practically every issue of life.

You may have thoroughly read your manual by now, or you may find it in the stack of things your grandma gave you. Whatever the case may be, it's a good day to see if it does have anything to say directly to you. Since the scriptures were designed to build you up, lighten your heart, and bring you a little closer to God, they are always timely and always important.

When the troubles of the world loom big, check the Guidebook and God will always meet you there!

A HEART IN NEED

Lord, I am a Bible reader, but I don't always look for help there when I have concerns. Remind me that You've already provided for my every need and given some wonderful direction for my life in those pages. Amen.

Over and Over Again

Everything that happens has happened before, and all that will be has already been—God does everything over and over again.

ECCLESIASTES 3:15 CEV

Philosophers have tried to explain the meaning of life for centuries. Theologians have another view, and scientists think they may hold the key to life's truths. We each try to understand the big questions because we want our lives to have meaning and purpose.

One of the wisest men who ever lived was King Solomon. He had asked God for the gift of wisdom and God gave it to him with joy. After observing the world for some time, Solomon came to the following conclusion:

"The best thing we can do is to enjoy eating, drinking, and working. I believe these are God's gifts to us, and no one enjoys eating and living more than I do. If we please God, he will make us wise, understanding, and happy. But if we sin, God will make us struggle for a living, then he will give all we own to someone who pleases him" (Ecclesiastes 2:24 CEV).

The wisdom to take from this is that we need to open up our hearts to enjoy what we have. We need to find the fun that comes with making breakfast, listening to the birds, hugging our children, and sharing moments with a friend. Let your heart rejoice in knowing you can do these amazing things over and over again, for these are the precious ways you give your life meaning.

A HEART TO DO IT ALL AGAIN

Lord, let me always draw from the special moments in my life to give each day more meaning. Thank You for shaping my heart to see Your faithfulness to me. Amen.

Chasing the Wind

It is better to enjoy what we have than to always want something else,
because that makes no more sense than chasing the wind.
ECCLESIASTES 6:9 CEV

Human beings are prone to having restless hearts. We achieve a goal, and then we wonder what to do next. We get the job we always wanted and then imagine we may be missing something else. We think the grass is always just slightly greener elsewhere, and so we make the assumption that we have to chase after happiness or it will pass us by.

It's good to seek new direction and learn about possibilities and ideas. It's good to keep growing and stimulating your imagination. Sometimes though, you get caught with your little net trying to chase dreams that you haven't fully prepared or planned. Sometimes you find yourself just chasing the wind.

Today is a good day to stop and check with God about your dreams and plans. See the beauty that exists right where you are now, and know that He is with you, shaping your heart to move you into a bright future. Start with a conversation with God and He'll help you know when to go after your dreams. Only with Him are you assured that you won't simply be chasing the wind.

A HEART OF GRATITUDE

Lord, remind me to be thankful for all that I have at this very moment, and to seek You with my whole heart to discover all that is still mine to explore. Amen.

A Heart to Remember

*"The eye is the lamp of the body. If your eyes are healthy,
your whole body will be full of light."*

MATTHEW 6:22 NIV

Sometimes it's good to start the day by simply remembering a few worthwhile things. Maybe these can get you started:

- Your kindness brings power.
- Your wisdom brings peace.
- Your heart brings love.
- Your work brings joy.
- Your perseverance brings patience.
- Your helping hand brings gratitude.
- Your prayer life brings self-control.
- Your daily Bible reading brings goodness.
- Your desire to please God brings faithfulness.

Your life is in God's hands. Let your head, your heart, and your eyes be full of light.

A HEART TO BE LIGHT

Lord, thank You for bringing real joy into my life through the gifts of Your ever-present Spirit. Shape my heart to always see Your love and light. Amen.

Humble Hearts

Pride leads to disgrace, but with humility comes wisdom.
PROVERBS 11:2 NLT

As important as it is to remember things that motivate you to grow, become stronger, and to live a more heart-shaped life, it's also important to forget some things that no longer serve you in a meaningful way. The following examples are only meant to clarify your thinking. You may add your own to this list if you'd like:

- Self-criticism—a little of this goes a long way.
- Worry—hand it over to God instead.
- Embarrassment—everybody has done something to blush about.
- Pride—it has never served you well.
- Gossip—a little of this goes further than you might expect.
- Anger—misdirected anger may cause you to lose, not win.
- Doubt—a little of this will totally put you in a fog.
- Procrastination—will never let you get things cleared up.
- Revenge—God knows any injustice, and He will take care of things.

Sometimes it's helpful to look at the things you are meant to change. Ask God to help you know the attitudes of your heart that need to be reconsidered. Humility brings a lot of wisdom, and it will never lead you to disgrace.

HEART LINES

Lord, help me to let go of those things that only cause further pain and unhappiness in my life. Let me surrender all those things to You and seek You with my whole heart. Amen.

Standing in the Light!

*The one who is the true light,
who gives light to everyone, was coming into the world.*

JOHN 1:9 NLT

Do you have enough light? Can you see everything around you clearly? It's interesting to observe that we actually make the choice about how much light we'll have in our lives. We choose to see the drab or we choose to see the beauty. It's not about the weather; it's about the climate inside our hearts.

Albert Schweitzer said, "Your life is something opaque, not transparent, as long as you look at it in an ordinary human way. But if you hold it up against the light of God's goodness, it shines and turns transparent, radiant and bright. And then you ask yourself in amazement: Is this really my own life I see before me?"

As you look at your life today, try holding it closer to the light of God's goodness. See if it makes you radiate with more joy as you recognize all He has done to give you peace and pleasure. You are His incredible light in the world, and He wants you to stand in utter delight in every way possible. Shine for Him today!

A LIGHT HEART

Lord, I am so grateful for Your constant beam of light that brings such joy to my heart and to my life. Let me never get too far from Your utter brilliance! Amen.

Better Times

Many people say, "Who will show us better times?" Let the smile
of your face shine on us, LORD. You have given me greater joy than
those who have abundant harvests of grain and new wine.

PSALM 4:6–7 NLT

If you're seeking "better times" and greater joy in your life, there's only one certain place to get it. You have to stand very close to God and seek the smile and radiance of His face. You have to align your heart with His in ways you may not have done before. When you do, better times are sure to be ahead.

You are incredibly blessed because every time you pray, every time you seek to draw closer to God, you have the smile of His face shining down on you. His radiating smile and steadfast love zero in on you. His love gives you greater joy than all the jewels at Tiffany's or all the grapes in the Sonoma Valley. You've got the best and the brightest, and nothing begins to compare with it.

If you're living in the shadows today, then it's time to come back out into the light and give God the glory. You're set to sparkle! You're set to have better times, and all you have to do is pray. Now that should make your heart skip a beat!

A BRILLIANT HEART

Lord, there is nothing more wonderful than sharing in Your light. Thanks for giving me Your grace and mercy and for helping me maintain some luster in Your presence. Amen.

Light Show

*Make your light shine, so that others will see the good
that you do and will praise your Father in heaven.*

MATTHEW 5:16 CEV

Edith Wharton is remembered for saying, "There are two ways of spreading light; to be the candle or the mirror that reflects it."

As a child of God, you have light to share, and others are in need of it. You may indeed be the candle, the floodlight, the flashlight—something that shines directly on those around you. You may also simply hold up the mirror of grace and with genuine kindness share your faithful light with others.

You don't have to be an evangelist, a church leader, or a lighthouse to be a beacon to those in need. You just have to have a willing heart to let your light shine so that others can discover the Source of your joy and inspiration.

Today, be a candle of inspiration, a beam of joy, a twinkle of blessing to someone around you. It can make a big difference to their heart and to yours.

A TWINKLING HEART

Lord, help me shine Your light in positive, warm, and loving ways to those I encounter today. Amen.

Child of Light

For you are all children of the light and of the day;
we don't belong to darkness and night.

1 THESSALONIANS 5:5 NLT

There's a beautiful Chinese proverb that talks about the light within you, and it radiates within your heart and soul. Look at it now in light of your faith in God, the Creator, and in His Son, Jesus. How can you be a child of this light today?

> *If there is light in the soul,*
> *There will be beauty in the person.*
> *If there is beauty in the person,*
> *There will be harmony in the house.*
> *If there is harmony in the house,*
> *There will be order in the nation.*
> *If there is order in the nation,*
> *There will be peace in the world.*

The Light of the World came so that we could reflect His love and His truth to others and so that we could carry it within ourselves to find His peace. Only this Light can create harmony in all you do today. Today, be the light! Illuminate the way for others to become heart-shaped and filled with peace.

HEART AND SOUL

Lord, help me to gently, freely, and lovingly shine Your light today for the sake of each person I meet. Amen.

Genuine Love

You must teach people to have genuine love,
as well as a good conscience and true faith.

1 TIMOTHY 1:5 CEV

Most of us think we understand what love is, and yet a quick look around the world might make us wonder what we really know about the subject. Maybe we need a refresher course or a little Love 101 seminar. Maybe we simply need to align our hearts with God's love for all of us.

Perhaps the problem rests in our understanding of genuine love versus artificial love. Love is bandied about as though it were the real thing in advertising, TV sitcoms, and even personal relationships. We identify with things we love, like chocolate, our dog, or our summer home in Colorado. We do all that, but we may still be confused about genuine love.

Starting with what you know about God's love, the love shared in your family, or the love between you and your spouse, spend some time this week and concentrate on the word, the idea, and the concept of love. Study it until you get to the place where you can happily identify real love or genuine love over all the imitations out there. The lesson may be a great step in shaping your heart to love even more.

A HEART OF LOVE

Lord, help me to understand Your love so that I can use it as a measure for how I need to love others and how I hope to be loved in return. Amen.

Neighbors and Other Strangers

"Love your neighbor as yourself."
MARK 12:31 NIV

If you've lived in your community a long time, chances are pretty good that you know some of your neighbors. Maybe you won't know them all, because things change, people move, and new ones come along, but you may have a nodding acquaintance with most of them. Apparently, according to the scriptures, these are the people you are meant to love.

A word like *love* causes an emotional response between people and is the reason our hearts connect to each other. The same word can also cause a response toward something we just enjoy. . .like chocolate or cream puffs.

If you don't know your neighbors, or the neighbors next to them, or the ones across town, how are you supposed to love them? More than that, how do you love your neighbor as yourself?

As you consider this scripture, think about ways you can simply get to know your neighbors better. Maybe in getting to know and love your neighbors, you'll learn a little more about loving yourself as well.

A NEIGHBORLY HEART

Lord, it's not easy to make the effort to love people I don't know. I have enough trouble with learning to love myself. Help me to be a better neighbor by seeing each person with a heart of love. Amen.

When You Reflect the Son

*You are like light for the whole world. . . . Make your light shine, so that others
will see the good that you do and will praise your Father in heaven.*

MATTHEW 5:14, 16 CEV

The stars shine just as brightly in the middle of the day when you don't stop to notice them. The moon steps back for the sunshine, but it's still there waiting to reflect more joy.

You're a little like that too. Your light is always available, and often it shines best in the darkness. You were designed to fill in the dark spaces and bring them light because you reflect the Son. You're like turning the switch on so everyone can see more clearly. You send your waves of love and grace out into the world and hope that the darkness will embrace your message. You are what it means to live a heart-shaped life.

As a child of God, you carry the light to every corner of the world that you encounter. You reflect Him like the moon and shine for everyone to see, or you shine His light like the sunshine and bring His warmth to those in great need of it.

You can't help but shine! It's the reason God shaped your heart with such love!

A HEART TO SHINE

Lord, it is such an honor to share Your grace and Your light with others. I'm awed that You have blessed me with the chance to be a twinkling star. Amen.

Chosen to Love

"You didn't choose me. I chose you. I appointed you to go and produce lasting fruit,
so that the Father will give you whatever you ask for, using my
name. This is my command: Love each other."
JOHN 15:16–17 NLT

Remember what it was like to be chosen for a special athletic competition, the marching band, or for a sought-after part in the school play? It was so exciting when the results came in and your name was on the list. It opened up the world for you and gave you a new opportunity to shine.

As an adult, you have a similar opportunity. You were chosen to play a special role, to shine a very special light. You may not remember trying out, but somewhere along the way you gave your heart to the Lord and you told Him you were interested in moving His cause forward. He looked at the jobs that needed to be done, and He said, "I want you and I have an amazing part for you to play!"

How are you doing with your part? Do you need to rehearse your lines and read the manuscript over and over so you know just what to say at the right time? The answer is yes! You need to prepare your heart every day because what you do makes such a difference.

Today, let God shape your heart to even greater love. After all, you were chosen to play this very part.

A LOVING HEART

Lord, prepare my heart today to be a better light. Grant me insights through Your Word and in my prayers. Let me shine for You. Amen.

The Spirit of Truth

"When the Spirit of truth comes, he will guide you into all truth.
He will not speak on his own but will tell you what he
has heard. He will tell you about the future."

JOHN 16:13 NLT

Most of us spend a lot of time thinking about the past, more often than not, beating ourselves up over poor decisions and past sins. Then we spend a lot of time worrying about the future and wondering if we'll have any success with our dreams. We do both of these things so much, we sometimes totally forget to actually live today and let God lovingly shape us one day at a time.

To live for today requires us to line our hearts up with the guidance we receive from the Holy Spirit. The Spirit of Truth can share with us all that the Father has in mind. He can give us insight into the future and even into the present. Isn't that pretty incredible? We are worrying about the future, when we have a Guide right here and now.

If you're limping along wondering if life is ever going to get you where you want to go, then stop what you're doing. Let go of every negative thought you have, and surrender to the guidance of the Spirit of Truth. It won't be long and you'll have some very clear answers and a much happier heart.

A TRUTHFUL HEART

Lord, it is awesome that You provide so well for my daily needs. You know everything about me, and so I come to you to claim more joy. Help me seek the Spirit of Truth today. Amen.

Love Yourself. Come On, You Can Do It!

"Love others as much as you love yourself."
MARK 12:31 CEV

This verse about loving others as much as you love yourself seems simple enough, but in truth, it's a bit troublesome. How you feel about yourself at any particular time has a lot to do with how loving you are to anyone else. When you're feeling good about who you are and what you're doing, you're willing to be giving, forgiving, and generous. That could mean you're being generous with yourself.

When you're downhearted and carrying your big judgment stick around with you, you treat people a little less kindly. Here's a thought: surrender your heart to God, the One who loves you unconditionally, and allow Him to enter your heart and mind each moment of your life. He'll help you get better at loving yourself.

So give your negative self a break, send your self-critic out for a rest, and see if you can discover why God loves you in the first place. Once you understand more fully the price He paid for you, maybe you'll see more ways to carry that love to others.

Your job today is to love yourself. Every time you do one loving thing, give yourself a point. Make a mark on the wall and celebrate that you are changing and loving yourself more because the God of the universe loves you so much He is shaping your heart. It's going to be a great day!

A HEART TO LOVE YOURSELF

Lord, You know I'm not very good at seeing the positive and lovable things about myself. Help me to accept how much You love me, and then help me to love others too. Amen.

Keep Love Growing

*May the Lord make your love for each other
and for everyone else grow by leaps and bounds.*

1 THESSALONIANS 3:12 CEV

Love likes a little action. In fact, love demands action. It isn't content to sit passively by, cheering from the sidelines, while everyone else is in playing the game. In fact, love usually wants to let everyone know of its presence, shouting out its existence as much as possible. Love is noisy!

If it's just quiet and demure, then love may not be feeling well. If you stop to think of the top three people you've ever loved, maybe a spouse, a sibling, or a child, didn't every one of them demand you to show your love? Didn't they all say in one form or another, "Prove it!"?

When you think about your love for God, the same principle may apply. Your love for Him should make you want to share it. It should make you feel happy and good and demand some action from you. It should cause you to want to be close to Him and have heart-to-heart conversations.

If you let your love grow and become more active, you may find yourself smiling a bit more and getting excited about life a bit more, because that's what love does when it's actively growing!

A HEART FOR BIG LOVE

Lord, I'm so thankful for the opportunities I have to grow in Your love and Your presence. Help me to act on that love in every way possible. Amen.

If Love Does Not Compute!

Love is more important than anything else.
It is what ties everything completely together.
COLOSSIANS 3:14 CEV

When we think of romantic love and Valentine's Day, we generally think that one plus one equals two, who together become one. Funny math, but somewhere in our psyches we get it. If we add God's love to that addition, then we form a threefold cord that makes the relationship even stronger.

That's how it is when everything is going well. For some reason though, we're often left wondering why love or its imitations just do not compute. We know in our heart of hearts that love must surely be the answer, but for some reason, the real thing is fragile and elusive.

Maybe the best way to compute love is to strive for the greatest love you can imagine and assign a number to it. God's love is a million gazillion. Add to that the love in your heart for those around you, and assign a love number to each of those relationships. Before you know it, you're seeing love grow everywhere you go.

If you need to have more love in your life, try giving more away as well. In the mathematics of love, the more you give away, the more you have left. Maybe you should get a new calculator!

A HEART TO COMPUTE LOVE

Lord, remind me that I am loved and that I have a lot of love around me all the time. Help me to compute love and compound it with interest. Amen.

Blessing Our Differences

*Each one of you is part of the body of Christ,
and you were chosen to live together in peace.*
COLOSSIANS 3:15 CEV

The good news is we're all different from each other. The bad news is we're all different from each other. However, the truth is, we're more alike than we are different.

We live in a world that applauds our uniqueness, our particular gifts and talents, and that's a good thing. It often gives rise to competitive attitudes and experiences, but in the realm of perfecting our skills, that's good too.

However, as human beings, we all have the same essential needs and we spend most of our time trying to create the best environment to have those needs fulfilled. We have a duty to ourselves to become all that God created us to be, and we have a duty to each other to share God's grace, Spirit, love, and compassion.

As the body of Christ, we are truly God's heart, mind, and representation on earth. Part of our mission is to share the Good News with passion and love! Today as you strive to become the best you that you can be, strive also to become more for Him. May God bless all that you are and all that you can be because you are uniquely designed, shaped, and loved by Him.

A HEART OF BLESSING

Lord, thank You for the many gifts You've given me. Help me to share those gifts in ways that will glorify You and show that You live always in my heart. Amen.

It's about Deep Love

Most important of all, continue to show deep love for each other,
for love covers a multitude of sins.

1 PETER 4:8 NLT

Did you ever notice that sometimes the worst side of you comes out when you least expect it? You're minding your own business and then someone walks by and you have a strange thought like, *Someone needs to help her pick out her clothes!* It's not a terrible judgment, but a judgment just the same. Before you know it, you lob another one at someone else. *Who does your hair?*

Mother Teresa said, "If you judge people, you have no time to love them." That's a pretty heart-shaped thought. We can easily get ourselves lost in determining the way other people should live their lives, as though we actually know, and not ever lift a hand to share God's love.

The point here is that we're learning to live in love, letting God shape our hearts to be more like His. Judging isn't our job. Loving is! As you go about your day today, stop yourself any time some little judgment is about to slip out and send a prayer of love instead. Better yet, extend the hand of God's fellowship.

A HEART THAT TRULY LOVES

Lord, I'm so critical about myself that I know I tend to do the same things to others without even thinking. Help me to be more loving both to those around me and to myself. Amen.

Putting Up with Each Other!

God loves you and has chosen you as his own special people. So be gentle, kind, humble, meek, and patient. Put up with each other, and forgive anyone who does you wrong, just as Christ has forgiven you.

COLOSSIANS 3:12–13 CEV

It's interesting to see a phrase like "put up with each other" in scripture. It's interesting because usually that comes with a sense of judgment as one of us is pretty sure we're right and we're "putting up with the other." It could be that that is precisely what is happening, or it could be that someone is just as genuinely "putting up with you."

Either way, this verse in Colossians helps us see that gentleness and humility are hallmarks that could let us give one another room to be who we are. Isn't that really what we all want? Don't we want to know that those around us accept us and love us just the way we are? Sure we test their patience and we beg their forgiveness; it's all part of recognizing that God loves and is working on us to make us better. He expects us to be patient with one another and love one another that way too.

As you practice kindness, gentleness, and humility, someone is sure to test you to see if you really mean it. You've been forgiven so that you can be a forgiving spirit in the world. Be gentle, there are a lot of battles going on out there. Everyone around you needs an encounter with someone who lives a more heart-shaped life.

A HEART OF GENTLENESS

Lord, help me to remember that other people put up with me just as often as I put up with them. Whatever I do today, help me to be full of Your kindness and love. Amen.

A Cup of Sugar, Please!

*Let love be your highest goal! But you should also desire
the special abilities the Spirit gives.*

1 CORINTHIANS 14:1 NLT

Did you ever need to borrow something from your neighbor because you had no time to run to the store? You have company coming in fifteen minutes and even though you thought you had everything set, you realize you're short one folding chair or the sugar bowl is empty. Those are the moments you're so grateful for good neighbors and you recognize how much little things can mean.

In fact, little things are important, and you may run into a snag in your thinking if you assume that because you only have a cup of sugar or a folding chair to offer, those things don't really count. The truth is that it all counts.

Each thing you do for others out of kindness, joy, or genuine willingness to share is a gift of the Spirit. It's part of your gentleness and joy, and something not to be overlooked. It's part of sharing your heart. Think about how happy you feel when someone does some special kindness for you. Doesn't it make your heart rejoice?

If all you have today is a cup of sugar to share, then sprinkle it among as many friends and neighbors as you can. You'll sweeten up everyone's life.

A HEART FOR THE LITTLE THINGS

Lord, I sometimes stop sharing things just because I don't think I have enough to offer. Help me to give from whatever I have, any time a need arises. Amen.

Love Talk

If I could speak all the languages of earth and of angels, but didn't love others, I would only be a noisy gong or a clanging cymbal.

1 CORINTHIANS 13:1 NLT

We can get distracted pretty easily. We're busy working on a special project, keeping our house spotless, or teaching Sunday school. We're singing in the choir, speaking at women's groups, or translating documents from French to English. Whatever it is we do, there's only one way to do it and you can be sure it's not just our way.

We need to do everything with a heart toward others. We need to do everything in love. We can have a PhD in science, math, or linguistics, but the language we speak and the work we do has no meaning apart from what our hearts are also doing. If your heart isn't connected to your work, you may as well be a noisy locomotive going uphill all the way.

The concept is simple enough, but the execution of it is not that easy. We take great pride in our successes, and that's okay as long as our goals are aligned with God's purpose and our hearts are reaching out to others.

Listen carefully to yourself today and try to discover your own love language. Are you a clanging cymbal or a symphony of love?

A HEART OF LOVE

Lord, let me remember always that my real work involves loving those You've put into my life. Amen.

Worth Waiting For

The faithful love of the LORD never ends! His mercies never cease.
Great is his faithfulness; his mercies begin afresh each morning.
LAMENTATIONS 3:22–23 NLT

Some decisions are life changing. Figuring out whether to accept a new job in a city that will take you away from your family, whether to have a baby, whether to marry, or how to invest your savings—what you decide can change everything.

How do you manage to determine your course of action? Hebrews 10:36 says, "Patient endurance is what you need now, so that you will continue to do God's will. Then you will receive all that he has promised."

Waiting on God's promise with patient endurance is the hard part. It often feels more like an endurance test than it does simply waiting. When your next decision really matters though, remember that the Lord's mercies are new every morning and that He is totally faithful to you. He is working to give you an open heart and mind so you recognize His hand in every decision you make. He will truly direct your steps if you give Him a chance.

He gives you unfailing, never-ending love, and He protects you when you seek His heart for the important matters of life.

A HEART FOR DECISIONS

Lord, it is not unusual for me to leap ahead of You and forget about waiting to hear what You would have me do. Help me today to wait patiently for You so I make good choices. Keep my heart aligned with Yours. Amen.

The Shifting Shadows

*Whatever is good and perfect is a gift coming down to us from God
our Father, who created all the lights in the heavens.
He never changes or casts a shifting shadow.*

JAMES 1:17 NLT

You may have friendships that run hot and cold. You never quite know what to expect from them. One day your friends are cheery and helpful and the next time you see them, they're like different people altogether and you're not sure why you even make an effort to keep the relationship.

Your friendship with life can be like that too. Everything is going along fine, rain or shine, you're moving with the beat and everything feels safe and secure, and then you find yourself on rocky ground and everything has shifted. You're confused, and you're left with only shifting shadows.

Everything changes! You change and circumstances change, but one very dependable thing is that the One who is watching over you, shaping you, and helping you to become the person you're meant to be, does not change. Your future then is based on the never-changing, always-the-same-today-and-tomorrow faith that you have in Jesus Christ. Build your life on the Rock, the One who is your eternal friend, and you won't have to worry when the sands of change start shifting under your feet. Reach up and give your whole heart to God.

A HEART FOR CHANGE

Lord, help me to look to you when things around me seem all out of whack. Help me to see my life as staying steady and strong in Your hand. Amen.

Adding to Your Style

*Clothe yourselves with tenderhearted mercy, kindness, humility,
gentleness, and patience. Make allowance for each other's
faults, and forgive anyone who offends you.*
COLOSSIANS 3:12–13 NLT

*Patience serves as a protection against wrongs as clothes do against
cold. For if you put on more clothes as the cold increases, it will have
no power to hurt you. So in like manner, you must grow in patience
when you meet with great wrongs, and they will be powerless to vex
your mind.*

—LEONARDO DA VINCI

This da Vinci quote is important to note. If you layer your outfits, you can put on more clothes when it's getting cold, or remove some of them if it's getting too warm, and either way, the weather around you won't affect you very much. In other words, you're prepared for whatever happens. He says in the same way you can prepare for things that cause you to need more patience.

If you think of patience as a scarf you always have with you, or a layer of protection you can wrap around you when things get irritating to your spirit, then you'll be ready to face most anything. If you look heart-first at any situation, even at those that require layers of patience, you'll be less apt to come unraveled throughout the day. Ask God to give you a patient and compassionate heart.

A HEART WRAPPED IN PATIENCE

Lord, I come undone pretty easily when things pile up and irritate me. Help me prepare for those things and dress my spirit and my heart in kindness, humility, and patience. Amen.

....

....

....

....

....

....

Lesson from Job

There once was a man named Job who lived in the land of Uz.
He was blameless—a man of complete integrity.

JOB 1:1 NLT

The lesson for us from Job is that spiritual warfare continues. It bombards us from television stations, radios, and social media. It even undermines our faith community. We may not see all the land mines that are out there to try to hinder our walk with God, but He does, and it's important that we pay close attention. Like Job, we hope to remain blameless and walk with God with integrity.

Remaining faithful when you're bombarded with life's setbacks is a challenge. If you've had to face miseries over and over again, you begin to wonder if God really knows you're there and if He hears your prayers and pleas for help.

The answer is that He does know and He cares. He's with you to help you discover a new path. Embrace your life challenges with patient endurance, knowing full well that God protects your heart and has your back. Believe in God, and in yourself, and know that all good things will be restored to you soon. Ask God to give you a heart of complete integrity.

AN HONEST HEART

Lord, when life hands me bad news, I hardly know what to believe. Help me to keep trusting and believing in You. Shape my thoughts and my actions to live with great integrity. Amen.

In His Presence

*You will show me the way of life, granting me the joy of your presence
and the pleasures of living with you forever.*

PSALM 16:11 NLT

God is with us and lives with us. He wants us to draw so close to Him that nothing can distract us or hinder our willingness to seek Him in all things. He wants us to know that the chaos and the turmoil, the doubt and the worry are not things we have to live with each day. We simply have to turn to Him with patient hearts and know that He will lift us up over the noise of life.

Take a deep breath and think about what you can do when negative thinking looms. Try some of these ideas to spur you on toward greater patience and positive thinking in the presence of God:

> P stands for peace, prayer, and positive spirit.
> A stands for attitude adjustment.
> T stands for thankfulness for all you have.
> I stands for insight and imitating Christ.
> E stands for expecting that all is well.
> N stands for not giving in to negative thoughts.
> C stands for caring about all those around you.
> E stands for experiencing more of God's grace.

When you're vexed, seek God's presence and read this list again. God will make sure your needs are met. Maybe then you'll spell patience with joy, knowing you are always in His presence.

A HEART FOR PATIENT JOY

Lord, be with me today as I work through the things that keep me stirred up and unable to quietly feel Your presence. Amen.

....

....

....

....

....

....

Bookmark This!

"May the LORD be good to you and give you peace."
NUMBERS 6:26 CEV

Peace is a beautiful word. It makes us think of Christmas cards with sparkling snow scenes and stars twinkling over Bethlehem. It inspires us to desire greater peace in the world. It beckons us to be peacemakers and people who always seek the good of others.

Teresa of Ávila offered wisdom on the subject of peace centuries ago, and it's a good one to carry with you or keep in your favorite book so you read it often. It says:

> *Let nothing disturb you,*
> *Nothing frighten you,*
> *All things pass*
> *And God never changes.*
> *When you endure things with patience,*
> *You attain all things that God can give you.*
> *When you have God,*
> *You lack for nothing.*

Peace then, is a thing to be found in the context of God. We may not find it in all situations as they exist here on earth, but we can find it in the place we also find safety and rest. . .in the arms of our Savior. When we find it there, we carry it with us in our hearts. May God bless your heart with His goodness and His peace today.

A HEART OF PEACE

Lord, grant me Your goodness and Your peace today, and let me share that peace with everyone I meet. Amen.

God's Children

God blesses those people who make peace.
They will be called his children!
MATTHEW 5:9 CEV

Tumult! Chaos! Uproar! When will it cease? Where is the peace?

Living in a world that is continually at war somewhere is totally unsatisfactory to those of us who would much rather wage peace across the planet. We're offended at the governments who don't treat all people with humanity. We are compassionate and socially conscious, and we need to become powerful peacemakers.

How do we stand up and be counted as peacemakers and children of God? We become the warriors of prayer, vigilantly seeking God's help to bring peace in the world, in the communities where we live, and in the hearts of each person we meet. We surrender our need for things and embrace our need for one another. We become Samaritans of the universe, knowing that life itself depends on us. We are leaders who defend the good and create a place for future generations to exist.

Let peace rule in your heart today as you pray for peace everywhere on the globe. Let God shape your heart to have even greater compassion on others until the victory of peace is won. You are one of God's children and He welcomes your prayers for all humankind.

THE HEART OF A CHILD OF PEACE

Lord, I know that many of Your children do not live in a peaceful and safe environment. Remind me to pray for them and for peace each day. Amen.

A Heart to Dance

May God our Father and the Lord Jesus Christ
give you grace and peace.
EPHESIANS 1:2 NLT

In some cultures, dance is a common form of worship. It is used to both glorify God and to seek His help. It is a way of dancing with a loving heart focused on God and His goodness.

Pull out your dancing shoes and offer prayers for more love in every community in the world. Come together as brothers and sisters of Christ and representatives of all of humanity. Tap into God's grace and His Spirit so that you make peace and love a priority. Do you hear the music yet? Can you feel grace, peace, and mercy all around you?

Come on! It doesn't matter what kind of dancer you are. It doesn't matter whether you have the right outfit or the right dance partner. You simply need to have the desire to worship God and let love reign in your heart and in your own community. Sing, dance, pray. . .it's about focusing your attention on an action that will keep your heart and mind on the God of all things possible. It's time to get in step!

Dance for joy today!

A DANCING HEART

Lord, I'm sure I'm not a good dancer, but I'm a good prayer, and I lift my voice and tap my feet with my brothers and sisters around the world, asking for Your gifts of peace, grace, mercy, and love. Amen.

Bits of Wisdom

Proverbs will teach you wisdom and self-control
and how to understand sayings with deep meanings.
PROVERBS 1:2 CEV

Marketing gurus count on you to remember their product by the great slogans and catchphrases they use to persuade you to buy everything from car insurance to the latest technological gadget. Once you've purchased their product, they want you to talk about it, wear their slogan on a T-shirt, and get the news out to other potential buyers. This is the way we communicate things we're excited about in the world.

The book of Proverbs is somewhat like those slogans. The Bible gives you bits of wisdom that you'll find useful and memorable. These are the slogans you'll recall when you need a good word; the ones that help keep you walking on the best path of life.

Thomas Carlyle said, "These wise sayings seem to have some strange power to discover our rich, hidden talents—those hidden seeds of greatness that God plants inside every one of us. Here's a hint as to how proverbs can be helpful to you. If you are already wise, you will become even wiser. And if you are smart, you will learn to understand proverbs and sayings, as well as words of wisdom and all kinds of riddles."

Open your heart today to exploring Proverbs, and commit one or two passages to memory. It will surely serve you well. As Proverbs 1:7 says, "Respect and obey the LORD! This is the beginning of knowledge. Only a fool rejects wisdom and good advice."

WORDS FOR A GOOD HEART

Lord, grant me wisdom in understanding more of the things that will help me live a life that honors You. Teach me to be wise in all I do. Amen.

The Hidden Treasure of Common Sense

Keep in tune with wisdom and think what it means to have common sense.
Beg as loud as you can for good common sense. Search for wisdom
as you would search for silver or hidden treasure.

PROVERBS 2:2–4 CEV

Do you ever wonder what happened to common sense? Does it seem like we've almost gotten too smart or too sophisticated (at least in our own minds) to be able to actually do the sensible and sometimes simple things? We're in such pursuit of lofty ideas and utter brilliance that we can totally lose sight of everyday garden-variety common sense.

Proverbs 2 grabs us and shakes us up a bit. It says, "Beg as loud as you can for good common sense." Even God knows we are apt to lose track of simple everyday commonsense things and that we'll have to call on Him to get them back. If you're a master at your computer but not so sure how to figure out your checkbook, or you're able to explain quantum theory to the masses, but you can't figure out what to wear with brown shoes, you're in a position to start begging. . .loudly!

Ask God to give you the kind of common sense that comes from the heart and acts in loving ways to those around you. Balance the savvy you have in doing a good job in the world with a degree of common sense wherever you are and you'll be truly blessed. In fact, you'll be wiser in every way!

A COMMONSENSE HEART

Lord, I don't always do things in the most sensible way. Help me to be wise in a very commonsense way, and help me to do all things with the right heart. Amen.

Advice about Advice

Without good advice everything goes wrong—
it takes careful planning for things to go right.
PROVERBS 15:22 CEV

When we're asked to give advice, we're sometimes uncertain as to whether we should tell someone what we really think. This is especially true if our advice is contrary to what we believe the other person wants to hear.

When we're the ones seeking advice, we're open to a genuine response that may not fit with our hopes and plans. If we're just seeking confirmation of our own direction, then any advice will meet our needs because we won't take it to heart anyway.

When you give advice though, seek to do the loving thing. Seek to listen with ears attuned to the Holy Spirit, and speak with a voice that is pleasing to God.

Your advice can bring God's desires to someone's attention. If you've ever watched a friend or a family member make a bad choice and wished later that you had said something in spite of the risk, you understand the challenge of not giving a heartfelt word at the right time. After prayerful consideration, give your best advice with love.

A HEART OF COUNSEL

Lord, help me to offer advice in a loving way when asked, and to seek advice from those who will help guide me according to Your will and purpose. Amen.

Today, Well Lived!

Don't brag about tomorrow! Each day brings its own surprises.
PROVERBS 27:1 CEV

Look to this day. . . . In it lie all the realities and verities of existence, the bliss of growth, the splendor of action, the glory of power. For yesterday is but a dream and tomorrow is only a vision. But today, well lived, makes every yesterday a dream of happiness and every tomorrow a vision of hope.

—SANSKRIT PROVERB

What is the prize that we are awarded with every sunrise? It's the one that allows us to start again, hearts fully connected to God, ears ready to listen, voices ready to share all we can to help make this a day that is well lived.

Yesterday cannot be reclaimed. Past joys, past friends, past relationships, are just that. . .passed on to the past! They are either to be enjoyed or let go so that you can truly live in today. Only God knows what tomorrow will bring, and so He doesn't need you to help figure things out.

Today is what God has given you. Today He has offered you the world, and He will rejoice if you live it well. Open your heart to this day with gusto! Be very conscious of seeing God's hand at work every place you go, and be His voice of love where you can. Live well today; it is a gift beyond measure.

A HEART FOR TODAY

Lord, thank You for loving me so much and giving me the gift of today. Help me to use it wisely and live it well. Amen.

Return to God Wholeheartedly

"I will give them hearts that will recognize me as the LORD. They will be my people, and I will be their God, for they will return to me wholeheartedly."

JEREMIAH 24:7 NLT

It's good to have people! We like to know that when we're in a fix or we need advice or help in some way, we know who to call. We have people!

It's good to have people, but today, the desire of your heart is for the Lord. He gave you a heart that allows you to recognize Him. You feel His presence and sense His direction. You turn your face to Him in prayer and know that He hears you and seeks only your good.

You may have had moments when you forgot that God was there to help you. You went on alone, walking through life somewhat asleep, somewhat unaware of what you were missing. The light was within you, but it was dimmed by your own hand.

This is a great day to return to the Lord, the God of your heart. This is your day to shout for joy that He lives within you and that His light will shine forever, guiding your steps and ensuring that you are never alone.

Give God your heart one more time. Give it wholeheartedly with reckless abandon, and let the Love of your life know you are so glad to be one of His people.

A HEART FOR GOD

Lord, nothing makes my heart happier than knowing You are with me. Please take me back one more time to walk more closely with You. Amen.

The Heart of Believing

*So I tell you to believe that you have received the things you
ask for in prayer, and God will give them to you.*

MARK 11:24 NCV

Prayer is a heart thing. You may have grown up with rules about prayer, or your church may define prayer for you, but those are only views of prayer at best. The truth of prayer rests between you and God. It's about your heart and your motivation and your faith. God hears all your prayers. He honors your requests, but He can do a lot more for you when you remove all doubt and are fully ready to receive the gifts and blessings He has for you.

Doubt blocks the way, making it difficult for God to act on your behalf. Drain off the doubt, give lots of room for the Holy Spirit, bow your head and put your requests before God with a giant believing heart. That's how God can most effectively help you.

If you're wondering if anything is too big or too small to ask God in prayer, think of it this way. If you're willing to pray, God is willing to answer. Nothing is too big or too small for the God who created mountains and hummingbirds. If you're having trouble believing, ask for greater faith in your prayers and read the Word to strengthen your spirit.

It's a new day to pray, and God is waiting to hear the needs of your heart.

A HEART TO PRAY

Lord, I do believe You're listening when I pray, but I sometimes struggle with believing that my concerns really matter. Thank You for loving me just as I am. Amen.

Please Hold!

Ask, and you will receive. Search, and you will find. Knock, and the door will be opened for you. Everyone who asks will receive. Everyone who searches will find. And the door will be opened for everyone who knocks.

MATTHEW 7:7–8 CEV

When you call for information about a service, often the first thing you hear is, "Please listen to the following options because our menu has changed." Then you listen, and because you can't speak to a real person, you try a few things and then are finally put through to an associate. After all the waiting and the listening, the person still can't always help answer your question. Technology is a wonderful thing, but if often leaves you "on hold" with nowhere to go next.

God does not put you *on hold!* When you ask, when you knock, when you search for Him, He answers. Sometimes you may not recognize the answer, but the truth is you are connected to God and He provides for your needs as quickly as possible.

If you're waiting for His answers, keep asking. Ask with all your heart and you will receive. Believe with everything you've got and you will hear His voice. Knock louder than you've ever knocked before. Give God time to answer in the best way for you. Sometimes you and He have to work out the answer together.

Give Him a call. . .His line is open to you. He hears your heart already, and He never puts you on hold.

A STEADFAST HEART

Lord, I am always knocking at Your door and I'm grateful just to know You're in when I call. I'll wait humbly for Your answers because only You know what is best for my life. Amen.

I Don't Feel like Praying

We also pray that you will be strengthened with all his glorious
power so you will have all the endurance and patience you need.

COLOSSIANS 1:11 NLT

Not in the mood to pray? Tapped out? Disillusioned? Maybe you simply feel like you don't know what more to say in prayer. Prayer isn't about your mood or about you having all the right words. Prayer is about your relationship with God, and that is a matter of the current state of your heart. After all, once you begin to pray, your heart reshapes to fit the mood perfectly. Mother Teresa said this about prayer:

> *Love to pray. Feel often during the day the need for prayer, and take the*
> *trouble to pray. Prayer enlarges the heart until it is capable of containing*
> *God's gift of Himself. Ask and seek and your heart will grow big enough to*
> *receive Him.*

What a wonderful thought! Even when you're not feeling quite up to praying, the prayer itself will expand your heart so that you can receive all that God intends just for you. Your heart is all that's needed for real prayer to happen, for a connection to be made. God sees your heart before Him and comes to relieve, receive, and bless its desires.

A HEART OPEN TO PRAYER

Lord, prayer is about love. Prayer is about the heart relationship we share. Help me to love You so much that I bring everything to You in prayer no matter what mood I happen to be in at the time. Amen.

Who Can Stop the Rain?

*The eyes of the LORD watch over those who do right,
and his ears are open to their prayers.*

1 PETER 3:12 NLT

Elijah, the ancient prophet, prayed that it would not rain. His prayer was answered and it didn't rain for three and a half years. When he prayed again for rain, the heavens opened up and the crops were restored. He believed God would honor his prayer. Elijah had a heart for prayer because he had a heart that was sold out for God. What mattered to God, mattered to Elijah every day of his life! God honored Elijah and inspired his work.

You may not have an interest in stopping the rain today, but you have a definite need for God to be with you, to open your heart, and to answer your fervent prayers. Keep your umbrella handy because you will receive what you pray for as long as your heart is ready to believe.

When you strive to live a heart-shaped life, you know that it's important to keep close to God and to do all you can to obey His guidance. He guides you out of love and out of a desire for you to both serve Him and have a personal relationship with Him. He guides you out of complete love and watches over you. Draw close to Him today. Who knows? He may even ask you to stop the rain with your prayers.

OPENHEARTED PRAYER

Lord, prayer has always been a mystery to me. I know You're listening, so help my heart to be open to pray about the right things. Help me to align my prayers and my heart with You every day. Amen.

Talk or Action

So, my dear brothers and sisters, be strong and immovable. Always work
enthusiastically for the Lord, for you know that nothing you
do for the Lord is ever useless.

1 CORINTHIANS 15:58 NLT

Sometimes we mean well, or we intend to do things for others, but for some reason we never actually get things done. We're talkers, but not doers. If all the talkers were put in a room, probably one doer would complete what had to be done before the talkers took a break for donuts and coffee.

God wants us to be doers. He wants us to serve one another with love, joy, and a heart fully connected to Him. He wants us to get past the chatter of what we will do and get out there and do something. When you start a new diet, you might research various options, buy all the right foods, and know exactly what it takes to make that diet work. Even then, you'd still be *talking* about dieting and not losing a pound. The truth is, the diet doesn't work at all if you don't do it.

If you sit in the living room all day while the Thanksgiving dinner is cooking, smell the great smells, and anticipate the delicious dessert, but you never get called to the table and miss the dinner, what good did anticipating it do you? Get out in the kitchen so you know you won't miss serving and being served. Then you'll be past the talk and into the walk, and the serving of the Lord as well. Ask God to shape your heart to have a greater desire to serve Him in every possible way.

A HEART TO SERVE

Lord, I know that I often mean to help out and somehow don't get around to it. Help me to serve with a willing and happy heart. Amen.

Making Life Count

You should be happy to give the poor what they need,
because then the LORD will make you successful in everything you do.
DEUTERONOMY 15:10 CEV

We want life to be about meaning, purpose, and the positive impact we can have on those around us. We don't necessarily want to be noted in history, but we'd like to feel deep within our own hearts that we made a difference. We want to feel successful in all we do.

God is gracious and gives us that opportunity every day. He provides for our needs and fills us up so we can open our hearts to others. We have a fulfilling and abundant life in Him each time we choose to share our hearts, skills, talents, and money with those around us.

Emily Dickinson expressed part of this idea in her poem:

> *If I can stop one heart from breaking,*
> *I shall not live in vain;*
> *If I can ease one life the aching,*
> *Or cool one pain.*
> *Or help one fainting robin*
> *Unto his nest again,*
> *I shall not live in vain.*

You can make life count for someone today. Show them your goodness and compassion; show them your heart. You will surely make a difference!

A HEART OF GOODNESS

Lord, I often think about those in need and I do my best to help, but I know I don't do it enough. Please let me live more abundantly in Your service, and open my heart to the needs of those around me. Amen.

A Heart for the Lord

There is just one body and one Spirit, just as you were called to one hope when you were called; one Lord, one faith, one baptism; one God and Father of all.

EPHESIANS 4:4–6 NIV

You may not recognize your value sometimes, but God always does. He knows that as He shapes your heart and mind, you'll get His work done. You're part of the family business and you signed up the day you accepted Jesus as your Lord and Savior.

Family businesses can go on for several generations or they can collapse in the first few months. What makes the difference is how well the family pulls together to get the job done. Each person has a unique role to play and it's very important to the success of the group.

Teresa of Avila said this: "Christ has no body now on earth but yours; yours are the only hands with which he can do his work, yours are the only feet with which he can go about the world, yours are the only eyes through which his compassion can shine forth upon a troubled world. Christ has no body on earth but yours."

You have a job to do and it begins with your heart. It is done in a way that helps others to see that Christ lives within you and that you are there to share His love. As an important member of His family, God blesses you because He counts on you!

A HEART OF CHRIST'S LOVE

Lord, help me to be Your hands and feet today. Help me to love others as You would love them, wherever I am today. Amen.

Making the Effort

*Work all the harder because [your]
efforts are helping other believers who are well loved.*

1 TIMOTHY 6:2 NLT

Some days you may wonder if the things you do are really worth the effort. You see each day pass with no real progress, and motivating yourself to get out there and try again just feels hopeless. Sometimes you have to figure out what it is you really want to bring to the job at hand; what part do you really want to play?

If you've worked on a committee, you know there are always people who do what is asked of them in a consistent and thoughtful way. Then there are the go-getters who get the job done almost single-handedly. Finally, there are those who attend the meetings but never seem to have a clue about what they can do to help.

Every committee, every job, every family has some nuance of these three people in the mix. Add to the mix, the person who feels the old ways of doing things have always worked and therefore change isn't needed. The go-getter seeks innovative ways to get things done and create possible solutions. The thoughtful volunteer is trying to keep the peace.

Whichever person you are, pray for God's guidance and grace to direct your heart and your steps as you serve Him and others. There's always room for you, and He knows exactly what role you need to play today. Your heart-shaped efforts will pay off.

A HEART TO MAKE AN EFFORT

Lord, help me to be of real value to any situation whether I'm on a committee or sharing time with my family. Let me make the effort out of love for You. Amen.

Opening a Can of Success

A longing fulfilled is sweet to the soul.
PROVERBS 13:19 NIV

We like instant gratification! We have high expectations to attain things easily. We go to the grocery store, buy a can of soup, take it home, pop it in the microwave oven in its own ready-made bowl, and eat it. We don't go to the grocery store, buy vegetables, chop them up, make a broth, and wait four hours for the cooking and then sit down with a bowl of soup and homemade bread. Well, we might, but we like things that are ready when we are.

Sometimes our frustration in prayer or getting God's guidance is that He doesn't always give in to our "instant gratification" life. Sometimes He wants us to learn a few special things along the way; sometimes He has to shape our hearts differently so we can understand what He already knows is best for us.

Success does come in cans, however. You succeed every time you say to God, "Yes, I can do that." Success warms up on the stove every time you try harder, go the extra mile, and believe you can really make it happen. Each time you believe you can accomplish something, you're that much closer to getting it done. If you're shopping for success today, look for the "cans," and even though they may not give you instant success, they will definitely help you in the long run. Your longings can indeed become blessings to your heart and soul.

A POSITIVE HEART

Lord, I do want to be successful in doing the work You've called me to do. Help me believe and trust that I can do all things through You. Amen.

Visions of Sugarplums

Commit to the LORD whatever you do, and he will establish your plans.
PROVERBS 16:3 NIV

Some of us are first-class dreamers. We have been carrying around visions of sugar-plums since we were kids, and those visions are still in our heads. Getting older doesn't mean you no longer have dreams. Dreams are the motivators, the gift givers. They help you find a path to walk, and with the grace of God, you have a chance to get there.

However, some dreamers assume that each thing must be in place before they can actually take a step toward their goal. If they want a new job, they have to have the perfect one before they can make a change. If they want to find a partner, he or she has to have a perfect set of characteristics before they can convince themselves they have the right one. If they want to create a recipe, they have to have every exact ingredient without any substitutions. This approach almost guarantees the person won't have to take the risk of going after the dream. Perfection will keep the door closed and every-thing will stay safe. The dream can just be a vision of sugarplums.

If you're dreaming for an outcome of something you really want, don't set up road-blocks to make it impossible. Set your prayers and your heart before God, and commit your dreams to Him. The outcome will be assured according to His will and purpose for your life.

A HEART THAT DREAMS

Lord, I know that I am often my worst enemy when it comes to completing the things I dream to achieve. Help me overcome my own fears and go after the dreams of my heart. Amen.

A Heart-Shaped Life

As long as he sought the LORD, God gave him success.

2 CHRONICLES 26:5 NIV

We often believe that success has something to do with money, power, or position. We imagine having more material things indicates our level of worldly success. Perhaps, but what happens if we seek to rise to the level of God's measure of success?

Ralph Waldo Emerson said this about success:

> *Success: To laugh often and much, to win the respect of intelligent people and the affection of children, to earn the appreciation of honest critics and endure the betrayal of false friends, to appreciate beauty, to find the best in others, to leave the world a bit better, whether by a healthy child, a garden patch, or a redeemed social condition; to know even one life has breathed easier because you lived. This is to have succeeded.*

This quote embodies what we truly mean by living a heart-shaped life. If your goals are to leave the world a bit better than you found it, or share love so that you've warmed the heart of at least one other soul, then you can count yourself among the successful and among the blessed. As you seek the Lord, He will continue to give you glorious opportunities to succeed abundantly.

A GREATER MEASURE OF HEART

Lord, please continue to shape my heart to show Your love, for that is where real success is found. Help me to succeed in ways that please You today. Amen.

Finding the Rainbow

I have placed my rainbow in the clouds.
It is the sign of my covenant with you and with all the earth.
GENESIS 9:13 NLT

After being sealed up in the ark for nearly a year, and weathering the rains that poured for forty days and nights, it had to be a pretty welcome sight to Noah and his family to see the rainbow appear in the sky. It was essentially the gift of God's forgiveness, and it meant that life would go on.

Life is often flooded with sorrows and it can feel damp and gray. Your heart longs for the sunshine and the promise of better days ahead. You need a rainbow to help motivate your direction and get your heart back on course. You grow weary of being stuck in the same place, seemingly going nowhere, and having no means to create change.

You may well be stuck, but remember that God isn't! He's busy planning a future hope for you. He sees the rain coming into your life, but He's preparing a place in the sun so you can smile again.

As you patiently wait for Him, open the doors to every opportunity to feel His presence. Pour out your concerns and let Him wash them away and create a bright new day for you. You will come upon your rainbow when you least expect it, and when your heart is fully prepared. Your Father has already placed it in the clouds.

A CLOUDY HEART

Lord, it is so hard for me to wait for Your direction when I'm anxious to make a change. Send me Your rainbow today, and give me the heart to see it. Amen.

Buzz! Thank You for Playing!

*Be an example to all believers in what you say, in the way you live,
in your love, your faith, and your purity.*

1 TIMOTHY 4:12 NLT

When you've made a number of wrong turns in life and you're looking for a new start and direction, you often have to start by letting go of what is in the past. Maybe you need to look at life like a game that gives you new opportunities and new choices to make once you decide to move on. You simply press the buzzer, say "Game over, thank you for playing," and try again. Taking an approach like that may make it easier to get back to the winning side of things.

Of course, the Sponsor of your game show is very invested in your choices and wants you to do the right things. He will help you establish your true course if you will just expand the playing field to include Him in more of your plays. He will help to get you in shape to try again. He will give you a more flexible perspective and a heart to pursue new dreams.

When we make poor choices, we don't have to beat ourselves up. We simply need to have the courage and the heart to move on. Get in the game and be an example to others. Let God help you make new choices and prepare your heart for a whole new game.

Ready, set, go!

PUT YOUR HEART INTO THE GAME

Lord, I'm hesitant to make new choices. I lose as often as I win. Help me remember to put more of my choices in Your hand and to follow my heart as You lead. Amen.

The Bear Went Over the Mountain

We live by believing and not by seeing.

2 CORINTHIANS 5:7 NLT

One of the songs from childhood is a silly song called "The Bear Went Over the Mountain." Now of course, we're not sure why the bear went over the mountain, but the song explains that he did so in order to "see what he could see."

Sometimes we too need a new perspective. We need to get a panoramic view before we can go on and get our lives together. G. K. Chesterton said, "One sees great things from the valley; only small things from the peak."

Maybe it helps then if we "go over the mountain" before we can actually see all the great things that there are for us to discover. We have to look up into the hills from the valley and ask God to join us there. We have to lift all of our old thoughts and ideas up to Him and ask that He would help us see clearly with a new heart and new vision. We have to look very intentionally for something new.

When your life stays on the plain, it may not require a lot of faith to go from day to day. When you move from a peak to a valley to another peak, you may focus on the movement, direction, and the One who always leads you safely over the next hurdle. Walk in confidence, fully trusting God's plans for you. As He shapes your heart, He'll shape your thoughts and guide you to the landscape that will serve you the best. Believing is seeing.

A HEART TO SEE CLEARLY

Lord, Your goodness keeps me moving forward and keeps me looking up. Help me to cross through the valleys and up toward the peaks in faithfulness and joy. Amen.

No Pat Answers!

"Be strong and courageous!"
2 CHRONICLES 32:7 NLT

Life throws you a lot of curves, and no matter how much you try, you can't always be prepared for them. Dealing with a personal crisis is hard work and takes a lot of faith. One thing you don't need is the person who tries to give you a pat answer for why this particular crisis happened to you. You don't need your own "friends of Job," who must have made him feel annoyed too.

When a crisis hits you, there's only one real place to go. Take it to God and ask for His help. Share your heart with Him and seek His strength and sit quietly in His presence. He will come and listen, and He will not try to give you any pat answers. He will talk you through the problem until you come to a solution or a conclusion that makes sense to you.

Be strong, courageous, and certain that He holds you powerfully in His hand. He cares more about you than anything in the world. He will help you in the ways that will serve your life and your spirit. When life throws you a curve, just duck, because God will be right there with a catcher's mitt.

Don't listen to anyone who tries to blame you or God for what has happened in your life. Trust that God knows your situation and is ready to comfort and bless you.

A TRUSTING HEART

Lord, it is so wonderful to know that You are always there, and even in the midst of life's ups and downs, You hear my prayers. Be with me today, and give me strength and courage. Amen.

A Matter of Trust

I trust in God's unfailing love for ever and ever.
PSALM 52:8 NIV

You've learned a few things about trust by now. You've learned about people and the kind of person you can trust. You've learned that you can't always trust someone by the way they look, what their job title is, or what they might promise. You've learned to look carefully and be discerning about places you are willing to put your trust.

You may be off to a good start if you trust yourself, but you don't want to stop there. Believe it or not, you'll disappoint yourself and you won't be sure if you should trust yourself the next time.

If you put your trust in friends, your pastor, or your family, you may be on even shakier ground. As soon as any one of them does something to let you down, moves away, or leaves you when you need them, your sense of trust may break down again.

If you put your trust in money or your job, you'll have to constantly protect those things because jobs can be lost and money disappears in ways you never expected.

You have only one place to dependably put your trust. God is the only one worthy of a lifetime of trust. You can't hope to recognize the good guys, or think you can rely totally on yourself. You have to look up and let your Redeemer safeguard your heart, mind, and soul. In God we trust is more than a slogan for you, more than a saying on a dollar bill; it's the one place to put your trust for today and always.

A HEART OF TRUST

Lord, help me to know in my heart when to trust myself or when to trust others. Most of all, help me to build my trust in You today. Amen.

God Almighty!

The instructions of the LORD are perfect, reviving the soul.
The decrees of the LORD are trustworthy, making wise the simple.
The commandments of the LORD are right, bringing joy to the heart.

PSALM 19:7–8 NLT

One of the principles of faith is to be willing to say out loud that you believe in God, the Father Almighty, Maker of heaven and earth. Along with that you confess that you believe in Jesus Christ, His only Son.

When you recite these creeds, something powerful happens. You've spoken something holy, and that bit of holiness is good for your soul. God designed you, and He offered you guidelines to live in His care and keeping. He offered you the laws and the commandments and the decrees that have been handed down generation after generation, and He did this for just one reason.

He did this so you would know that no matter how old you are, or what generation you were born into, or what the laws of the day might be, you are covered. Your sins are covered. Your life is covered. Your heart is covered.

This covering is yours eternally and it is a witness to your heart and soul each time you say it aloud. Each time you speak the words that say, "I believe," then God is able to show up. He shows up in big ways and changes your path. He looks at you and reminds you that you can count on His presence, that He is totally trustworthy.

Today, lift up your heart to God Almighty. Lift up your dreams and disillusions. Lift up your doubts and your worries. Let your heart stand firm in your love for the Lord.

A HEART FOR GOD

Lord, help me to stand firm in You. I thank You for guarding me, guiding me, and loving me so much. Amen.

Right Choices! Wrong Choices!

We are the people he watches over, the flock under his care.
If only you would listen to his voice today! The LORD says,
"Don't harden your hearts."

PSALM 95:7–8 NLT

Living a heart-shaped life is about being willing to listen to God, surrender to His counsel, and let Him in to everything you do. You cannot develop a softer heart without seeking His voice for each decision and concern you have. You are pliable like soft clay when you are in His hands. That's the best place to be because He can shape you and remake your life into something beautiful, no matter what has gone on before.

A soft heart is not a weak heart! It's a heart that knows where its strength lies. It's a heart that rests solely in the care and keeping of Jesus. That's what you do each day, each morning when you surrender your life to Him so that He can tenderly watch over you.

If you get a signal that you're making a wrong choice or moving in a direction that takes you away from the Shepherd, stop everything. Seek God with your whole heart and He will lead you forward because you're safe in His hands.

Erich Fromm said, "Our capacity to choose changes constantly with our practice of life. The longer we continue to make the wrong decisions, the more our heart hardens; the more often we make the right decisions, the more our heart softens or better, perhaps, comes alive."

Let the Holy Spirit guide your heart into the decisions you must make today.

A SOFT HEART

Lord, I know if I'm making a decision that isn't healthy or wise for myself, but I don't always have the strength to step away from it. Please guide me with Your love today. Amen.

No One Quite like You

Pay careful attention to your own work, for then you will get the satisfaction of
a job well done, and you won't need to compare yourself to anyone else.
For we are each responsible for our own conduct.

GALATIANS 6:4–5 NLT

Humans love to compare things. We like to compare ourselves with others to gauge whether we're doing well. We like to set ourselves apart one minute and join into groups where we can compete a bit more the next. We set milestones for our achievements, checking to see if we're aging better than others, if we have more toys than the next person, or if we are more brilliant than others at our place of business. We push, we strive, we compete, over and over again.

This is one way to look at your life, but maybe there's a better way. Maybe you could appreciate the fact that God designed you as a unique individual with specific talents and an almighty purpose. Maybe you could align your heart more closely to God's to figure out how you're really doing.

He knows you well and wants you to feel pleased with your achievements. He wants you to strive to be more for Him, competing only with yourself because of your love for Him. After you do a little happy dance for the things you accomplished today, He wants you to move on and challenge your heart again to grow even bigger in His grace.

A UNIQUE HEART

Lord, forgive me when I look to the world to figure out whether I'm doing well or not.
Help me to only look to You for the measure of success that fulfills Your purpose for
me. Amen.

Your Worry Quotient

Give all your worries and cares to God, for he cares about you.

1 PETER 5:7 NLT

What's your worry personality? Do you worry about everything, even making up things to be concerned about when you don't have quite enough on your plate for the day? Or are you the kind of person who lets everything just roll off your back, taking it in stride, never really hassling yourself about things till they actually get there? Most of us are somewhere in between these two worry personalities. We accept worry as a sort of natural thing to do. But is it?

Matthew 6:25 says, *"That is why I tell you not to worry about everyday life—whether you have enough food and drink, or enough clothes to wear."*

Worry is one of those matters of the heart that often reflects your faith. If you believe God is taking care of you, then you know the basics are covered and you trust things are going okay. If you aren't sure if God is taking care of you, you're not sure anything is really covered. You hope it is, but you give in to worry just the same.

God will take care of you. In fact, He's always caring for you, and all you have to do is believe that He is. Nothing will come into your life that will surprise Him, and He will do all He can to help you with anything and everything. Raise your faith, not your doubts. Sweep out the worries and relax in God's care. Give your heart a rest today and let worry bother someone else.

A WORRY-FREE HEART

Lord, it isn't easy to step aside from worry. Help me to raise my faith and trust and believe in You. My heart needs a rest. Amen.

The Last Straw

Don't worry about tomorrow. It will take care of itself.
You have enough to worry about today.
MATTHEW 6:34 CEV

Do you remember the scarecrow in the *Wizard of Oz*? When Dorothy first discovers him he is hanging on the fence trying to figure out how to get down, which way to go, and hoping he won't fall apart in the process. The longer he hangs there, the more certain he is that he'll never accomplish anything, and it appears he's not even making the crows nervous.

Dorothy gets him down from the fence and helps him pull himself together. She reminds him that he is great and just needs some direction and more confidence. Even though he isn't sure he's capable of making a decision because of his "hay"-wired brain, he follows Dorothy anyway. He knows that he still has the last straw of faith.

Some of us are like that. We allow life's worries to become so important that we lose our way. We fall apart, and we're not sure which way to go anymore. We think we just aren't smart enough, attractive enough, or capable enough to become what God intended us to become. We're down to the last straw.

If your worries have shaken you up like that, then stuff a little more faith into your system and take your shaky legs and walk toward God. He's ready even now to renew and strengthen you, and He'll gladly give you a new heart as well.

A HEART TO TRY AGAIN

Lord, I need Your help to get my life together now. Please renew my heart and my spirit, and meet me on the path to direct my steps toward Your will and purpose. Amen.

You Are a Child of God

"God [made the nations] so that they would seek him and perhaps reach out for him and find him, though he is not far from any one of us. 'For in him we live and move and have our being.' As some of your own poets have said, 'We are his offspring.' "

ACTS 17:27–28 NIV

This is a good time of year to reflect on what it means to be sons and daughters of God. After all, we're preparing for the birth of the Christ Child, God's only Son, knowing that through Him we too become God's heirs. It's a glorious thought, and one we have to wrap our arms around to truly understand.

You are a child of God! That's right, the living Creator of the universe, the Redeemer, the Savior, the Holy One, has made you His own. He watches over you like a loving parent, concerned for your well-being, protecting your heart and your way of life. He is a Father like no other!

This special season of the year reminds us to seek God's Son in ways that we may miss during the other calendar months. We want to draw closer to Him, tiptoe up to the manger and peek in, and bring Him our gifts.

As you go through Advent, remind yourself of what it means to give the one gift you truly have to give to your Father in heaven. Give Him your heart.

A HEART FOR GOD

Lord, thank You for making me Your own child. Thank You for the multitude of gifts You've given me. Help me to share those gifts and my heart with others. Amen.

Too Smart to Be Wise?

Teach us to use wisely all the time we have.
PSALM 90:12 CEV

We don't talk a lot these days about people with great wisdom. We make note of those with intelligence, business savvy, or genius IQ, but not wisdom. Is it possible to be too smart to be really wise?

In past generations, the great thinkers, philosophers, and theologians were sought out to lead, guide, and offer insight to those around them. They were revered and trusted. Today, we're so bombarded with talkers, it's hard to know if any of them are actually brilliant, much less wise.

Proverbs 3:16–18 talks about wisdom in the metaphor of an enlightened woman. It says this: *"In her right hand Wisdom holds a long life, and in her left hand are wealth and honor. Wisdom makes life pleasant and leads us safely along. Wisdom is a life-giving tree, the source of happiness for all who hold on to her."*

Wisdom provides a long life, and it's one that is pleasant and safe. Wisdom brings honor and substance. Wisdom is a source of happiness, a life-giving tree. Wisdom doesn't have to have a PhD or an Ivy League education. It simply has to stay connected to the Source of all life. When you're trying to determine the best ways to follow your heart, it's good to seek truth and be aligned with God's plans for you. The fear or the adoration or the surrender of the spirit to God is the true beginning of wisdom.

This would be a simple word to the wise.

A HEART OF WISDOM

Lord, help me to seek Your wisdom in all that I do. Keep me ever connected to Your life-giving Source of all wisdom and grant me a more loving heart. Amen.

A Wise Old Owl

If you love Wisdom and don't reject her, she will watch over you.
PROVERBS 4:6 CEV

It's fun to think of wisdom as a wise old owl perched on a tree right above your house, watching what goes on and looking for opportunities to share her insights with you. A little poem by Edward Hersey Richards was written in wisdom's honor:

> *A wise old owl sat on an oak,*
> *The more he saw, the less he spoke;*
> *The less he spoke, the more he heard:*
> *Why aren't we like that wise old bird?*

If part of wisdom is knowing when to keep quiet and when to speak up, we can appreciate the task set before us. Often, we speak up too quickly and later we wish we had waited before sharing our thoughts. There's an old adage that says we have two ears and one mouth so we can listen twice as much as we speak.

Today, try listening with your heart. Let others have the floor, and respond only as you must. Listen beyond the words, beyond the situation, and see if you can hear the truth of all the chatter going on around you. Listen the way you would hope God Himself would listen to you, with heartfelt sympathy and patience.

A LISTENING HEART

Lord, sometimes I'm so quick to get my thoughts on the table that I'm not very good at listening to those around me. Today, help me to be a thoughtful listener. Amen.

Peace from the Wild Side

The heavens declare the glory of God; the skies proclaim the work of his hands.
PSALM 19:1 NIV

Wherever you live, you have opportunities to get out in nature, smell the fresh air, and walk among the flowers and foliage. Okay, some of you have to do this in a city park, but most of you can get away and enjoy creation as God intended it.

John Muir wrote, "Climb the mountains and get their good tidings. Nature's peace will flow into you as sunshine flows into trees. The winds will blow their own freshness into you, and the storms their energy, while cares will drop off like autumn leaves."

If you haven't experienced the good tidings coming your way from the mountaintops, or the freshness of the winds that clear out the noise in your head, then make today an opportunity to let God speak to your heart with clarity and power. You might be impressed with what you learn from the sound of a winging bird or the rippling waters of a creek bed. You may even hear the still, small voice of God speaking your name.

May His peace prevail in your heart today.

A QUIET HEART

Lord, walk with me through the beauty of all You've created, and speak to me in whispers that only the mountains and rivers know at every rising of the sun. Amen.

Your Job and Your Work!

Do your work willingly, as though you were serving the Lord himself.
COLOSSIANS 3:23 CEV

You've probably heard the old line that goes something like, "A lot of people stop looking for work once they find a job." It's lightly humorous and sadly truthful.

Your job is what you're trained to do in a specific way. It's your livelihood and a gift to you from God. It is part of the way you recognize your purpose in life. No doubt, you do it well. However, even if you were to lose that job, you'd still have work to do.

Your work is what you were born to do. For some people, it ties very closely to their chosen professions. For others, it's the work that feeds those around them in heart, soul, and mind through gifts of kindness, friendship, and love. It's the work you do for God, and so He always provides people in your midst who need to see His love in action. He brought you on for the job the day you asked Him to be your Savior. He has work that only you can do.

God loves it when you do your work, but He wants your heart to be reshaped in ways that allow you to volunteer your services. He's called you and delights in your service.

One thing is for sure, you'll never get laid off from His work.

A WORK OF THE HEART

Lord, help me to see all the work I do as something I do for You. Bless those around me, and open opportunities for Your work to continue everywhere. Amen.

'Tis the Season!

"Prepare the way for the LORD's coming! Clear the road for him!"
MATTHEW 3:3 NLT

With Christmas just ten days away, most Christians are at the height of preparation for the Lord's coming. Church services, caroling, baking cookies, and sharing time with friends all become part of the beauty, joy, and wonder of the season. Add to that the time it takes to write out your Christmas cards, remember family and friends you haven't had a chance to connect with all year, and make Uncle Ted's favorite yule log cake, and you might begin to wonder if it's really worth it for one special day!

Everything you do to prepare for the Lord's coming is worth it. At Christmas you focus on giving, sharing, and loving. You give to charities, work in soup kitchens, remember the homeless. . .you become the hands and feet of Christ. You become an ambassador of the heart of God. You prepare the way for Him to come and bring greater joy! It's worth it!

This year as you make room for Him to enter anew into your heart and mind, enjoy the many gifts of the season. Serve Him with fresh enthusiasm, thanksgiving, and glad tidings. Prepare the way for the Lord!

A WORTHY HEART

Lord, I always have childlike excitement at Christmas. I ask that You would inspire my heart to create the spirit of Christmas anywhere I am. Amen.

More books with "heart" you'll love!

The Heart-Shaped Life Daily Devotional

Readers will be motivated to live a "heart-shaped" life with this devotional from Barbour Publishing. With refreshing thoughts, prayers, and scripture selections, *The Heart-Shaped Life Daily Devotional* will help readers discover the best path to the good life. . .which is LOVE.

Hardback / 978-1-68322-009-1 / $14.99

Prayers for a Woman's Heart Creative Devotional

Fifty-two heartfelt devotional-length prayers complemented by fifty-two unique coloring pages on quality stock will encourage and delight your soul through beautiful design and refreshing insights. As you read the weekly prayer, meditate on the scriptures, and unlock your creativity, you will be drawn to experience an intimate connection to your heavenly Father.

Paperback / 978-1-68322-722-9 / $9.99

The Bible Promise Book: 500 Scriptures to Bless a Woman's Heart

Barbour's Bible Promise Books are perennial bestsellers, with millions of copies in print. *The Bible Promise Book®* is available in a lovely paperback edition featuring 500 scripture selections plus encouraging prayer starters to bless your heart. With 50 topics that matter most to you—including Comfort, Love, Faith, Worry, Worship, Courage, Joy, and Contentment—you can quickly and easily locate a topic that will speak to your needs.

Paperback / 978-1-68322-729-8 / $5.99